SECRETS
The Wallace Family

James M. McCracken

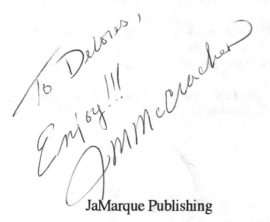

To Delores!
Enjoy!!!
JMMcCracken

JaMarque Publishing

Secrets: The Wallace Family

Copyright © 1998 by James M. McCracken

IBSN 0-9667853-0-4

Printed in the United States of America

JaMarque Publishing, PO Box 5211, Oregon City, Oregon 97045-8211

To two very special people who, through their friendship, have taught me to believe in myself.

Acknowledgments

With heartfelt appreciation to Marcia Klinge, for her encouraging a shy teenaged boy to write; and to Dennis Blakesley, Bruce Fiebach, Patrick Huff, Trudy Kay, Michael Anne Maslow, Eric Meese, Mary Newman and Tamera Somers for all of the encouragement they gave me over the years that kept me writing.

THE REUNION

The warm mid-July breeze blew gently through the spreading oak trees of the backyard. Beneath, in the shadows of the many branches, the lighthearted sounds of laughter and splashing drifted up from the inground swimming pool.

"Okay! Okay!" laughed the thin, graying haired man as he shielded his face from the barrage of water. "I give up."

"Carl Andrew Wallace." The familiar stern female voice thundered down on the two men. "You get out of that swimming pool and get into the house immediately."

The smile faded from Carl's face. He recognized that tone in his wife's voice. He had heard it several times in the passed two months since Steven had moved back home.

"I'm sorry, son," he apologized. Lately it seemed as though he had been apologizing a lot. Carl turned around and made his way to the steps; the water in the pool swirled around him.

"That's okay, Dad," Steven nodded. He knew why his mother was upset but he still felt bad for his father.

"I guess your mother is upset with me again," Carl said to try to release the tension as he watched his wife disappear into the house.

"Maybe I should talk to her again?" Steven handed his father a towel. "I'm not a little boy anymore. She doesn't have to worry about me."

Carl looked at his eldest son and remembered the little boy with freckles he had once known not so long ago. Now, this young man, taller than himself, thin and mustached with a touch of gray by his ears stood before him. Carl smiled to himself. Time had flown by so quickly.

"She's your mother, Steven. It's her job to worry about you and all of your sisters and brother. It has nothing to do with your age. To her, you will always be her little boy." Carl smiled as he dried himself off.

"Well, I thought she understood. I don't want to be babied. I want to-"

"I know," Carl interrupted him, not wanting to hear those words again. "She does understand, but her heart does not. This isn't easy for your mother. Hell, it isn't easy for me."

Steven looked at his father and for the first time suddenly realized that his father was human, with feelings. He quickly searched his memory and could not remember any time he had seen his father cry. He had always been strong, manly, cool and calm no matter what the situation. Steven put his arm around his father's shoulders and gave him a one-armed hug.

"But you seem to be handling it fine," Steven

reassured him.

"Yeah, I do, don't I." Carl feigned a smile. Inside his chest tightened and his throat ached as he fought back the tears in his eyes. "Well," he breathed loudly. "Let's get out of these wet clothes before the rest of the family arrives."

"Sure." Steven kept his arm over his father's shoulders. "I love you, Dad."

Carl clinched his teeth and fought harder to keep from letting the tears fill his eyes. He turned and hugged Steven tightly until the flood of emotion passed.

"Let's go." His voice was a mere whisper.

The two walked quietly into the house.

Steven smiled to himself as he reflected on the fun he and his father were having in the swimming pool moments ago. He cherished fondly the many memories of the fun they had shared as he was growing up. The many fishing trips, the baseball games. In recent years those moments seemed to be fewer. So this morning was very special to him.

Slowly he walked back to his bedroom after his shower. His long terry cloth bathrobe felt warm against his skin. As he walked in the open hallway above the foyer, he became aware of the voices coming from his parents' bedroom behind him. Slowly he lowered the towel he had been using to dry his reddish-brown hair. As he stopped and turned around, he cocked his head to listen. He recognized his mother's voice. She sounded upset. He strained to listen.

Inside the bedroom, Carl sat on the dressing bench at the foot of their queen-size bed. He listened to his wife as he finished tying his shoelaces. He understood her frustration and anger, but it seemed little help as she paced the floor in front of him.

"Ruth," Carl sighed. "He's not a baby anymore."

"I know that!" She snapped in indignation. "I'm not crazy. Is it a crime for a mother to want to hold onto her children for as long as she can?"

"No." Carl shook his head and sat back. He did not like keeping secrets from his children. For years he and Ruth had raised them to be open and honest with each other and them. Now one of them was asking them to keep silent. It was a hard thing to ask of them and it was proving to be an even harder thing for them to do.

"This isn't about you or me," Carl spoke softly. "This is about respecting the wishes of our son."

"Well, I can't do it!" Ruth said emphatically as she stopped in front of him and let her tears fall. "He's asking too much of me, I tell you. I can't. It's just too hard. Tell me what other mother would agree to such a thing?"

Carl quickly stood up and took his wife in his arms. She held him tightly as she buried her face in his chest and sobbed.

"It's not fair."

"It's his life, Ruth. We have no choice but to accept it." Carl held her trembling body in his arms as though to protect her from the pain. "I know it's hard, but we have to respect his wishes otherwise we will lose him, forever."

"Carl, it's tearing me up inside. I don't know if I can." She continued to cry and protest.

"I know, Honey. I know." Carl fought back his own tears. He had to be strong for her. He could not let her see him cry even though he wanted to so desperately. In his heart he knew that everything she was saying was true. This was not fair.

Steven turned away from the doorway and walked slowly back to his bedroom. He stared blankly about the bedroom at the familiar pine wood paneled walls, the bookcase with books and memorabilia from his childhood days, the things he had left behind when he had moved out on his own. Here everything was, just as he had left it, waiting for him to return. He looked at the suitcases and boxes next to his old writing desk under the window. It was true. He had returned but not for long.

His mind kept going over his parents' conversation. He knew what he was asking them to do was hard, but it was just as hard for him to tell them. Telling them meant he had to admit it to himself and that was something he had fought for two years not to do. He did not want to hurt anyone, especially them, but if the rest of the family knew, it would tear the family apart. That was something he could not bear to let happen. The family had always been the most important thing to him.

Steven walked over to his bed and sat down. He smiled at the sight of the photograph of his older sister and best friend, Tamera, and himself that sat on his nightstand. It was taken on the day of his High School graduation. His heart ached at the thought of not seeing her again. Tears filled his eyes for a moment but he shook them away.

"No!" he firmly breathed out loud. "No."

The front doorbell chimed in the open foyer. Before

anyone could answer, the door opened and a young, wavy brown haired, bearded man stepped inside.

"Dad? Mom?" He called out in a deep husky voice.

"Bradley!" Ruth answered with open arms as she hurried to greet her son. "I'm so happy all of you could make it." She kissed his bearded cheek.

"Where is everyone?" Bradley looked about the foyer and open staircase.

"Well, your father and Steven are out back. As for the rest of the family, they haven't arrived yet," she answered, distracted by the cute, brown haired little boy peeking out from behind his mother's skirt. "My how you've grown, Benji," she cooed at her grandson.

Benjamin smiled and buried his face in his mother's skirt nearly knocking her to the floor.

"Benji!" Amanda snapped as she tried to balance the cake box and keep from falling over. "Bradley, here." She nodded toward their son.

Bradley smiled and playfully picked up his son, swinging him into the air. He was totally oblivious to his wife's annoyed tone.

Ruth looked at her daughter-in-law, surprised by her harshness. Amanda was usually a happy, carefree person. Never before had Ruth heard a cross word or angry tone come out of her. She excused it without further thought.

"Here, let me take that for you, dear." Ruth reached out for the cake box.

"Thank-you, Mom." Amanda smiled with a relieved sigh. "So, how are you doing?"

"I'm fine." Ruth smiled back and tried to sound convincing. "Why don't we all go out back. You know, I think your father could use a hand with that gas barbecuer you gave him last Fall. I still don't think he has the hang of it yet."

"Sure." Bradley laughed and hurried off ahead of them.

Amanda slowly closed the front door. Her heart pounded in her chest as she tried to muster up the courage to talk about her feelings.

"Mom," Her voice was soft. "Can I talk to you, alone, for a moment?"

Ruth turned around and looked at her daughter-in-law. Her smile faded as she looked into Amanda's dark brown eyes. She could tell that something was wrong and now the sound of Amanda's sharp tone a moment ago came echoing back in her ears.

"Sure. Let's go into the parlor."

Amanda walked across the small cozy living room off the foyer and stood facing the fireplace mantle. Among the many framed pictures of the family was a photograph of Bradley and her on their wedding day three years ago. The sight of it stuck her like a sharp pin. She turned away quickly.

Ruth sat down on the edge of the love seat and held the cake box on her lap. Quietly she studied Amanda, searching for some clue as to what was troubling her. Amanda's long brown hair was neatly combed and held back out of her face by a butterfly hair comb. Her skirt hung loosely about her almost too thin waist. Amanda clasped her trembling hands tightly in front of her. Ruth began to feel anxious and concerned.

"What is it, honey?" She reached out to her with her soft words.

"Well," Amanda fidgeted. "You know Bradley

better than I do. I mean, when he was a teenager and dating. What were they like?"

"They?" Ruth looked at her puzzled.

"You know, his girl friends." Amanda looked at her hands and the ring on her finger. "Were they thin and pretty?"

"They were just girls and actually there were only two." Ruth set the cake box on the coffee table. "What's this sudden interest in Bradley's old girl friends."

"Well," Amanda spoke in a weak whisper. "Bradley and I haven't been getting along so well lately. He's been distant to me. I know I haven't been able to lose all the weight I gained after Benji was born and I can't help but think that maybe that is why. Patty told me that the girls he dated were like fashion models, toothpicks."

"Oh, honey," Ruth smiled reassuringly. "Bradley loves you. He married you, not them."

"I know," Amanda shrugged. "But, maybe he'd be happier with one of them instead."

"That's nonsense, Amanda. Bradley is very happy and he loves you. Your weight doesn't matter to him. You could be fifty pounds over-weight and he'd still love you."

Amanda's eyes filled with tears and she turned away.

"No, he wouldn't."

Ruth was becoming worried about her daughter-in-law. She could tell something much more serious was going on in her young little head and she didn't know how to help her.

"Amanda," she reached out again. "Talk to him,

you will see. Bradley loves you dearly. He understands it's hard for women to lose weight. He doesn't care about that."

"You'll see." Amanda looked at her. "He'll leave me just like my father left my mother when she couldn't lose weight after having the six of us."

Ruth was shocked by the anger in Amanda's voice.

"Amanda, I don't know anything about your parents, but Bradley is not like that. Trust me, I know him and deep down you know it too."

"I'm pregnant again." Amanda burst into tears. "I am going to get fat and he's going to leave me. I know it. I can feel it. I lie awake at night and I can't sleep because I'm afraid he'll leave if I do."

Ruth held back her joyous thoughts of another grandchild around the house and tried to figure out how to reassure her daughter-in-law.

"Amanda, I don't know what I can say to make you see that you are wrong. Bradley is not going to leave you."

"Mom, I don't want to have this baby. I can't get fat again." Tears streamed down Amanda's cheeks. "I can't."

Amanda's words hit Ruth's ears like a sharp slap. Her joy instantly gave way to shock then fear. She slowly stood up and walked over to Amanda. Cautiously she took her shoulders in her hands and fought the urge to shake her.

"Amanda, dear girl, you have to talk to your husband. You will see that he will understand and you have no reason to be afraid. Everything is going to be fine. You have to promise me, now, that before you do anything, you will talk to Bradley. Promise me."

Amanda looked into her mother-in-law's golden brown eyes and nodded.

"I promise." She wiped the tears from her eyes.

"We all love you so much Amanda." Ruth hugged her tightly. "You are the best thing that has happened to Bradley. He knows that too. Now, go upstairs and freshen up." Ruth kissed Amanda on the forehead and smiled.

"Okay." Amanda forced a smile then hurried back into the foyer. She paused for a second at the foot of the stairs as though she were about to say something then changed her mind and hurried up to the powder room.

Ruth picked up the cake box and walked into the foyer. Silently she watched Amanda close the door. This is not over, she thought to herself. There was a bigger problem brewing in the head of her daughter-in-law, if only she knew how to reach her.

Tamera carefully made her way around the side of the house and into the back yard. She did not want to come to this family gathering because she did not want to face Steven; but at the last minute she gave into her husband Daniel's insistence. Her heart pounded as she saw Carl, Bradley and Steven huddled around the barbecuer. She took a deep breath.

"Hello, everybody," she called as she walked closer.

Steven turned around at the sound of her voice. Immediately he smiled and ran around the swimming pool to greet her. As their eyes met, he froze.

"I'll go set this stuff down on the table." The tall, thin, dark haired man kissed Tamera's cheek and took the grocery bag from her arms.

"Thank-you, Dan," she said without taking her eyes off Steven. "Make sure Nicholas gets out here. I don't want him messing around out front," she quickly added.

"Gotcha," Daniel nodded. "Hey, Steven." He smiled as he brushed passed him.

"Hi, Dan." Steven smiled at his brother-in-law. He then turned his attention back to his dearest sister. Her long blonde hair was curled away from her rosy cheeked round face. Her soft blue eyes were filled with tears behind her pink tinted glasses. Steven's smile faded.

"Who told you?"

"Mom," she answered flatly then quickly added, "But even if she hadn't, I would still have known. I can tell by the look in your eyes. We've been too close for me not to have known." She wiped the tears from her cheek.

"Don't cry, please." Steven fought back his own tears. This was exactly what he had wanted to avoid. He did not want to hurt her.

"How dare you ask that of me!" Tamera choked and struggled to keep from raising her voice. "I love you, damn it!" The tears began to fall too quickly to wipe them all away.

"Please, Tamera," Steven pleaded and stepped closer. "If you cry, it will only hurt Mom and Dad more."

"I don't care. I can't help it." Tamera stepped back and dried her eyes.

"Did you tell anyone else?" Steven lowered his voice to a faint whisper.

"No. I didn't tell anyone," she answered him smugly but then the tears began to fall again. "But how? Why? It's not fair."

"Life isn't fair. At least that is what you've always told me." Steven tried to smile and catch her eyes.

"Oh, that's really comforting. Throw that in my face after all these years." Tamera fought back her smile. "How can you joke and tease at a time like this? Besides, I said that to get my own way when we were kids." She looked up at him.

"Who said we ever grew up?" Steven smiled at her.

Tamera shook her head and took a deep breath.

"So, what am I supposed to do, Steven? What are we all supposed to do?"

"There's nothing you can do, or anyone else for that matter. Just be happy for me."

"I don't know if I can." Tamera strained to speak again fighting back her tears.

"Please, try. I don't want you to cry. I love you."

Tamera stepped closer to him.

"I love you, too," she said and hugged him tightly.

"Hey. Hey." A voice came up from behind them. "Knock that off you two. What will the neighbors think?"

Tamera immediately released her bear hug on Steven and turned her back to her older sister, Morgan. She hated how Morgan was always needling her. If it was not about her weight it was about some other perceived character flaw. Today she was not up to dealing with her. Quickly Tamera tried to dry her eyes.

"I'll be right back," she said as she hurried off into the house.

"What's her problem?" Morgan asked curtly, unaware of her harsh tone. "I was only teasing," she added.

"Nothing," Steven sighed and looked at his eldest sister. Her short, sandy brown hair was dyed and permed to hide the gray. Even though she was the eldest, she was the shortest in the family, taking after their aunt on their father's side of the family.

Like Tamera, Steven always hated how Morgan treated him as though he were still a child. Her condescending looks and tone always irritated him; but today, he was willing to forgive all of that and he realized then that he really did love her. He was happy that she and her family had come.

"So, little brother, don't I get a hug?" She insisted more than asked.

"Of course." Steven smiled and hugged her, ignoring the familiar tone in her voice.

"So, What's the big idea getting the family together?" Morgan looked up at him. She loved him in her own awkward way. Being five years older than he, it was hard for her to see past the many years of baby sitting and taking care of him and the rest of the family. She did resent those lost teenage years and maybe even him a little.

"Oh, nothing special. I just thought that it would be kind of fun, that's all. So, where's your other half?" Steven tried to change the subject.

Morgan's back stiffened at the sound of those words but she tried not to let it be noticed.

"Chuck's coming," she answered and hoped he would not pursue the conversation.

"And where are the two love birds?" Steven continued.

"See for yourself." Morgan sighed a quiet sigh. "Here they come." She glanced over her shoulder and then made her exit.

"Hi, Dad!" She called ahead as she continued over to the picnic table.

"Uncle Steven," Ariel beamed as she escorted her tall, long sandy blonde haired fiance' over to him. "I'd like you to finally meet the guy I've told you so much about. Uncle Steven, this is my fiance' Mark Jones. Mark, this is my Uncle Steven."

"It's good to finally meet you, Mark." Steven held out his hand and smiled.

"The same, sir." Mark shook Steven's hand politely but distractedly. He really did not want to be there, much less have to talk to anyone. His mind kept wandering to the gig he and his band played the night before and the one that was coming up this weekend.

"Please, just call me Steven. I may be thirty-eight, but I'm really not old enough to be called, 'sir' yet." Steven smiled at Mark. He could tell by the look in Mark's eyes that his thoughts were far away. "So, how are the wedding plans coming?" Steven asked and watched Mark for his reaction.

Mark's eyes snapped back to the present.

"Oh, don't ask," he spoke up before Ariel could. "That is, unless you have a week to listen."

"Well, I don't." Steven laughed lightheartedly. "We can talk about that later. So, where is your father? Your mom said he was coming. Isn't he with you?" Steven looked beyond them, indirectly hoping they would drop the conversation. Ariel was too dreamy-eyed over Mark to carry on an adult conversation just yet. She seemed to be getting worse as the wedding date drew nearer. On the other hand, there was something definitely going on in Mark's head that puzzled Steven, but he did not have the energy to think about that now.

"Daddy?" Ariel looked over her shoulder. "Yeah, he's here. He drove up just after us. He must still be out front. Do you want us to go and get him?"

"No. He'll be here soon enough." Steven stepped aside and ushered Ariel and Mark passed him. "Let's go join the rest of the family, okay?"

Steven followed them around the swimming pool to the back yard.

"Dad." Bradley nudged Carl slightly to get his attention. "Can I talk to you for a second?"

"Sure." Carl looked up from the grill and from cooking the hamburger patties. "What's on you mind, son?" He asked.

"Not here, Dad," Bradley half whispered.

Carl looked at Bradley again. This time he could see that something was troubling him. "Hey, Dan, you any good at barbecuing?"

"Yeah, I've done it a couple times." Daniel nodded as though trying to convince himself.

"How about watching this for me for a minute?"

"No problem, Dad." Daniel stood up from the table and from his conversation with Morgan.

Carl and Bradley started around the opposite side of the swimming pool heading toward the house as Tamera rounded the other side to join the family.

"What's up son?" Carl inquired.

"Let's go over there first." Bradley motioned toward the patio chairs.

The two men walked over to the chairs on the deck and sat down. Bradley sat forward and leaned on the patio table in front of him as he stared across the pool at the family. Carl studied his youngest son's dark brown eyes, trying to figure out what was bothering him. When Bradley was a boy, his face was an open book. Carl could always tell what was on his mind. But now, at thirty-six, Bradley was not so easy. This time Carl came up with a blank. He looked over at the family and then beyond them where Amanda was pushing Benjamin in the swing.

"So, are you going to tell me what this is all about?" Carl broke the silence.

"I wish I knew, Dad. Something is bothering Amanda and I don't know how to talk to her about it. Everything I say is the wrong thing." Bradley turned his attention to his father. "Have you noticed how thin she is?"

Carl nodded in response.

"Well, she still thinks she's fat. I try to tell her she isn't but she then says I'm lying. I don't know what's going on in her head, but I'm really worried about her."

"Have you thought about counseling?" Carl shrugged not knowing exactly how to answer his son. "I know-"

"Out of the question," Bradley interrupted. "She won't do it. She thinks I'm the one with the problem."

Carl turned and looked at Amanda and tried to come up with a solution but his mind was a total blank. He turned back to Bradley and again looked into his eyes. He was waiting for some words of wisdom to make it all better, but Carl was out of them. He had never dealt with a situation like this before or had he? He smiled at his thoughts.

"You need to find some way to talk to her, today,"

he said and continued to smile.

Bradley looked curiously at his father. He saw nothing in their conversation to be smiling about.

"Why? What's up?"

"Oh, I was just thinking about the times your mother would become overly concerned about her weight and nine months later she was over it."

Bradley's eyes widened at the thought. A smile spread across his lips.

"You think?"

"I can't say for certain, but it's possible." Carl beamed at the thought of having another grandchild.

"You're right." Bradley nodded. "I will talk to her, today."

"Good. So how's work going?" Carl changed the subject as the two of them stood up.

"Things are a little slow right now." Bradley shrugged as the two started back around the swimming pool. "The big wigs say things should be picking up soon; but, I tell you, I hope they're right otherwise we're looking at layoffs for sure."

"Tamera! Dan!" A deep voice thundered from around the corner of the house interrupting everyone's conversations. As if in unison, everyone turned around to see what was going on as Chuck appeared tugging on Nicholas' arm.

Tamera quickly shot an angry glare at Daniel.

"I thought I told you to make sure he was back here," she hissed as she jumped up from her chair. Again Daniel had not done as she had asked. She could not take time to figure out who was worse, Nicholas or Daniel. Right now her attention was required to deal with her over-bearing brother-in-law and her son.

"What have you done now?" She snapped at Nicholas. "I thought I told you to get yourself back here when you got out of the car."

"I wasn't doing anything, ma." The brown-eyed teenager with long, dyed black haired twisted in his uncle's tight grip.

"Come on you little liar, tell the truth for a change." Chuck tightened his hold on Nicholas' thin arm.

"Stop it! You're hurting me." Nicholas winced. "I wasn't hurting anything."

"You can take your hands off my son, Chuck. I will handle this." Tamera glared momentarily at her brother-in-law. She never did like him. Ever since that day twenty five years ago when he and Morgan began dating. She was all of fourteen and just beginning to show a chest. When Morgan was not looking, Chuck would always try to slip his hands up her blouse teasingly. Then there was another reason too. One she kept secret for all these years and yet, one she threatened to tell if he did not watch his step.

Chuck sensed Tamera's anger at him and he was not about to back down.

"You'd better, Tamera, because the next time I'll just call the police." Chuck jerked Nicholas' arm as he released his grip.

"You can keep your hands off my son, Chuck, or I'll be the one calling the police." Tamera glared as he walked nearer to her.

"Pardon me, I didn't know he was your son," he said under his breath but loud enough for Tamera to hear.

A cold chill and almost a panic sensation ran up

Tamera's spine as the words hit her ears. She stood fast and continued to glare at Chuck as he casually strutted over to the table. Tamera shook the feeling from her mind.

"I hate that jerk!" Nicholas hissed as he rubbed his arm.

Tamera swung around and faced Nicholas.

"You mind you mouth, young man. Now, for the last time, what were you doing out front?"

"Nothing," Nicholas answered defiantly.

Without warning or hesitation, Tamera drew back and slapped his face. Nicholas' head jerked sharply at the impact. Immediately he covered his red cheek with his hand and fought back the tears in his eyes. His cheek stung, but it was more the embarrassment that hurt and he was not about to let her know she had gotten to him.

"Don't lie to me." Tamera continued her interrogation. "Why is your uncle ready to call the police if you were just 'doing nothing?' Do you want to end up in a juvenile home? Because, that's exactly where you will end up if you slip up just one more time, young man."

"Why do you always take everyone else's side? Why do you always believe them? Why don't you ever believe me, your own son, for once? I wish you weren't my mother," Nicholas protested.

The words rang in Tamera's ears and echoed down to her heart. She looked at the boy in front of her. The sunlight caught the gold dangling ear ring and flashed the light back into her eyes. His black leather jacket and unkempt looking hair did not escape her notice. Her mind flashed with images of the day she had brought him home from the hospital. He was so tiny and helpless. She promised herself then that no one would ever hurt her baby. Where did that baby go? She looked into his eyes and her anger faded. Tears filled her eyes and she spoke softly, "Don't say that."

"Then believe me for a change." Nicholas kept up his anger and hurt.

"Give me a reason to, Nick. Talk to me. Tell me the truth. What were you doing?"

Nicholas studied his mother's eyes for a moment.

"Okay," He breathed cautiously. "I was sitting in Uncle Steven's car." He paused for a reaction anticipating her to fly into another rage as she had so often done in the passed few months. Nothing. She just stood there and listened. "I found some papers and you won't believe what they say."

"I already know," Tamera interrupted him. Her heart pounded as she realized what papers he might be referring to.

"But Mom, they say Uncle Steven-"

"I said that I already know." Tamera grabbed his arm and pulled him closer to her. He winced as he prepared himself for another slap.

"You are to keep this between you and me. Do you understand me?" She whispered sternly. "Not a word of it to anyone, not even your father."

"Shouldn't we at least ask Uncle Steven about it?" He protested and tried to get free of her tight hold.

"No. Absolutely not!" Tamera could not believe her ears. "Out of respect for your uncle, you are to keep this between us. He doesn't want the family to know. So, keep your mouth shut. Am I making myself clear? I am very serious here, Nick."

"Yes, but I don't understand what the harm would be in telling everyone." Nicholas twisted free from her hold and rubbed his arm again.

"Your Uncle Steven wants it this way and we have to abide by his wishes. In time the rest of the family will be told, okay?"

"That's cool," Nicholas nodded.

Tamera looked at her son and shook her head. She felt old at that moment and being thirty-nine, looking at her fourteen year old son.

"Cool?" She smiled and repeated. "That's not exactly what I would have said. Now, why don't you go see your cousin Ariel and stay out of your Uncle Chuck's way and out of trouble."

"Okay," Nicholas answered halfheartedly. He really did not like being around Ariel and Mark, not lately. They were getting too serious and did not want to have fun just hanging out anymore. However, it was only for the afternoon, he could suffer through it for that long.

Tamera watched him walk over to the table and sit down. She glanced over to Daniel. When their eyes met, he turned around and joined Carl and Bradley at the barbecuer. Tamera sighed out loud to herself.

"Looks as though you have your hands full." Ruth walked up behind her.

"Oh!" Tamera gave a start and turned around to face her mother. "That's an understatement, Mom. I don't know what to do with that boy. Everything I try doesn't seem to be getting through to him. He just doesn't see what serious trouble he is in."

"He's just a boy. He'll grow out of it. You all did." Ruth smiled sympathetically. "Here, give me a hand with this stuff." She handed Tamera a tray of vegetables and dip.

"Well, none of us ever got into this kind of trouble. So, why my son? I don't understand it. Some people say that it is hereditary, that the bad genes from a parent can be passed on so the child turns out bad. It's probably from Dan's side of the family. That has to be it."

"I doubt that very much, Tamera." Ruth laughed out loud as they started over to the table. "Times are changing. Nowadays, kids are not taught to respect authority let alone their parents. Even those who are taught can get mixed up in the wrong crowd and in the excitement of the moment do stupid things. What Nick did, shoplifting a compact disc, that's pretty tame stuff compared to the other kids out there. Kids in gangs are actually killing one another. They're stealing cars and doing god knows what else. It's a good thing Nick was caught now. Maybe it will keep him from doing much worse; but Tamera, honey, you have to lighten up on him. Don't drive him away from you or he will run to them."

"I'll try." Tamera nodded silently as she thought about her mother's advice. Over the years while Nick was growing up she had solicited Ruth's advice on several occasions. She was happy in knowing that she still could.

Ruth smiled to herself as they put the trays down on the table. She could not help but remember the young teen-aged rebel Tamera was in her youth. Although she never found herself in serious trouble, she did her share of not following the social norms. Just as Tamera grew up, Nicholas would too.

Slowly Bradley approached the swing set. His palms were sweaty and his stomach was nervous. He could not decide how he was going to bring up the subject with Amanda, but he knew he had to. It could not wait.

"Amanda, can we talk for a second?" He asked cautiously.

"Sure," Amanda nodded. "I've been wanting to talk to you, too."

Bradley was surprised by her eagerness. He watched her as she slowed the swing to a gentle stop and then helped Benjamin down from the wooden seat.

"Go see Grandma for Mommy," she cooed into his little ear and pointed across the yard toward the picnic table.

Without a word, Benjamin smiled and scurried off as fast as his little legs would go. Bradley and Amanda watched him until they were sure he would not hear them. Slowly Bradley turned to her.

"Amanda," he began again. "I've been meaning to talk to you. It's about us. Lately we don't talk anymore, we just argue. It has to stop."

"I know," Amanda interrupted him. "I've been thinking about that too. If you want a divorce, I understand. You can have it," She sighed and looked at the ground.

"What? Oh, god, no!" Bradley gasped as though he had been punched in the stomach. Tears immediately filled his eyes. This was not going at all as he had thought it would. He took her shoulders in his hands. "Why would you say such a thing as that? Whatever gave you that idea?"

"Because I'm getting fat. I'm not as thin as I was when we were married." Amanda tried to avoid looking at him. She felt ashamed of her weight and embarrassed.

"Amanda, you are thin. In fact you weigh less now that before we were married. You have your wedding dress at home in a box, try it on, you'll see." Bradley was becoming frightened at the thought of his wife being seriously ill. For the first time words like anorexia and bulimia entered his thoughts. This could not be happening. This only happens to teenagers, not women in their early thirties.

"Amanda, I love you. I am worried about you. You are losing too much weight. You have to get help. I don't want to lose you."

Amanda choked and burst into tears as she fell into his strong arms.

"What's wrong? Honey, please talk to me," Bradley pleaded as he cradled her tightly.

"I," she tried to speak. "I'm pregnant."

"What?" Bradley's eyes lit up and he could not stop from smiling. "That's wonderful. That's fantastic. We're going to have another baby." Bradley pulled Amanda away from his chest and looked at her. She continued to cry. Her body trembled. "Aren't you happy?" He tried not to smile seeing her tears.

"I don't want to get fat again." She shook her head. Bradley froze. "I don't want this baby."

Bradley could not believe his ears. How could she not want their child? He was numb. Words left him. His mind was a blank. He looked at her and she stopped crying as she looked at him.

"Say something." She slapped him with her words.

"What?" Bradley released his hold on her. "What do you want me to say? It's okay to get an abortion? Is that what you want? I can't." Bradley tried to control his feelings of hurt and anger and fear at the thought.

"I just don't want to be fat. I can't. I don't want to be like my mother." Amanda began to cry again.

"Amanda, honey," Bradley sighed in relief, realizing what was really behind this. "I'm not like your father. I am not going anywhere. I love you. I'm not leaving you. We will be fine." He took her chin in his hand and raised her head to look into her eyes. "I'm not leaving. I love you," he repeated. "Everything will be fine. You'll see. Are you okay?"

Amanda nodded her head but inside she was beginning to feel nauseous. She really did not want to be obese, not like her mother. She remembered how, as a child in school, the other children would bully and tease her about her mother's weight. She could not remember when it started, but she did not want her children to go through what she had. Now that Bradley knew about the pregnancy, she knew he would never allow her to give it up. Part of her felt secure in that fact and happy about the prospect of holding a baby in her arms again; but the other part of her was frightened at the idea of getting fat again.

Bradley looked at his wife still remembering her words. He had to ask her just one more question, but he was afraid of her answer.

"So, do you still not want to go through with this?"

"You are sure you won't leave me?" Amanda looked up at him.

"Yes," he answered without hesitation.

Amanda looked at her flat stomach, fighting her fears, and then back at Bradley. Slowly she reached up and gently stroked his beard.

"Then, it looks like we're going to have a baby."

Bradley smiled as his anxieties melted.

"I love you, Mrs. Bradley Wallace." He kissed her and for the first time in a long time and she kissed him back. "Let's go tell the others the great news," Bradley said as he held her.

"Not just yet." Amanda pulled back. "Today is for Steven."

Bradley looked at her curiously. What did she mean by that? This was a family gathering. He could not think about that now and shrugged off her comment.

"Okay. We'll tell them later." He conceded.

Ruth set the glass of lemonade down on the table and picked up another and began to fill it. She smiled to herself at the noisy chatter around the table as Ariel and Mark told Steven about the concert they had just attended. When she had finished filling the last glass, Ruth turned back toward the house. Out of the corner of her eye she noticed Nicholas. He was standing alone under a tree and staring off deep in thought. Slowly she walked over to him.

"Hi, Nicky," she smiled as she stood beside him. "What are you thinking about?"

"Oh, nothing," he shrugged and ran a hand through his hair.

"You seem to be doing a lot of that today." Ruth smiled and tried to catch his eyes. As she looked at her grandson, she remembered the little boy who was so full of energy and whom you could not shut up. Anything you asked him, he would have an answer; but now, something was troubling him. Something that he was not willing to talk about. Ruth hated the feeling of helplessness that it gave her and she hated seeing one of her children or even grandchildren troubled.

"Are you sure there isn't something you would like to talk about? You know I'm a good listener," she prodded.

"Yeah, Grandma," he breathed and glanced over at his mother as she visited with the others at the table. "I'm sure."

"Okay honey," she smiled and stroked his hair. "If you change your mind, I'll be in the house."

"Thank-you, Grandma," Nicholas nodded and turned away. He wanted to talk to someone. He needed to. The trouble was he promised his mother he would not say a word. What could be so horrible about what he found. Slowly he pulled the paper out of his pocket and looked at it again. He smiled to himself as he read it. Then carefully he folded it up and put it back in his pocket.

Ruth continued to think about Nicholas as she walked up onto the deck and headed for the back door. Her thoughts shifted as she noticed Morgan sitting at the patio table watching the family silently.

"How about giving me a hand in the kitchen with the salad?" Ruth asked as she stood over Morgan.

"Sure," Morgan nodded. She stood up and straighten her blue jeans.

Ruth patiently waited and shook her head. Her eldest daughter was so different from the rest. Morgan was so full of anger and bitterness that it was reflected in her eyes and in the lines that were appearing around her pursed lips. Ruth noticed it immediately when she brought Tamera home from the hospital thirty nine years ago. Even though Morgan was only four, she immediately took a disliking to her sister, and after that with each new sibling those feelings were amplified. Ruth had tried to spend extra time with her in those years, but Morgan had already shut her out. It was not until she became engaged to Chuck that Morgan let down the wall at least part of the way between them.

"So, how are the wedding plans coming along?" Ruth tried to make conversation.

"Not well at all to tell you the truth," Morgan shrugged disgustedly. "I can't seem to get Ariel to sit down for five seconds to finalize the guest list, the flowers, anything. We are already too late to rent a hall for the reception. I don't know what we're going to do. The wedding is only three months away. I just don't understand what's gotten into her." Morgan cast one last look at Ariel just before she closed the back door behind them.

"Sounds like a serious case of love." Ruth smiled. "And so familiar, too."

"What did you mean by that?" Morgan snapped sharply as she stepped up to the kitchen counter.

"Oh, don't be so defensive." Ruth laughed playfully which angered Morgan more. "I seem to recall another young girl who was so in love she couldn't sit still. That's all." Ruth took the bowl of chopped lettuce and vegetables out of the refrigerator.

"Well, I was never like that," Morgan said indignantly. "Ariel hangs on Mark all of the time. She's forever holding his hand, rubbing his back, giggling and carrying on so. She's eighteen and getting married. She should grow up!"

"Yes, she should and she will, just as you have settled down; but Morgan, it will take time. Give her a chance." Ruth handed Morgan the salad spoon and fork. "So, what kind of work does Mark do?"

"Don't even get me started. Why Chuck agreed to this marriage is beyond me. The boy says he's a musician and it takes time to build up a reputation. So, I guess they plan on living off of Ariel's income from her waitressing. I just don't know." Morgan shook her head and shrugged as she tossed the salad.

"So, what do his parents think?" Ruth continued to fill the salad dressing shaker.

"Oh, they are useless," Morgan hissed and wiped the counter with the kitchen cloth. "They are too busy with their golf or flying around the countryside to be bothered with their twenty-one year old bum of a son."

"Well, let's just hope Ariel knows what she is getting into and hope for the best." Ruth shook her head and handed the salad dressing and salad to Morgan. "I'll get the plates and be right out."

Morgan started for the back door and then turned back around deep in thought.

"Mom, why was it so important to Steven to get the family together?" she asked.

Ruth stiffened as the words hit her ears. It was a good thing she had her back to Morgan, she thought to herself.

"Oh, nothing special," she shrugged.

"You know, there's something different about him. Is there something wrong?" Morgan persisted in her questions.

"No, there's nothing the matter. You just haven't

seen him for a while. That's all." Ruth did not turn around. "I'll be right out." She said and hoped that Morgan would not pursue the conversation and leave.

"You're probably right." Morgan nodded.

The sound of the back door closing brought a sigh of relief to Ruth. She turned around and wiped the tears from her eyes. "I can't do this," she sighed out loud to herself.

"Can't do what, Mom?" A soft voice came back at her.

Ruth jumped and looked up to see her youngest daughter, Patricia, standing in the doorway.

"Oh, you scared me!" She breathed out loud. "Don't do that again."

Patricia smiled and gave her mother a hug. Her long auburn hair and soft brown eyes were the image of her mother in younger years.

"What can't you do?" Patricia repeated as she stepped back and looked at her mother.

"Oh, nothing." Ruth shrugged and tried to think of something fast. "I can't carry all of this by myself." She lied.

Patricia knew she was lying. She was standing in the doorway listening to Morgan's questions and watching her mother's reactions, but she was not going to call her on it. She knew in time she would find out. This family was not one to hold onto secrets. That thought comforted her as well as frightened her.

"So, how's the news business these days?" Ruth asked. She was so proud of her daughter's accomplishments. She had worked hard and was finally a reporter for the local television news station.

"Oh, they're great." Patricia smiled. "We just

finished up with a big story involving fraud and embezzlement right here in town. It hasn't made for very happy businessmen but for the people they defrauded it has meant justice. I just hope they get put away for a good many years."

"Well, I'm so very proud of you." Ruth hugged her again. "Let's go out back."

"Tamera, let's go for a walk," Daniel said as he took hold of her arm and lifted her to her feet.

"Sure, honey," she smiled. "What is it?"

"Let's just go over there by the swing so we can be alone, first." Daniel's tone was calm but determined as they slowly walked away from the gathering.

"Hey you two, don't go too far," Carl called after them.

"We won't, Dad," Daniel answered his father-in-law.

"Okay, so what's up?" Tamera turned around to face Daniel as they reached the swing. She was beginning to become annoyed at being escorted off as she had been.

"Tamera," Daniel looked into her eyes pleadingly. "You have to ease up on the boy. This was only his first offense. Even the judge recognized that."

Tamera looked into the brown eyes of her husband. She could tell he was being serious and almost pleading, but still she was annoyed.

"Is that what this is all about?" She snapped. "If I'm being hard on Nicholas, it's because I just don't want there to be a second. He has to learn that if he steals things, then he will have to pay the consequences."

"Damn it, Tamera." Daniel tried to keep from raising his voice and not lose his temper. "Nick knows he did wrong. He was sentenced by the judge and has forty hours of community service left to do. Let him do his time and forget about it. He's only fourteen years old for crying out loud. He shouldn't be branded for life for one lousy mistake." Daniel tried to reason with her.

Tamera listened to her husband but the words were not sinking in. She was distracted by a flood of emotions and being torn in every direction by Nicholas, by Daniel and by Steven.

"If you don't ease up on him, we will lose him. Children tend to live up or down to the expectations of their parents. Treat him like a criminal, he'll be one. Is that what you want?"

"Of course not," Tamera spoke in an indignant whisper. She looked at the ground and bit her tongue.

"Then back off." Daniel took Tamera by the shoulders and tried to force her to look at him. "Nicholas is beginning to think you don't love him anymore. Is that what you want?"

"No." Tamera looked up at Daniel, at his kind, gentle face framed by his dark brown hair. "I just-. It's just that-." Tamera stammered not being able to find the words.

"What? What is it?" Daniel tried to encourage her. He knew that for the passed couple of months she had been very edgy and moody. He knew something was bothering her but he could not tell what it was. When ever he had tried to bring up the conversation, she did not want to talk about it. Now, maybe she would.

"I'll try," Tamera nodded.

"That's all I'm asking." Daniel put his arms

around his wife and gave her a gentle yet firm hug. He realized she was not going to talk anymore. Her secret was going to stay hidden for a bit longer. "I love you, Tam cat." Daniel kissed her forehead.

"I love you, too, Danny." She smiled up at him and kissed him.

"Let's get back to the family." Daniel turned and walked arm in arm with his wife back toward the table.

Off in the distance Tamera spotted Nicholas alone sitting under a tree. She released Daniel's arm.

"I'll be right back," she told Daniel and left him at the table.

Nicholas watched his mother approach but he did not stand up. He kept snapping a twig between his fingers and watched the pieces fall to the ground between his legs.

"Nick, honey," Tamera spoke softly. "I'm sorry I've been so hard on you. I just love you so much. You do understand that don't you?"

Nicholas looked up. "Yeah, I guess."

"Come here." Tamera held out her hand. Nicholas dropped the rest of the twig and stood up. Tamera hugged him and kissed his cheek then looked him in the eyes. "I know I've been hard on you, but I do love you," she repeated. "Come on, let's go eat."

Nicholas smiled faintly and looked down as they walked over to the table.

Ruth and Patricia set the plates and hamburger buns down on the picnic table. She smiled as she looked around the table at her children and grandchildren. Her eyes stopped when she looked at Steven. He sat quietly next to Bradley blindly staring off into nothing.

"Okay everyone, line up over here to get your hamburgers," Carl called out in a loud voice.

As everyone rose and grabbed a plate, Ruth leaned over to whisper into Steven's ear. "You look tired, honey. I'll get your dinner. You rest, all right?"

"All right." Steven repeated. He blinked and nodded his head. "Mom," Steven called before she could turn away. "Do you have a second?"

"Sure, dear," she smiled.

Steven slowly and unsteadily rose to his feet. Ruth took his hand and walked with him to a quiet tree away form the rest of the family.

Still holding his hand, she looked at her son. His face was pale beneath his brown hair and reddish brown mustache. A couple of premature gray streaks accented his temples and made him look more like his father. Tiny beads of sweat dotted his forehead. She wiped them away with her fingertips as she remembered the sensitive little boy from so long ago. He had always cared so much for everyone in the family. Always the one everyone could count on for a shoulder to cry on or a listening ear, even for her. Her heart ached as she looked at him now.

"Are you okay, honey?"

Steven looked at his mother but could not think.

"I don't know," he said softly. "My head hurts a bit. I think I've been in the sun too long."

"Well, if you need to rest, why don't you go upstairs and lie down on your bed for awhile?"

"No, it'll pass and I'll be fine." Steven took a deep breath and began to sound more confident. The pain in his head eased for a moment. "Mom, I know this has been really hard for you, my asking you to keep my secret. I just want you to know that I'm sorry for putting you through this. Truly, I am."

Ruth took a deep breath and looked away from her son to fight the lump that rose in her throat. She smiled an unsteady smile as she looked back at him.

"Steven, I'm trying to understand, but this is not an easy thing for any parent to accept and have to deal with." Her eyes began to tear. "But, I love you so very much and I'm trying."

"I know, Mama." Steven's throat tightened as he fought back his own tears. "I'm sorry."

"It's not your fault, son. You didn't have a choice in this." Ruth reached out to him and hugged him close to her heart. "Sometimes, we just have to accept what we are handed. It's hard but we will get through this."

"I love you, Mama." A tear fell from Steven's eyes and he quickly wiped it away as he pulled back and stood in front of his mother. As he stood there struggling to hold onto his composure his thoughts raced trying to find words.

Ruth noticed that there was something going on in his mind. She was curious as to what, but she remained silent allowing him time to tell her in his own way.

"Mom," he began slowly and then stopped. He looked at the ground avoiding eye contact with her. "Did you ever do something that you wish you didn't? I mean, that you wish you could change?"

Ruth looked at him confused. "Well, I guess just about everyone has made mistakes but it's all part of growing up."

"No. It wasn't a mistake exactly." Steven shook his head. "Remember when I was away at college?"

"Oh, heavens," Ruth smiled. "That was nearly

seventeen years ago. Sure, I remember. Why?"

Steven continued to look at the ground and struggle with his thoughts. The pain in his head returned with bigger force.

"Oh, never mind," he shrugged. "It doesn't matter now. Just foolish thinking." Steven looked around. "I wonder what's keeping Patty."

Ruth looked at her son sharply. Her smile instantly gone.

"Steven, she's right over there. She arrived a few minutes ago. She carried out the plates, don't you remember?"

Steven's expression was blank.

"Oh, okay," he nodded, not really seeing anyone, the pain had become more intense. The tiny beads of sweat reappeared on his forehead. His mouth was slightly open as he tried to catch his breath.

Ruth's heart began to race as she looked at her son. She felt so helpless.

"Steven!" She spoke sharply.

He continued to struggle with his breath.

"Steven," Ruth repeated and put her arm around him tightly. She could feel him tremble and then he relaxed and shook his head.

"What is it? What's the matter? Are you okay?" She barraged him with questions excitedly.

"I'm fine," Steven smiled to put her mind at ease. "I just couldn't seem to catch my breath. That's all. I'm okay now but I think I should sit down."

"Okay." Ruth nodded warily and wiped the sweat beads from his forehead again. "I love you." She smiled as she kissed his cheek. "Come on, dinner is waiting."

"Hey you two," Carl called out from the head of the picnic table as Ruth and Steven returned to the group. "Where have you been? Your burgers are getting cold."

"Just talking." Ruth smiled. "I need to go into the house for a second. I'll be right back."

Carl kissed her cheek as she passed by him.

"Is everything all right?" He whispered.

Ruth looked over at Steven as he sat down at the table. A concerned look came over her as she shrugged.

"I don't know." She tugged on his arm to get him to step back from the table, away from the family. Then she whispered into his ear. "There's something troubling him that happened, from what I can gather, when he was back East at college."

"But that was a long time ago." Carl looked at Steven but kept his voice soft. "What is it?"

"I don't know." Ruth shrugged. "He stopped before telling me. I'm sure he'll tell us when he's ready. Well, I'll be right back."

"Don't be long," Carl said and took a bite of his burger.

"Mom," Bradley called haltingly to her and then looked back at Amanda. "You sure it's okay?"

Amanda nodded. Bradley kissed her cheek and then smiled proudly.

"Before you go, Amanda and I have an announcement to make. I'm lousy at keeping secrets and especially this one." He smiled again at Amanda. She feigned a smile back.

Ruth stepped over to Carl's side again and put her arm around his thin waist. Carl smiled at her.

"Go ahead, Brad," she encouraged anticipating the announcement.

"Well," Bradley put his arm around Amanda. "Amanda and I are going to add one more Wallace to our family."

"What kind of announcement is that supposed to be?" Morgan scoffed.

"Amanda is pregnant, stupid," he said bluntly. "We're having another baby."

Morgan glared at Bradley and turned around and walked away as the table erupted in chatter. Everyone began to congratulate Amanda and Bradley at once.

Ruth watched Morgan for a moment then turned her attention back to Amanda. She could tell Amanda was not as excited about having a baby as Bradley. Her feigned smile seemed so obvious to Ruth. Still Amanda tried to put up a front, if only for Bradley.

Ruth tugged on Carl's arm again.

"I think we're in for some rough times with Amanda," she whispered.

"What?" Carl looked at her confused.

"Look at her plate." Ruth motioned with her head toward Amanda's plate. There untouched lay a sliver of a carrot stick, a few small pieces of lettuce and a small stock of celery. "We had a little talk earlier today and she seems to be preoccupied about her weight and the idea of getting fat."

Carl looked at Amanda's plate and then back at Amanda. "Oh for crying out loud! As if we don't have enough to deal with already," he sighed. "You don't think she could be anorexic, do you?"

"I don't know that much about it, but what I do know is if she isn't, she's on her way and the baby is the one that will suffer." Ruth kept her eyes on Amanda.

"It's funny." Carl shook his head. "Bradley talked to me about this very thing earlier too. He said he was concerned about her. I suggested he talk to her, but I guess I'll have to have another talk with him."

"Not today, dear." Ruth gave his had a gentle squeeze. "Let them enjoy this moment. We'll have plenty of time later to talk to them. Well, I have to go in the house and check on the dessert, strawberry pie with fresh whipped cream."

"Oh boy." Carl smiled and watched her walk back to the house.

"So, when's the baby due?" Ariel spoke over the din of the ongoing chatter.

Bradley looked at Amanda and laughed. "I was so happy, I forgot to ask. When is our little bundle of joy due?"

Amanda smiled politely at Ariel. "The first of February."

"Oh, that's wonderful," Ariel cooed and put her head on Mark's shoulder. "I can't wait until Mark and I have a baby. I think it will be so cool to be a mom."

Morgan, who was now standing behind Ariel, choked on her lemonade spiked with vodka that she had snuck in inside her purse. She tried to cover up when she saw everyone looking at her.

"Those darned ice cubes get me every time."

Ariel ignored her and continued to cuddle Mark's arm. She was used to her mother's jabs. She knew all too well how her mother felt about Mark and this whole wedding thing but she did not care. She was happy that finally she would be free of her mother and her mood swings. Lately living with her had become a real hell for Ariel. She used to wonder why her mother never had any other children. Perhaps if she had she would not be so controlling. Perhaps her aunt Tamera could shed some light on the subject. Ariel made a mental note to ask her later.

"So, Benji." Steven smiled across the table at his nephew seated next to Amanda. "What do you think about having a new baby brother or sister?"

Benjamin just smiled and kicked his feet as he continued to nibble on his hamburger.

"I'm really happy for you two." Steven looked up at his younger brother. Steven was proud of the way that Bradley had grown into a responsible husband and father. When they were younger, Steven had his doubts due to the type of girls Bradley would bring home but that all changed when he met Amanda. Steven only wished he could find the right words to tell him.

"Well, one of these days it'll be your turn." Bradley smiled at him. "The only problem is, we have to find you a wife first."

"Yeah." Steven smiled and looked over at Tamera. As their eyes met, her smile faded. Without a word she pushed her plate away and left the table. Steven watched her in silence.

Patricia, who had been sitting silently taking in the conversations and how everyone was interacting, stood up from the table and headed into the house to find Ruth.

"So, you seem pretty quiet, Chuck." Daniel changed the subject. "How's that job down at the mill going?"

"Oh, it's going." Chuck nodded and took another drink from his glass. "I've been offered a job as a long haul driver. It means more money, way more, but it means I'd be gone weeks on end. Now that Ariel is going to be moving out soon, I don't know what to say."

"Oh, that's a hard one to call," Daniel teased. He and Chuck were good friends despite the fact that neither Tamera or Morgan liked each other. Truth be told, they barely tolerated each other's presence. "Is the pay really that much more?"

"In a word," Chuck paused playfully. "Yes. A whole lot more." He grinned.

"Then why don't you just take it!" Morgan snapped and threw her plate on the table. She glared at her husband as she turned around and stormed off.

"Oops." Daniel ducked his head as he watched Morgan head for the swing set. "I didn't mean to start any trouble." He apologized.

"Don't worry." Chuck brushed it off and smiled as he stood up to follow her. "She's been really moody lately, with the wedding plans and all. Women stuff."

"I hear you." Daniel nodded and watched Chuck hurry after Morgan.

"I think I'll take Benji inside and clean him up. It's about time for his nap," Amanda announced. "Come on, honey." She took away his napkin and wiped his face before picking him up.

"You can put him in Patty's old bedroom," Carl called after her. "Well, Nick, you've been awfully quiet. You feeling okay?" Carl sat down next to his grandson.

"Yeah," he shrugged. "I've just been doing a lot of thinking. That's all."

"About what?" Carl tried to pursue the strained conversation.

Nicholas looked around the table at everyone staring

at him. He quickly looked down and shook his head.

"Nothing. I really don't want to talk right now, Grandpa. I'm sorry." He quickly stood up and headed for the house.

Carl watched Nicholas for a moment and then turned to the rest of the family at the table.

"Well, this little party is falling apart fast," he teased. "I hope it wasn't my cooking."

"No, Dad." Bradley spoke up as he looked around the table at the empty chairs. "It's something else."

Steven tried not to look up at him.

Morgan leaned against the oak tree with her back to the house and family. Chuck walked up to her and stood silently at her side.

"That was just brilliant." Morgan began in a disgusted tone.

Chuck set his jaw firmly. He hated the way she always put him on the defensive, making him out to be the bad guy; especially since he had done nothing wrong.

"What are you talking about?" He came back at her with the same tone.

"I thought we had an agreement that we wouldn't tell the family until after Ariel's wedding. I should have know you couldn't be trusted."

"Just what did you mean by that crack?" Chuck was not backing down, not this time.

Morgan turned around to face him. Her brown eyes were fixed angrily on him.

"You know full well what I'm talking about," she hissed in a lower tone so that the family would not hear. "You lied to me about fooling around with that tramp at work."

As Chuck looked at her, he suddenly relaxed and gave a disbelieving laugh.

"Oh, you are a fine piece of work yourself, Morgan." He shook his head and then set his jaw again. "I wouldn't have fooled around as you put it, if I hadn't caught you and that college boy that you were supposed to be tutoring. Did he get his problems worked out?"

Morgan looked at him. Suddenly she felt the loss of control in this argument and that made her uneasy. She was used to always being on the offensive side ever since she was a child. This was a new feeling for her and she did not like it. Without warning, she slapped Chuck's face. His head snapped at the impact but he quickly recovered.

"That's good," he smirked. "The only problem, my dear wife, is that you were supposed to be tutoring him in grammar!" Chuck slapped her with his words. "Oh, and as for the family, you don't have to worry. I didn't tell them anything. They still think that we are happily married. So your precious image hasn't been tarnished." Chuck finished.

Morgan did not say a word. For the first time, she was totally void of a comeback. Slowly she turned away and stared blindly into the distance.

"Well, aren't you even going to thank me for that?" Chuck softened his tone but continued his jabs.

Morgan remained silent.

"Honestly, I don't understand you." Chuck shook his head and ran his hand over his short dark brown hair in frustration. Morgan's silence was beginning to stir guilt feelings in him and that angered him. "I didn't want to fool around on you, Morgan, but how was I supposed to feel catching the two of you as I did? For god's sake, Morgan, you were in our bed. Do you know how much that hurt me? Do you even care?"

"You still don't get it, do you?" Morgan spoke calmly. The hostility gone from her voice. "You shut me out of your life years ago. You put your job first. You had no time for me let alone Ariel. I practically had to raise her on my own . I spent days without anyone to talk to. You weren't there and then Ariel was off doing this and that. So when this young man showed an interest in me, well, I felt alive again."

"I was working to buy you that big house and all that furniture you said you desperately needed." Chuck felt his anger leave and his heart aching to hold his wife in his arms and tell her he was sorry.

"The only thing I ever wanted, ever needed was you. I just wanted to spend time with my husband. That's all." Morgan turned around to face him. Tears had filled her eyes, not the fake ones she had used on him many times before; this time they were real. He gently wiped them away.

"I'm sorry I hurt you. I didn't mean to," she apologized and reached out to him. He held her tightly in his strong arms as she sobbed into his chest.

"All I want is you, too." He kissed the top of her head. "I'm sorry, babe. I know, what do you say after this wedding is over the two of us take a vacation alone. We can go where ever you want. It'll be like starting over, a second honeymoon. How does that sound?"

"That sounds wonderful." Morgan looked up into his brown eyes and smiled. "I love you, Chuck."

He smiled and kissed her as though for the first time.

"Mom," Patricia spoke softly as she sat down at the kitchen counter.

Ruth turned around. She placed the second chilled strawberry pie on the tray.

"What's on your mind?" She asked but continued to ready the dessert.

Patricia watched her mother as she opened the refrigerator to get the whipped cream. She noticed how Ruth avoided eye contact with her and how nervous she seemed.

"Mom, what's going on here? Everyone is acting strangely. Bradley and Amanda, Morgan and Chuck, Tamera and Dan; even Steven is acting a bit differently."

Ruth kept her back to Patricia. Right now she did not care for the profession her daughter had chosen. It was like having a detective around, studying every move, every word spoken. Ruth took a deep breath and turned around, closing the refrigerator door.

"I don't know. Now, come on let's go have dessert."

Patricia was not convinced but she would wait. Maybe in time it would all work out.

Tamera walked back to the picnic table and looked around.

"Where's Nick?"

"He just went for a walk." Daniel took her hand. "It's okay. He's just wanting to think. He'll be fine."

"If you say so." Tamera sighed out loud, too tired to keep fighting.

"I do. Now, sit down here with the family for a while." He pulled gently on her arm. She let herself slip into the chair beside him.

"Well, look what we have here," Ruth announced as she, Patricia and Amanda walked up to the table. "Who wants dessert?"

"I'll cut it, Mom." Patricia volunteered and counted the heads around the table.

"Thank-you," Ruth sighed and sat down next to Carl. She was grateful to have a moment to rest. He gently rubbed her back.

"Benji is sound asleep." Amanda kissed Bradley's cheek as she sat down next to him at the table. "I still can't get over how much he has grown. It seems like only yesterday he was just a baby." She smiled and put her hand on her stomach.

"Well, soon you'll have another little bundle to care for and believe me, you thought you had your hands full already." Ruth said playfully.

"I welcome the challenge." Amanda smiled to herself. For the first time, she meant it and was happy at the thought of being pregnant. "I can't wait until this one is born. Nothing compares to the smell of a baby."

"I guess that's one of those parent things," Steven teased and pinched his nose.

"Oh, you." Amanda laughed and threw a wadded up napkin at him. "Just you wait. Someday it'll be your turn and boy, will you pay."

Ruth and Carl cast a silent look at Steven.

"Yeah." Steven feigned a smile. "Someday. Oh, none for me, Patty." He turned to his sister and held up a halting hand as she tried to give him a slice of pie. "I've got to go lay down for a while. My head is really hurting." He looked over at Ruth. "Mom, come wake me up in a few minutes?"

"Sure," Ruth nodded. "Do you want me to go with you now?"

"No. I'm okay, really. It's just another one of those stupid headaches coming on. I'll take a couple aspirin and a short nap. I'll be fine." Steven reassured her with a smile.

"Okay, dear." Ruth gave his hand a gentle squeeze then let go. "I love you," she said softly.

"I love you, too." Steven kissed her cheek.

"You have a nice rest, son," Carl added as Steven started toward the house.

"I will," He called back without turning around.

Amanda, Bradley and Patricia watched Steven disappear into the house. All three turned and looked at Ruth and Carl. They saw the concerned looks on their faces. Bradley looked at Amanda as if asking her what was going on. She shrugged. They looked at Patricia. She shook her head and set down the pie server.

"All right, this has gone on long enough," she spoke up in an authoritative voice. "There is something going on here that you are not telling us." She looked directly at her parents and sat down.

Ruth cast a quick look at Tamera as if to ask for help. The look did not go unnoticed.

"That does it." Bradley was becoming irritated. "What is going on here?"

"Tamera, do you know what this is about?" Daniel asked his wife as he himself became concerned.

"I don't know what you're all talking about." Tamera slammed her hands down on the table as she stood up and hurried off to the front yard. Daniel watched her leave and now was confused.

"Mom, Dad, please." He looked at Ruth and Carl. "We have a right to know why we were asked here?"

"I can't do this anymore." Ruth looked at Carl. Tears filled her eyes. "I know I promised Steven, but enough is enough."

"What's wrong with Steven?" Patricia looked at her mother in shock.

Ruth continued to look at Carl. He looked around the table at his family's concerned and worried faces. He looked back at Ruth and nodded silently.

Nicholas nervously approached the closed bedroom door. With a deep breath he knocked lightly and waited for a response. Silence. His heart pounded in his chest. His hands sweat with nervousness. What was he going to say? How was he going to bring up the conversation? He slowly pulled out the folded paper from his pocket and stared at it. Will Steven be angry? Will his mother? She had told him not to talk to Steven about it. He wanted to turn and leave, but he had to know the reason why it was such a big secret. He folded the paper back up and tucked it away.

"Uncle Steven?" Nicholas called as he knocked again.

"It's open. Come in," Steven called faintly from inside.

Slowly Nicholas opened the door and stepped inside the bedroom. The shades were drawn to block out the afternoon sunlight, but still the room was filled with a soft honey glow. Steven sat up on one elbow as he lay on his bed.

"What is it, Nick?" He asked.

"Can I talk to you for a second?" His voice was

sheepish.

"Sure. Grab that chair by the desk and pull it around. What's on your mind?" Steven sat up on the bed and rubbed his forehead.

Nicholas pulled the chair around to face Steven and sat down. He rubbed his hands together and kept looking at the floor. "I've been doing a lot of thinking today."

"I've noticed," Steven nodded. "Is everything okay?"

"Not really." He shrugged. "Ever since this thing with the mall happened, Mom seems to be on my case for everything. I feel really bad about what happened. I know that taking that disc was wrong and I told her that I am sorry. I just don't think she believes me."

"Yeah," Steven nodded. "I know she has been hard on you, but she does love you very much. She doesn't want to lose you, too." Steven reached out and stroked Nicholas' hair. "Your mother has had it pretty rough in her life. Try to go easy on her and be patient with her for me?"

"I guess." Nicholas reluctantly agreed. "But why won't she believe me?"

Steven smiled and thought for a moment.

"Maybe you have to do more than tell her. Maybe you have to show her. Take a look at yourself in the mirror." He nodded toward the mirror on the dresser beside them.

Nicholas looked at his reflection.

"So?"

"Would you honestly believe that that person is sorry for shoplifting? Take a look at your hair. The way you're dressed. Does that reflect someone who has truly changed? I know I probably sound old fashioned, but I have been there; well not exactly there, but I went through a long hair stage myself. The point is, you have to let the person you are inside show through on the outside. Otherwise you are sending a mixed signal."

Nicholas did not say a word. At first he felt defensive about what his uncle was saying, but then he began to think about it and it made sense.

"Nick, if you want to convince your mother you've changed, show her. You'll be surprised at the outcome." Steven smiled again. This time Nicholas smiled back.

"I will," he nodded.

"Good." Steven smiled to himself as the pain in his head increased. "Nick, I really need to lay down for a while."

"Okay." Nicholas stood up and put the chair back. As he started for the door he stuck his hand in his pocket and felt the paper. His heart began to pound again and he stopped and turned back. "Uncle Steven?"

Steven lay back on one elbow again and squinted as the pain persisted.

"Is there something else?"

"Kind of." Nicholas started back into the room and pulled out the paper. "This afternoon I was sitting in your car and, well, I found this paper." He unfolded the paper to show Steven.

Steven recognized it immediately. "I see," he said flatly. "Have you said anything to anyone?"

"No," Nicholas quickly answered. "Well, I started to tell Mom but she said she already knew and that you wanted to keep it a secret."

Steven realized Tamera did not know this secret and released a shaky breath.

"Thank-you."

"Uncle Steven," Nicholas spoke softly. "Why keep it a secret?"

"I guess," Steven looked at his nephew and shrugged. "It's just that it happened so long ago. I was in college and it was my last year. A group of us flew to Las Vegas to celebrate. We got drunk and did some pretty stupid things. This was one of them. It can even happen to grown ups, Nick. We all can do pretty stupid things sometimes."

Nicholas nodded trying to understand.

"Here. You better have this." He reached out the paper to Steven.

"No." Steven put up a halting hand. "You can keep it. When ever you feel like you are alone, pull it out and look at it. It will remind you that even your Uncle Steven did some pretty stupid things."

Nicholas nodded and half smiled.

"Do you ever wonder what would have happened -"

"Sometimes," Steven interrupted him. "But, it's too late for that." The pain was intense. "Go. Please."

Nicholas nodded and folded the paper and put it back in his pocket. He turned around just before closing the door.

"I love you, Uncle Steven."

Steven lay quietly on the bed. Still.

Nicholas closed the door.

"So, there you are." Daniel walked up to the front door steps.

Tamera did not respond. She continued to stare blindly across the street. Her thoughts kept going back to when she and Steven were children. The time they built the snowman in the front yard and dressed it up in Carl's new hat and scarf. They sure caught the dickens. Then the time they were fired from picking blackberries one summer because they kept laughing too much. Steven had always been able to make her laugh no matter what the situation, but not this time.

"Why didn't you tell me?" Daniel asked and slipped his arm around her.

"It wouldn't have done any good. There's nothing anyone can do about it. It's just one of those things." Tamera shrugged as though giving up.

"Maybe so, but at least I would have understood what's been bothering you. We could have faced this thing together." Daniel turned her around to face him. "I know how close you and Steven are. This news is not the kind of thing you can keep bottled up inside. I make a pretty good listener, too, you know."

Tamera did not say a word. She could not. A lump tightened in her throat as tears welled up in her blue eyes. She fell into Daniel's arms and cried.

"I love him so much, Dan. It hurts so much."

"I know," He said and held her.

The front door opened beside them. Daniel looked up but Tamera did not. She continued to cry on his chest. Nicholas froze in the doorway when he saw his parents.

"What's wrong?" He asked as he looked at his mother.

"Nothing," Tamera sighed and straightened up and wiped the tears from her eyes. "Where have you been?"

"Well, I," Nicholas stammered and then decided to tell the truth even if he were to get in trouble. "I was just upstairs talking to Uncle Steven," he answered softly as he closed the front door behind him. "I needed to talk to him about the -" He looked at his father then back at Tamera. "You know."

"I thought I told you not to." Tamera snapped then just as quickly caught herself.

"I know you did." Nicholas looked at the ground for a moment. "But, Mom, I had to. I just don't understand how this could have been kept a secret for so long. Oh, I'm sorry." Nicholas looked at this father in horror at spilling the beans.

"It's all right, son." Daniel put a reassuring hand on his shoulder. "I know."

"You do?" Nicholas looked at him surprised.

"Yes. Your grandmother just filled us all in on what is going on."

"Oh, that's a relief," Nicholas sighed and then thought for a moment. "You know, I think we should throw him a party."

"What?" Tamera looked up at Nicholas in shock.

"Yeah, a party." Nicholas looked at her.

"Oh, Nicholas, how could you say such a thing?" Tamera snapped angrily. "This is not the time for a party."

"But-" Nicholas looked at her confused.

"Your mother is right, Nick. That was a very insensitive thing to say," Daniel added. "I think you better not say that in front of your grandparents."

"I don't understand. You guys had one. I've seen the pictures. I don't see why Uncle Steven shouldn't have one."

"Nicholas, I don't want to hear another word from you." Tamera shook her head in disbelief at her son's coldness.

"I give up." Nicholas looked at his parents and shook his head. "I just can't win with either one of you. Nothing I say is ever right." With that, Nicholas ran off clutching the paper in his coat pocket.

Tamera watched him disappear around the corner of the house and sighed.

"I just don't know what's gotten into that boy."

A hush hung over the picnic table as Bradley, Amanda, Patricia, Ariel and Mark took in the news. Ruth looked at her family and held tightly to Carl's hand. She wondered if she had done the right thing in telling them, but she could not ignore the feeling of relief that grew inside her. It actually gave her a second wind, a burst of strength.

"I don't know what to say." Bradley stared in disbelief. "How could he have kept this a secret from us all this time.?"

"You would have thought we would have had some clue before now," Patricia added.

"So, that is the reason this reunion was so important to him." Amanda realized out loud as she leaned against Bradley for support.

"Yes." Ruth nodded in acknowledgement. "But you can't let on that you know. Steven would be very upset if he knew that we told all of you."

"I can't believe you kept this a secret for this long, Mom." Patricia looked at her mother in concern. "This isn't the sort of thing that would be easy to not talk about. It must have been rough for both of you." She looked sympathetically at her father.

Carl looked at the table with tear filled eyes. He tried not to think about it for so long. Avoiding admitting it to himself totally. Not wanting to think that far ahead, but now, he was. He hated that feeling, that pain in his chest.

"So, what's up?" Nicholas said as he walked up to the table and looked at all the sullen faces.

Ariel looked up at him.

"Grandma just told us about Uncle Steven," she said.

"Isn't it neat." Nicholas smiled and tried to lighten the heavy mood, much to the surprise of everyone at the table.

Ariel jumped to her feet and slapped him across the face.

"No, it isn't neat and it's nothing to joke about." She burst into tears as she ran off around the house to the front yard.

Mark looked around for a moment then silently hurried after her.

Ruth looked at her grandson angrily. She could not believe he had said such a thing.

"What?" Nicholas looked at their angry faces. "Did I say something wrong?"

"I need to go check on Benji." Amanda stood up to break the silent tension. "Mom, do you want me to check on Steven?"

"No." Ruth looked at her daughter-in-law. "I'll let him rest a bit longer. Oh, don't forget to put the child gate up. It's in Steven's closet, so be quiet, please."

"Okay." Amanda kissed Bradley on his furry cheek and headed off toward the house.

"It would be so easy for Benji to fall down those stairs." Ruth thought out loud. "I don't think I could take much more today."

"That goes double for me," Bradley agreed. "What an emotional roller coaster. First the news about the baby and then this. It almost makes me feel guilty about being happy today."

Nicholas sat down at the table and continued to look at the faces of his family. He could not understand why everyone was so upset over the news about Steven. This should be a happy time. Why were they all so sad?

Patricia looked beyond Bradley at Morgan and Chuck in the distance. They were still hugging and kissing each other by the swing just like two love struck teenagers.

"Do you suppose we should tell Morgan and Chuck?" She asked and motioned with her head in their direction.

"Not now." Carl looked and shook his head. "There's plenty of time to tell them later. They've had enough of a rough time already. Let them have their moment to patch things up."

"Yeah, I guess you're right," Patricia agreed and looked back at Nicholas. "So, you seem to be taking all of this well."

Nicholas looked up at his aunt as she sat on the back of her wooden lawn chair.

"Oh, just leave me alone," he mumbled and jumped to his feet and headed for the house.

Patricia stood up to follow him but Ruth grabbed her arm.

"Let him go," she said haltingly. "He's been acting kind of different today. Give him some space."

Suddenly a scream came from inside the house. Instantly everyone at the table froze in shock.

Bradley jumped to his feet.

"Ohmygod, Benji!" He ran for the back door practically knocking Nicholas to the ground as he pushed passed him.

Ruth looked at Carl as a wave of panic came over her. They both jumped to their feet and headed for the house.

"Please, God, not today," Ruth whispered out loud to herself as she ran into the house.

"Amanda!" Bradley called out, his voice echoing ahead of him. As he entered the foyer, Daniel and Tamera entered through the front door followed by Ariel and Mark. Bradley's heart pounded in his chest and his throat tightened as he turned toward the stairs.

"Amanda!" He screamed as he started up the stairs. Suddenly, he froze on the steps as he saw Amanda standing in the open doorway of Steven's room.

"Oh, God, no!" Carl choked and yelled as his eyes filled with tears instantly. "Steven!" He screamed in a raspy hoarse voice. He cleared the stairs in three leaps and stood in the doorway. Ruth was right beside him as he entered the bedroom.

"Oh, God, not my boy. Not my boy." Carl's heavy sobs echoed throughout the house. Slowly he fell to his knees beside the bed.

Steven lay quiet. Motionless. His hands were cold as Carl took them in his. Tears fell uncontrolled. Carl's chest heaved as he sobbed out loud.

Ruth reached down and felt Steven's cold wrist for a pulse. Slowly she reached up and stroked his hair. A single, silent tear fell from her eyes as she looked at her son.

"Oh, Steven, my baby," she whispered then bent

down and kissed his lifeless forehead. "I love you."

Downstairs, in the foyer, Morgan and Chuck looked around at everyone confused.

"What's going on? Who screamed?"

Amanda looked up from Bradley's arms at her sister-in-law.

"Steven is dead," she choked then buried her face in Bradley chest and sobbed.

"What?" Morgan looked disbelievingly at her. "You liar," she hissed. "This isn't funny."

"It's true, Morgan." Daniel spoke up as he hung up the telephone receiver from calling the ambulance. "Steven found out months ago that he had an inoperable brain tumor. The doctors told him last month he only had a few days left."

"No." Morgan said flatly and turned her face away from him and looked at him out of the corner of her eyes. "You are lying." Morgan slowly moved toward the stairs, not taking her eyes off Daniel.

"You're all lying!" She screamed and darted up the stairs.

"Morgan," Chuck called as he reached out for her and missed.

Tears filled her eyes and blurred her vision of her parents standing by Steven's bed. "No." Her voice was a faint whisper as she collapsed against the threshold and cried.

Carl walked over to her and helped her to her feet.

"It's okay," he whispered to her as he guided her back down the stairs.

"Chuck," Carl said almost as though a question as they reached the foyer.

"I'll take her, Dad." Chuck took Morgan in his

arms and helped her into the parlor.

"I've got to call the ah-" Carl fumbled for the word. "Ah-"

"Dad, I've already called the ambulance and they are on their way." Daniel put his arm around his suddenly frail and vulnerable father-in-law.

Carl immediately grabbed him and sobbed uncontrollably and out loud.

"No. No. No." He kept repeating over and over.

Daniel held him tightly and looked across the room. Patricia stood holding onto Ariel and Mark. Their faces all wet with tears. He looked up at the stairs just in time to see Tamera step into Steven's bedroom doorway.

Tamera paused as she saw Ruth stretch a sheet over Steven's lifeless body.

"Mama," she spoke softly. "May I see him, please?"

Ruth turned around with the sheet still in her hands. She looked at her daughter in silence.

"I need to see him." Tamera slowly walked into the room. "I didn't get to tell him good-bye. I-I didn't get to tell him how much I loved him." Tamera crept closer to the bed. "I did love him, Mama. I-I, Mama, no!" Tamera fell into Ruth's arms and cried.

"It's okay, honey." Ruth held her daughter and stared at the wall. "It's okay," she said softly yet firmly. "Steven knew you loved him and he loved you, too."

"He can't be dead, Mama. He can't." Tamera's body trembled with grief.

"Let him go. He's not in pain anymore." Ruth slowly guided Tamera out of the room and back down the stairs.

Ruth slowly closed the front door as the black hearse disappeared down the street. She turned around and leaned against the front door. Her eyes wandered up the stairs to the open bedroom door. The sheet that shrouded Steven hung over the rail. The house seemed cold, quiet, empty. Steven was gone. One moment he was alive, laughing and enjoying the family; the next, he was dead.

She folded her arms over her chest and took a slow deep breath. Her eyes were dry, void of tears. She could not cry. The pain was too deep. Every muscle, every bone in her body ached from the pain, but still no tears. Her son was dead but she could not cry.

Slowly she walked over to the parlor. As she stood in the doorway, she looked at each one of her children. Tamera sat next to Daniel on the love seat under the front window. Bradley quieted Benjamin, gently rocking him back and forth in his arms as he sat on the arm of the old wing back chair where Amanda was sitting. Amanda stared at the coffee table, content to rest her hand on Bradley's back. Morgan stood wrapped in Chuck's arms, resting her head on his chest silently crying. Ariel sat curled up in the chair in front of Ruth. Her shoulders quivered as she quietly cried. Mark stood behind her, feeling lost and out of place as he looked at the floor.

Ruth turned without a word and walked over to the kitchen. Carl stood staring out at the swimming pool. In his mind he kept seeing and remembering the fun he and Steven had splashing about earlier that morning. He was grateful for the memory even though it hurt so much to remember. Quietly he cried.

Ruth slipped her hand in his and stood beside him. He put his head gently against hers and sighed a quivering sigh. The two stood and looked out at the back yard.

"It's going to be okay," Ruth softly assured him. "We are going to be okay."

Nicholas quietly looked about the bedroom at the top of the stairs. The room was dark as evening fast approached. Tears filled his eyes and dampened his cheeks.

"Why?" He cried softly. "Why didn't you tell me, Uncle Steven?"

Slowly he pulled the folded paper out of his pocket. He wiped his nose and tried to dry his tears as he read the large letters at the top of the paper, "Certificate of Marriage." He folded it back up and tucked it away in his pocket and cried.

THE REHEARSAL

A crisp breeze gently blew through the tall oak trees in the front yard. Slowly the colorful autumn leaves drifted down to dot the carefully manicured front lawn. The flower beds that lined the driveway and walk were pruned and ready for the coming winter.

Ruth glanced at the catering truck parked in the street in front of her house as she opened the car door. She looked up at the second story bedroom window as the faint sounds of hammering touched her ears. She sighed outloud to herself and shook her head. While her mind understood, her heart did not. Turning back to the car, she scooped up the packages in her arms and carefully closed the door with her hip.

Juggling the packages to keep from dropping them, she made her way up the front walk to the door. She rang the doorbell with her elbow then stepped back to look up at the bedroom window. The pounding continued. With a heavy sigh, she rang the doorbell again and waited. Nothing.

"Carl." She clinched her teeth as she tried to balance the packages while she dug through her purse for the house key.

"Here, let me help you with that, Mrs. Wallace." A deep voice came up behind her.

Ruth turned around and looked at the thin, tan, dark haired, young man in coveralls.

"Thank-you, Luke," she smiled and handed him the packages. "How are things going out back?"

"Not bad," he nodded and smiled at her politely.

Ruth took her keys out of her purse and quickly unlocked the front door.

"Thank-you, so much. I really appreciate it," she said as she held the door open for him.

"Sounds like Mr. Wallace is tearing the place apart up there." Luke looked up at the open hallway above him as he walked into the foyer.

"That it does." Ruth frowned as she looked up at the closed bedroom door. "You can put those down on the kitchen counter in there." Ruth pointed in the direction of the open doorway. "Thanks again. I'll be out in just a few minutes."

"You're quite welcome, ma'am." Luke nodded and walked into the other room.

Ruth shut the front door the walked over to the table under the stairs. She paused as she set her keys down and looked at the wilted flowers. The sympathy card was still attached. Tears welled up in her eyes and just as quickly disappeared. It had been only three months since Steven's death, yet it seemed like only yesterday. She looked at the rest of the table and noticed that something was missing; however, the constant pounding of the hammer upstairs made it difficult for her to think.

"Carl, what have you done?" She said out loud to herself and shook her head.

Without giving it any more thought, she headed for the kitchen. Just as she was about to leave the foyer, the front doorbell chimed.

"Now, what?" She returned to the front door and opened it.

"Hi, Mom," Morgan greeted her with a smile.

"Well, hello, you two. Come on in," Ruth invited and stepped aside and let her daughter and granddaughter enter.

Morgan ushered Ariel into the foyer ahead of her.

"I really appreciate your letting me stay here tonight, Grandma," Ariel beamed. Her blue eyes sparkled with excitement.

"Don't be silly. You are always welcome here." Ruth smiled warmly and closed the door. "Besides, it only makes sense for you to stay here the night, since the wedding is here tomorrow afternoon. Why don't you take your things upstairs to the guest bedroom then come on in the kitchen. Oh, Patty will be spending the night here too, so you'll have to share the room."

"Thank-you, Grandma." Ariel smiled and started up the stairs.

Morgan and Ruth watched her ascend the open staircase. Suddenly Morgan became aware of the hammering and looked at the closed bedroom door at the top of the stairs.

"What's with all that noise?" She asked in a demanding sort of tone.

"It's your father." Ruth shook her head in disgust. She turned and headed back into the kitchen. "He's been remodeling Steven's bedroom. He said he just couldn't take the constant reminder any longer."

Morgan looked at her mother. She could tell that she was not in agreement about the change.

"I'm sorry."

"Please, I'll be fine." Ruth put out a halting hand. "I hope you're going to give me a hand with cooking tonight. You know, I just can't understand that boy's parents. They have known for months about this wedding. How is it that they won't be here?"

"I don't know," Morgan sighed. "Mark said that his father was called away on business at the last minute and that his mother had to go and help him."

"Well, I know that if it were my son getting married, I would be there," Ruth said matter-of-factly.

"You know, this wedding is fast becoming expensive, with us having to provide the rehearsal dinner too. You would think with all their money they could let go with a little. Afterall, it is their son's wedding too." Morgan began to unpack the grocery bag.

"Well, at least we will make it nice for Ariel." Ruth resigned herself as she took the roast from the refrigerator for the night's dinner. "I hope everyone likes roast beef."

Morgan smiled. She loved her mother's roast beef. It brought back so many nice memories of Sunday dinners around the table when she was growing up. She had not thought about those in years.

"Well, I do," she nodded then thought out loud. "Mom, what happened to the family picture that was on the table in the foyer?"

That is it. That is what is missing. Ruth thought

to herself.

"I don't know," she wondered out loud. "Your father must have done something with it."

"Oh, not this again," Morgan said disgustedly. "You remember when Grandpa Wallace died. Dad went through the house and threw away everything that reminded him of Grandpa. Now, he's doing it again."

"Losing a child is never easy," Ruth spoke firmly not happy with Morgan's lack of empathy. "We all handle our grief differently. Your father will deal with it in his own time and three months is not that long ago."

"True," Morgan sighed and put the groceries away. "I still can't believe he's really gone."

"Tell me about it. It all doesn't make sense." Ruth shook her head. She set the oven temperature and then washed her hands.

"What doesn't make sense?" Morgan paused and watched her mother. Was there something more she had failed to tell her about the day Steven died?

"Oh, I don't know exactly." Ruth shrugged then silently continued to season the roast.

Morgan studied her mother's expression for a moment. She could tell that something was troubling her and it made her more curious.

"What is it?" She prodded.

"Did Steven ever tell you about his college days?" Ruth asked without looking at Morgan.

"Mom, Steven and I rarely talked. If anyone would know about that time in his life, Tamera would. Why?"

"Well, he started to tell me something that afternoon but he stopped short of actually coming out with it. I've already asked the other kids and he hadn't said a word to them. So, I thought that maybe he might have said something to you. That's all." Ruth lifted the roasting pan from the counter and placed it in the oven. The conversation came to an abrupt halt.

Morgan watched Ruth for a moment, her mind wondered what other secrets the family was keeping from her. She shrugged it off and then changed the subject.

"I really appreciate you letting Ariel have her wedding and reception here."

"It's no problem." Ruth picked up the silk flowers on the breakfast nook table and began to arrange them in a vase.

"Ariel has so many memories of our family get-togethers here and of swimming out back in the summer. She thinks of this as her second home. I know it means a lot to her," Morgan continued.

"Actually, I have an ulterior motive for wanting it here. I want to have a happy memory of a family gathering here to think about. Our last one didn't turn out exactly as I would have liked."

A silence came over the kitchen as Ruth continued to arrange the flowers and Morgan went about preparing the rest of the night's dinner.

"Hello," Amanda called as she opened the back door.

Ruth turned around and smiled at her pregnant daughter-in-law. Amanda had her long dark brown hair tied back with a silk scarf that matched her smock. As she walked over to them, she moved with a slight waddle.

"So, how's it going out there?" Ruth glanced out at the canopy covering the backyard.

"So far, so good." Amanda nodded. "They would

like you to come out if you have a second or two. The
caterers want to be sure the tables are how you want
them before they begin putting the chairs out."

"Okay, dear. I'll be right out." Ruth put the last
of the flowers in the vase and cocked her head as she
looked at them. "That should do it. While I'm out
there, would you put this vase on the table in the foyer
for me, Amanda. You can throw out the dead flowers
from Steven's funeral. I think we can do without those
now."

"Sure, Mom." Amanda took the crystal vase of
flowers from Ruth and started off for the foyer.

"Well, Morgan," Ruth sighed heavily. "Let's go
take a look."

The two walked out the back door leaving the
kitchen quiet and empty.

Amanda set the vase of flowers down on the small
table in the foyer. She stretched her back and rolled her
shoulders to ease her tired muscles. She picked up the
vase of dead flowers and turned around to start back to
the kitchen when she froze. Across the foyer, she had
caught a glimpse of herself in a mirror. Slowly she
walked over to it.

As she stood there looking at her reflection, she
gently felt her stomach. Her smile faded as she looked
at her round figure. Suddenly she heard the voice of her
mother echoing in her head, "You're fat. He's going to
leave you, too. All men are alike." A wave of panic
swept through her followed by a flood of emotions.
She even found herself hating the child she was carrying
for causing her to be so big. She tried to hold in her
stomach to flatten her figure, but it was not working.

Just then the front door opened and Bradley walked in.

"Bradley!" Amanda gasped and jumped, nearly dropping the vase of dead flowers.

"Hi, honey." He closed the door behind himself without noticing Amanda's startled expression. He walked over to her and gave her a kiss.

"Mmmm, so how is my lovely wife today?" He breathed as he wrapped his strong arms around her and held her in a firm bear hug.

"Tired," she sighed. "I didn't realize how much work would be involved with helping Mom and Morgan with this wedding."

"Yeah." Bradley nodded. "Well, thank heaven it is almost over." He said flatly. He was not thrilled with the idea of Ariel and Mark getting married, but he did not know why. "So, is that Dad I hear?" Bradley cocked his head and listened to the hammering above them.

"He's been at it all week. I don't know what he's doing up there but whatever it is, I hope he doesn't plan on keeping it up tomorrow."

"I'll go see what he's up to." Bradley released her.

"Well, I've got to get back outside. Let me know when it's time to pick up Benji from the day care," Amanda said as she disappeared into the kitchen.

Bradley turned his attention to the hammering and started up the stairs. Cautiously he opened the bedroom door and peered inside. White chalky dust from the sheets of drywall covered the tarps protecting the carpet on the floor in the empty room.

"So, how's it going, Dad?" Bradley asked softly so as not to startle Carl.

"Don't just stand there." Carl looked over his shoulder as he tried to hold the panel of drywall in place. "Give me a hand, Steven," he said and froze at his own words. "I'm sorry, Brad," he apologized.

"No problem, Dad." Bradley quickly grabbed a hammer from the tool box near the door and a handful of nails and hurried to help lift the last sheet of drywall into place. "What would you have done if I hadn't come along?" He asked playfully.

"I never thought of that." Carl paused and then began to hammer again. Bradley smiled to himself and joined in at the opposite end.

When they were finished, Bradley put his hammer back in the tool box and looked around the bedroom. The familiar pine wood panels were gone. The furniture was gone. There was nothing left to remind them that this was once Steven's bedroom.

"Dad, let's take a break," Bradley suggested almost pleadingly.

"Oh," Carl wiped the sweat from his brow with a heavy exhalation. "I guess I am about due for one. So, what do you think?" Carl looked around the room proudly.

"I guess it's fine." Bradley shrugged. "Dad, I know why you are doing this. It's not going to work."

Carl looked at his son and then looked away. He felt his anger rise inside himself at the sound of those words. It will work. It has to work. He told himself as he bit his tongue.

"I don't know what you're talking about. Your mother has wanted this to be her sewing room for years. I just never got around to it."

"Dad, mother already has a sewing room. It's

Morgan's old bedroom in the basement. This has to do with Steven. You think that by remodeling this room, he will not have existed."

"No." Carl turned around sharply and looked out the window. "It has nothing to do with Steven," he lied more to himself than to Bradley. His words echoed Steven's name in the empty room and then fell to a deafening silence. A flood of emotions bombarded him, love, grief, anger. His shoulders slumped under the unseen weights.

"Yes, it does have to do with Steven," he admitted. "I just can't take remembering him. It hurts too much."

"I know what you mean, Dad." Bradley walked over to his father and put his arm around his shoulders. "I miss him, too. I never really knew how much he meant to me, until now. I don't have a big brother anymore."

"It's more than that, Brad." Carl shook his head. "He didn't tell us everything. There was more."

Bradley looked at his father curiously. "What do you mean? What have you found out?"

"Nothing." Carl shook his head and straightened his back suddenly realizing he had said too much. "Never mind."

"Dad. You can't leave me hanging here." Bradley looked at his father and dropped his arm back to his side. Carl did not look back as he turned and walked over to the door.

"I'm through in here for a while. I need some fresh air." He said and then disappeared down the stairs.

Bradley looked around the room confused at what had just happened. He turned and looked out the window at the front yard.

"Mom," he said out loud to himself as he saw the

catering truck. Without another moment's wait, he turned and hurried out of the bedroom.

Ariel and Morgan stayed back out of the way as Ruth directed the caterers where to move the tables. Morgan smiled to herself as she remembered her wedding and how her mother was so nervous about how everything would turn out. Now, Ruth was confident and calm. Time had certainly changed her.

"Everything is going as planned," Ruth reported as she walked over to them.

"A lot smoother than my wedding," Morgan teased.

"Yes." Ruth smiled. "This time I'm making sure they don't get any chairs near the swimming pool. So, tell Chuck's mother not to worry."

"She'll be happy to hear that," Morgan laughed out loud.

"What's so funny?" Ariel cast a confused look at the two of them.

"Oh, at your mother's wedding, your Grandma Fletcher went to stand up but her chair was too close to the swimming pool. She went over backwards, dress over her head, right into the water." Ruth laughed when she recounted the story. "It wasn't funny then, but now we can laugh."

Morgan laughed as she looked across the swimming pool at the workers. Suddenly, her smile vanished and her heart began to beat faster as she stared at the young worker.

"Mom." Bradley walked over to the small gathering. "Do you have a moment? I really need to talk to you kind of privately." He looked at Morgan who continued to stare across the pool.

She turned around and looked at everyone staring at her.

"What?" She said innocently, trying to keep from blushing at being caught with her thoughts.

"Is something wrong, dear?" Ruth touched Morgan's hand and then looked over at Luke.

"No," Morgan answered a little too eagerly. "Everything's fine."

"Are you sure?" Ruth questioned. She could tell when Morgan was lying.

"Yes," she repeated, annoyed at being questioned. "Come on, Ariel. I want you to try on your dress before everyone else arrives here for the rehearsal."

"Thank-you, Morgan." Bradley smiled at her.

Morgan gave him a confused glare, not sure what he meant by that remark.

"What's on your mind, honey?" Ruth asked and folded her arms over her chest as she continued to look at Luke and the other men move the tables to where she had instructed.

"I had a talk with Dad just now and I'm really confused. I thought you might know what's going on," he began.

"What do you mean?" Ruth turned and gave him her full attention.

"I was just upstairs helping Dad for a second in Steven's room. Did you know he tore out the paneling?" Bradley looked at her with tear filled eyes.

"Yes," she nodded her head. "So?" She tried to encourage him to continue.

"Well, I told him that changing the room wouldn't help him forget Steven. That's when he implied there was something else Steven didn't tell us. Do you know what he's talking about?" Bradley studied his mother's eyes. Her short auburn hair was flipped back away from her face. She looked away from him, avoiding his eyes.

"I'll talk to your father," she finally gave an answer after a long silence. "He's got some strange ideas. Don't worry about it."

"All right," Bradley nodded but his curiosity was not satisfied. He watched Ruth walk over to the canopy in silence.

"Hi, Morgan," Tamera greeted as Morgan opened the front door for her.

"Hi," Morgan returned flatly. "Mom's out back." She offered coldly then headed up the stairs again, leaving Tamera to close the door behind her family.

"What's with her?" Daniel frowned as he looked up the stairs as Morgan disappeared into the guest bedroom.

"Who cares?" Tamera shrugged. "Let's go see what's happening out back."

Before Tamera could say another word, a loud bang from a hammer thundered from upstairs. Tamera jumped and looked up at the open door of Steven's bedroom. Something was different but she did not know what. There seemed to be more light coming out of the room than usual.

"Dan, you both go on. I want to see what's going on upstairs." She did not wait for a reply before heading for the stairs.

"Well, son," Daniel sighed and shook his head. "Here we go again. Come on, let's go out back." He put his arm around his tall, thin teenaged son and the two went their way.

Slowly Tamera approached the open doorway and peered inside. She froze at the sight of the room. Across the room Carl put his hammer in his belt loop and continued to spackle over the nails. He was aware of Tamera behind him. Even with all the dust in the air, he could still smell her perfume, a fresh floral scent mixed with hair spray.

"Dad?" Tamera questioned. "What have you done?"

She was in shock. For as long as she could remember, that room had always been Steven's bedroom. Even when he had moved out after returning from college seventeen years ago, the room had remained Steven's. Everything was just as he had left it. No one else's bedroom had remained like his. Morgan's basement room was converted into a sewing room. Bradley's room was turned back into the attic. Even the bedroom she and Patricia shared was changed.

"What does it look like?" Carl answered with a snap in his voice.

"But this is Steven's room." Tamera protested, still waiting for an answer to help her understand why the sudden need to remodel the bedroom. "Why?"

"This is my house and I will do with it as I see fit." Carl snapped and turned around to face her. "I'm not going to explain myself to you or to your brother. Is that clear?"

Tamera recoiled at Carl's sudden burst of anger. Her eyes immediately welled with tears behind her glasses. She opened her mouth as though to speak in her own defense but turned around and ran from the room as the tears fell.

Carl stood his ground with his teeth clinched. Slowly he looked around the bedroom.

"This is not Steven's room," he said out loud to himself as though expelling the memories from the four walls. Then, just as suddenly as his anger flared, it was gone and his eyes welled with tears. He dropped the putty knife and plastic jar of spackle as he slid down the wall and sat on the floor. "Damn, you, Steven," he breathed. "Why? Why, Steven?" Tears began to streak down his white dusted cheeks. He bowed his head and let them fall.

"Okay, Ariel, let's see what you look like." Morgan said as she stared out the window at the workers in the backyard.

"Mom, are you sure this was measured right?" Ariel asked, squirming as she stepped from behind the antique dressing screen.

"Yes." Morgan answered without looking at her. "All brides feel bloated on their wedding day, so the seamstress made it a little larger. You'll be fine."

Ariel looked at her mother, disgusted at her lack of interest in the dress. She turned and looked at her reflection in the full length mirror that hung on the back of the door. Slowly she ran her hand over her stomach feeling how tight the lace appliqued bodice felt. She turned to look at herself from the side to see if her stomach was noticeable. Her eyes followed the white satin flow of the long skirt and train.

"I can't believe this is actually happening." Ariel stared at her reflection. "I've dreamt about this day ever since I was a little girl." She continued thoughtfully, mesmerized by her reflection. "Somehow, though, I thought it would feel differently. What if I don't really love Mark? Should I still marry him?"

Morgan continued to stare intently at the workers below. She had not heard a word of what Ariel was saying. Her hands began to sweat and her heart pounded nervously as she stared from the window.

"Mother!" Ariel snapped disgustedly. "You haven't heard a word of what I've been saying."

Morgan turned around and faced her daughter for the first time. She instantly forgot about the men working outside as she was captivated by the sight of her little girl.

"You are so beautiful," she gasped. Tears filled her blue eyes. She could not help but smile proudly at her daughter. "I'm sorry, what were you saying?"

The moment was gone for Ariel. She did not want to talk about her fears anymore. Instead she became curious about what was occupying her mother's attention. She walked over to the window and looked out.

"Nothing, Mom." She shrugged then turned around. "Is there something wrong?"

"No. Why?" Morgan fidgeted nervously and then innocently answered.

"Well, you seem to be preoccupied with the caterers." Ariel took another look out the window. "Is something wrong? Do you not like them?" She pried as she stepped away from the window.

"No." Morgan answered too quickly. "I mean," she fidgeted again. "I don't know any of them, so how could I not like them. I'll be down in the kitchen. You get changed."

Before Ariel could say another word, Morgan hurried out the door and shut it behind her. Ariel turned back to the window now more curious than before.

Tamera closed the back door behind her quietly and walked over to Daniel. He stood with his hands deep in his jeans pockets and watched the hub of activity on the other side of the swimming pool. Tamera wiped the tears from her eyes and stared blankly out at the back yard. Daniel turned to her and smiled, not noticing her tears at first. Gently he slipped his hand in hers and gave it a little squeeze.

"So, what's up, Tam cat?" He smiled at her.

"Dad is tearing apart Steven's room," she sighed and a tear fell from her eyes. "I don't know what's gotten into him. When I asked him what he was doing, he snapped at me. He said he wasn't going to explain himself to anyone, anymore. Honestly, he's not acting like himself at all."

"You know," Daniel smiled an understanding sympathetic smile at her. "Losing Steven was hard on him as well as you. Perhaps this is what he felt he had to do. You know as well as I that your father loved Steven. Maybe keeping his room was more than he could bear."

"I know, but still-" Tamera protested.

"Tamera, we all handle our grief differently, you remember." Daniel tried to ease her concerns.

"Yes. I remember." Tamera looked at the ground. "I just don't understand how he could do it. That was the one place when I would come over here where I felt like I could still be close to Steven."

"Did you ever think, it could have been the same for Dad? Maybe that is why he felt he had to do it. To let go. To get on with his life. Losing a child is, no matter how young or old, the hardest thing to face. You know that." Daniel wrapped his arms around her protectively.

Tamera's eyes filled with tears.

"I don't want to forget him." She began to cry.

"You won't. Just like we haven't forgotten about Danny." Tears filled Daniel's eyes as he held Tamera in his arms.

Tamera stopped crying as she remembered that morning so many years ago. She had put her precious little baby boy to bed. He smiled and cooed at her. The twinkle in his big blue eyes. His soft blonde hair. He was so beautiful. Their son. She only left him for a couple of hours. She was so tired. She could not stay awake another minute. She will never forget the moment when she woke and went to check on him. It had been permanently engraved in her memory along with the pains of guilt. He was so cold. His rosy cheeks were blue. The sparkle was gone from his eyes as he stared lifelessly at the ceiling. "I should never have left him. If only I had stayed awake. If only I had stayed with him a little while longer." She had beat herself up for years. Tears fell from her eyes as the memories and guilt came flooding back. She tightened her hold on Daniel and sobbed out loud for her son and for Steven.

"It'll be okay." Daniel gently stroked her blonde hair. "You'll see, in time, everything will be all right."

Nicholas stood back and watched Bradley as he sat quietly in a lawn chair beside the swimming pool. He kept going over in his mind whether or not to talk to his uncle. The two had never been very close over the years. In fact, Bradley had never taken the time to even talk to him in as long as Nicholas could remember. Still, the folded up paper in his pocket was too much for him to keep to himself. He had to talk to someone. Cautiously he approached Bradley.

"Uncle Brad." His voice was steady even though inside he was shaking. He did not know why his uncle made him feel that way, but he did.

Bradley turned his head and looked at his nephew. A smile spread across his face.

"Nick?" He teasingly questioned. "Is that really you? You look great. It's good to see you looking more like a young man."

Nicholas felt his short hair. It had only been a month since he had his long hair cut off. He still was not used to people reacting to it.

"Thanks." He blushed. "Uncle Brad, are you busy?"

"No." Bradley opened his hands as if to say, does it look like it? "Pull up a chair and sit a spell."

Nicholas slid a lawn chair over next to Bradley and sat down. He leaned forward and rubbed his hands together nervously. He had never felt this uncomfortable talking with Steven. That is, except for that one day last summer, but he had good reason then. Now, he was not so sure.

"So, what is on your mind?" Bradley studied his nephew. He would be the first to admit that he did not know Nicholas very well. The two had never really spent much time if any at all together. He did not have an excuse since they both lived only a mile away from each other. His only reason that he could think of now was that he did not like the rebellious direction Nicholas' life seemed to be headed. With his long hair, black clothing and ear ring, Bradley did not want his son, Benjamin, to follow Nicholas' bad example. However, even he knew that was only a cop out. Benjamin was only two. No, the more the thought about it, the more he realized it had more to do with his relationship with Tamera than actually Nicholas himself. He and Tamera were not very close. They were separated by four years and those four years were as insurmountable as leaping the Grand Canyon.

"I just wanted to talk to you about Uncle Steven." Nicholas said cautiously. "That is, if you don't mind."

Bradley felt a wave of anxiety sweep over him at the sound of Steven's name. They may not have been close in age, being only three years apart, but they were close none-the-less. When they were younger, he remembered how he always looked up to Steven. Steven was always popular in school because of his wit and being a good listener. People were drawn to him. They opened up to him. Even in the family. Bradley knew that if he ever needed to talk to someone, Steven was always there ready to listen. Steven seemed to be the glue that held the family together. Sure, Ruth and Carl were there, but it was Steven that kept the peace between the siblings. Now, he was gone. The loss was felt by all and it hurt even three months later.

"Okay." Bradley tried to hide the quiver in his voice with a cough. "What did you want to talk about?"

"I really loved Uncle Steven but sometimes I get so angry with him." Nicholas spoke softly. "I miss him and I know that Mom does too. At night I can hear her crying in her bedroom. I hate seeing her like that and that's what makes me angry. Is that wrong?"

Bradley smiled to himself because he understood

just how Nicholas felt. He had those feelings too at times.

"No, Nick." He shook his head. "Those are the normal feelings. They are part of what people call the grieving process. Death is hard for all of us to understand, let alone accept. One minute the person you love is sitting right beside you laughing and talking and the next-" Bradley bit his lip and turned his head away from Nicholas as he fought back his tears.

"Why does it have to hurt so much?" Nicholas continued.

"I don't know." Bradley looked at him with dampened eyes. "What I do know is that in time, the pain you are feeling will fade away and you will be able to remember your Uncle Steven without the tears." Bradley's words were more for himself than for Nicholas.

"I don't think I'll ever be able to do that," Nicholas sighed and hung his head and took out the paper from his pocket. "There's something more," he said without looking up.

Bradley looked at the folded piece of paper in Nicholas' hands. His curiosity was piqued. He waited for Nicholas to continue.

"The day that Uncle Steven died, he made me promise not to tell anyone about this. I don't know if I should say anything now, but it's too hard to keep it to myself. I don't know what to do." Nicholas fumbled with the paper.

"Nick, I don't think your Uncle Steven would mind you telling now. Whatever it is, it won't hurt him anymore," Bradley urged. He could not help but wonder if this is what his mother and father were not saying.

"Here." Nicholas unfolded the paper. "He gave me this and told me to keep it as a reminder that even he had made some mistakes when he was young." He handed the paper to Bradley.

Bradley took it and eagerly read it. His mouth dropped open as he read the marriage certificate dated nearly seventeen years ago. He had no idea. How could Steven have kept this a secret for so long?

Carl emerged from the dusty upstairs bedroom and wiped the sweat from his brow. The bedroom was now ready to be painted. Soon things would be different, better. The memories that were stored up in those four walls would finally be erased as if Steven had never existed. Everything was going to be all right, Carl nodded to himself proudly and then shut the door.

The house was quiet. The hallway and foyer below were deserted. In the distance Carl could hear the faint sounds of voices in the front yard as he descended the staircase. When he reached the foyer, he glanced into the parlor. His eyes went straight to the portrait of Steven on the mantle above the fireplace. A sudden pain jolted him. He had not erased Steven from the house completely. Slowly he walked over and picked up the framed photograph. Gently he stroked the glass over Steven's face with his thumb. A tear came to his eyes. He shook it away.

"Damn you," he whispered under his breath.

He turned around with the portrait in his hands and walked back into the foyer. He did not notice Morgan standing in the archway to the kitchen. She watched him curiously, silently. He walked over to the coat closet, opened the door and laid the portrait on top of the others on the shelf. He closed the door and gave a silent sigh of relief.

Morgan slowly inched her way into the foyer as she watched Carl disappear into the family room. She tiptoed into the parlor to look at the mantle. Her eyes scanned the many pictures as she tried to figure out which one was missing. She knew in her heart which one it was but she had to see for herself.

Suddenly a shadow that moved across the window overlooking the front yard caught Morgan's attention. Slowly she walked over to the window and drew back the sheer curtain to peer out. Her eyes widened and her heart pounded in her chest as panic and fear filled her whole being. There walking across the front lawn toward the catering truck was Luke. Morgan quickly ran to the front door and threw it open. Luke turned around and smiled as Morgan ran over to him.

"What do you think you are doing here?" Her temper grew with each step closer. "Are you trying to ruin everything?" She snapped.

Luke's smile faded and he realized he resented her tone.

"I happen to be working here, if it's any of your business. What are you doing here?"

"This happens to be my parent's home and my daughter's wedding." Morgan hissed back.

A smile spread across Luke's face at the thought.

"What is so funny?" Morgan demanded.

"Oh, I was just thinking about the irony of it all." Luke folded his arms over his youthful yet muscular chest. "You take me to bed and your husband gets me expelled from college. Four months later I land a catering job and wind up doing your daughter's wedding.

Who would have guessed our paths would have crossed again, so soon."

"Well, you're fired. Get out of here." Morgan snapped.

"You don't have the authority." Luke shook his head and laughed to himself. "I'm not working for you; but, we could always see what your mother, Mrs. Wallace, has to say on the subject. If she wants to fire me after she learns about your nasty little affair, seducing a poor naive teenaged boy-"

Suddenly Morgan slapped Luke across the face, silencing him. He quickly brought his hand to his cheek and smiled at her.

"I owe you one for that," he threatened. "You and your husband have messed up my life enough. Now it's pay back time."

Morgan began to shake as a wave of panic overwhelmed her. She knew one word of this to her mother would destroy the fragile relationship she had with her. Slowly she backed away from Luke.

"Just get out of here," she breathed as she hurried back to the house.

"When I am finished." Luke smiled and continued toward his truck.

Morgan turned around when she reached the front door only to bump into Patricia who had been observing the whole confrontation.

"Well, hello, Morgan." Patricia drew back from her sister.

"Oh, shut up!" Morgan snapped in her usual bossy tone and started around her to the door.

"So, you and Luke was it." Patricia nodded to herself and smiled.

Morgan spun around in the open doorway. She looked into her sister's dark brown eyes as her heart beat faster.

"I don't know what you are talking about," she lied.

"Oh, I know all about your little affair." Patricia smiled. "You see, I work with Luke's father down at the station. He doesn't realize that you are my sister, though, and I didn't tell him."

A feeling of nausea swept through Morgan as she realized her secret was out. She glared at Patricia and tried to figure out a way to keep her from telling anyone.

"Well, I don't care if you know." Morgan lied again. "What do you plan to do, tell Mom and Dad?"

"I might." Patricia smiled at the power she suddenly had over her eldest sister. For as long as she could remember, Morgan had always treated her like a child, bossing her around. It felt good to finally have an equalizer, as it were. "But, I'm not going to, just yet. Telling them today would only hurt Ariel. I'll wait and when the time is right, if you are not nicer to me, I'll spill my guts."

Morgan did not say a word as she shut the door in Patricia's face. Ever since Patricia was born, she loathed her. All those Friday nights spent staying home baby sitting when her friends were out partying and having a good time. All the time being blamed for Patricia's scrapes and bruises. "Why weren't you watching her?" Ruth's voice echoed in her ears. "You're supposed to watch after your sisters and brothers. Afterall, you are the oldest." Morgan hated Patricia even more when she saw how Ariel and her were becoming close friends. When Ariel chose Patricia to be her maid of honor, that was more than Morgan could take. Now this. Morgan leaned against the front door to catch her breath before returning to the kitchen.

Patricia opened the front door confidently. The house was quiet. The smell of the roast beef filled the house. It felt strange to be spending the night here again, but it felt good. Safe. She clinched her over night bag tighter and headed up the stairs.

As she reached the top of the stairs, the sunlight shone through Steven's bedroom window into the hallway. It caught her attention. She put her bag down and walked over to the doorway. A chill ran up her spine as she looked around the remodeled room. He was really gone. Steven had been the only one who understood her. The only one whom she could go to for support and a listening ear. He had never judged her, never condemned her for how she lived her life. He had been the only one whom she could trust with her secret, but now, she was all alone. Gently she rubbed her shoulder and turned away.

"Aunt Patty!" Ariel shrieked and ran out of the guest bedroom. "You made it," she beamed happily.

Patricia smiled and forced her memories back into the closet of her mind.

"Of course I did," she laughed and hugged her niece.

Amanda walked Benjamin around to the back of the house. His little hands were held out as though to balance himself as his little legs hurried to keep up with his mother's pace. Once he had rounded the corner of the house and caught sight of Bradley standing beside the swimming pool, he squealed and ran to him.

"Benji!" Amanda screamed seeing only the

swimming pool.

Bradley turned around just in time to reach down and scoop up his son and swing him into the air.

"How's my boy?" He smiled up at him. Benjamin just giggled and wrapped his arms around his father's neck.

Amanda tightened her jaw as she walked over to them. Again Bradley had ignored her disciplining of Benjamin and his chance to reinforce her authority.

"Hi, honey." Bradley kissed her cheek. "Was traffic bad?"

Amanda relaxed and smiled, pushing her anger aside for the moment.

"Hi. No, it wasn't too terrible." She slipped her arm around his waist and looked out at the back yard. "Looks like Mom has everything under control here."

"Yes. They're through for the night. They'll be back first thing in the morning to put out the table cloths and flowers. This sure brings back the memories, doesn't it?" He sighed and lost himself in his thoughts.

"I'll say." Amanda agreed and looked at the canopy and tables. She was suddenly swept back three years to their wedding day. She remembered how thin she looked in her long white satin and lace wedding gown. Her dieting for weeks had paid off. She had stared at her reflection in the mirror, pleased with how she looked and hoped that Bradley would be too. Lost in her memories, she slowly slid her hand down across her round belly. Suddenly, the unfamiliar form jolted her mind back to the present. She looked down at her rounding stomach and a rush of nausea swept over her.

"I'll be right back," she excused herself and ran into

the house.

Bradley turned and gave a confused look at the back door as it shut.

"Well, Benji," he frowned at his son. "Was it something I said? Come on, let's go inside."

Bradley carried his son into the house. Thoughts of that morning's conversation with Carl and later with Nicholas kept creeping back into his mind. He could not shake the feeling of confusion as to why Steven had never said anything about being married and even further, why his mother did not come out and tell him.

"Boy, something sure smells wonderful." Bradley took a slow deep breath as he entered the kitchen.

Morgan pushed the roast back into the oven and closed the door.

"It's dinner," she said flatly and dropped the hot mitts on the counter beside the stove.

Bradley put Benjamin down and sat down on a stool at the breakfast bar. He looked at the green salad in front of him and reached over when Morgan was not looking and stole a carrot stick. As he bit down on it, Morgan spun around.

"Brad, that's for dinner," she snapped and grabbed the salad bowl from in front of him. "If you are going to pick at everything, then get out of the kitchen."

"So, where's Mom?" Bradley changed the subject.

"She's upstairs with Dad, why?" Morgan asked not really caring to hear the answer.

"Oh, I don't know." He shrugged and glanced over his shoulder at Benjamin and Nicholas in the family room. "Have you noticed Dad has been acting strangely?"

"As a matter of fact," Morgan raised an eyebrow. "I

have. Why? What's up?"

Now she was curious and interested in what Bradley was saying. Without thinking she picked up a carrot stick from the counter and bit it.

"For starters," Bradley noticed and smiled at her. "Why are all the pictures of Steven missing and why the sudden need to remodel Steven's bedroom?"

"I don't know." Morgan shrugged and folded her arms over her chest. She glanced out the window at the back yard where Ariel and Tamera were talking. Suddenly, she was distracted by the sight and her conversation with Bradley was over.

"Aunt Tamera," Ariel leaned across the table as she sat in one of the folding chairs. "Aunt Patty said that I should talk to you."

Tamera glanced back at the house.

"Oh?" She smiled. "About what?"

"Well, I have this problem and I don't know what to do. Please don't tell me to talk to my mother, I've tried and she wont listen, you know? Anyway, it's not like I'm the first one this has happened to." Ariel fidgeted.

"Just spit it out, Ariel. What's the matter?" Tamera looked at her niece and grew concerned and yet very confused.

"I'm pregnant." Ariel looked up at Tamera.

The words hit Tamera hard and caught her totally off guard. She tried to hide her shock from Ariel as she fumbled for something to say.

"Ah, do you, are you absolutely sure?"

"Yes." Ariel looked at her hands and nodded. "I took one of those in home pregnancy tests a couple of weeks ago."

"Oh, well, honey," Tamera relaxed a bit from the initial shock. "You know those tests can be wrong. You really-"

"I know." Ariel interrupted her. "That's why I took it again. It still came out positive."

"I see." Tamera looked around the back yard at the tables and chairs. She looked back and smiled at Ariel. "Hey, you're getting married tomorrow. So, no problem. After you are married then -" Tamera stopped and looked at Ariel who was avoiding eye contact. "Oh, now what?"

"I don't think Mark wants this baby." Ariel looked up at her aunt with tear filled eyes.

"What?" Tamera raised her voice slightly. This was beginning to sound all too familiar.

"Mark is just getting started with his music career. His group just signed a contract yesterday with a record company. They will be cutting an album and doing some tours and a baby would be, well, in the way?" A tear fell from Ariel's eyes. "I think I should have an abortion."

The words hit Tamera like a blow to the chest. Her mind flashed back nearly twenty-four years ago. The memories flooded her mind. She looked at the house and then back at Ariel.

"Ariel, there's something I think you should know," she began cautiously. "When your mother was eighteen, before she was married, she became pregnant."

"She was? What happened?" Ariel looked at her aunt with wide eyes of shock and surprise.

"Well," Tamera bit her lip as she tried to gather her thoughts. "Your father and her were dating for nearly a year and they were fooling around. Your mom discovered she was pregnant and your father wasn't ready to settle down, so, she had an abortion."

Ariel sat back in her chair. She was overwhelmed by the news.

"Your father drove her to a clinic fifty miles away so that no one would know. Since she was eighteen, they didn't need your grandparents' consent. The doctors really messed things up for your mom. So much so, that she wasn't sure if she'd ever have any children. They couldn't say anything to anyone and so they couldn't take any legal action. Your grandparents don't know. I only found out because I over heard your parents talking about it. So, Ariel, don't do it. Even if you don't have the same trouble as your mother, there will be the emotional scars, the haunting memories."

Ariel looked at her aunt not knowing what to say. She was in shock. She could have had an older brother or sister afterall. She looked down at the table again.

"Ariel, talk to Mark. The two of you can work it out." Tamera encouraged.

"But, Aunt Tamera, he's going on the road and if I'm pregnant, I can't travel like that." Ariel explained.

"Ariel," Tamera looked at her niece and said firmly. "You don't have to go with him. You could stay here with his parents or with your grandparents and have this child. Mark can get his music career going and when the child is old enough to travel, then you can go. Believe me, if you abort this baby, you will regret it for the rest of your life."

"I'll think about it, Aunt Tamera." Ariel said, not totally convinced. She stood up and started for the house. It was not exactly the words she had wanted to hear, but the shocking news about her mother overshadowed her thoughts.

Tamera watched her niece for a moment and then shook her head. She was not sure if she had reached her but she hoped beyond all hope that she had at least slowed her down. Maybe knowing what her mother had done would stop her. Slowly she stood up from the table and started back to the house.

"So aren't you the least bit concerned about Dad?" Bradley stared at his sister.

Morgan turned away from the window as Ariel rushed through the back door and into the foyer.

"Not really," she said distractedly. "Brad, I've got too much work to do right now. Why don't you find out what it's about and get back to me."

"Fine. Thanks for your help." Bradley watched Morgan who stood with her back to him as he reached across the counter and took an olive from the opened can. He quickly popped it into his mouth. "I'll bet you and Chuck will be glad to have tomorrow over so you two can go on your trip."

"You can say that again." Morgan nodded and continued to peel the potatoes.

"So, where are you two going?" Bradley snatched another olive.

"Chuck and I are taking a cruise up the coast to Alaska," she sighed in delightful anticipation. "I've always wanted to go there. I've heard that Alaska is so beautiful during the Fall. I cannot believe that I'm finally going to get my chance to see it for myself. If you take another olive, I'll peel your fingers."

Bradley quickly sat back and pulled his hand back

sharply.

"How did you know?"

"I can see your reflection in the window."

Bradley looked outside. The sun was setting and it was starting to get darker.

"So, how long will you be gone?" He continued his conversation.

"Three weeks. Chuck and I want to spend a while up there sightseeing before we fly back." Morgan continued in a pleasant tone.

"That's wonderful, but, not to burst your bubble, won't it be dark for most of the day?"

"And your point is?" Morgan smiled over her shoulder at her brother.

"Oh, you are wicked." Bradley laughed out loud. "I really hope you two enjoy yourselves." He meant that sincerely. He liked his sister when she was not being bossy or acting like someone with a chip on her shoulder, angry all of the time. Those moments, however, were rare. Still, he hoped that one day she would change and be more pleasant like she was at this moment.

"Well, I best see what Amanda is up to. I'll get out of your way. See you later." Bradley rose and walked out of the room.

"Bradley!" The familiar voice called from the parlor as he headed toward the stairs.

"Patty?" Bradley smiled as he recognized her voice. He quickly walked over to her and wrapped his arms around her in a bear hug, lifting her off the floor.

Patricia let out a controlled gasp as the tight grip pressed against her ribs. Bradley felt her tense up in his arms and quickly released his hold.

"What's wrong?" He looked at her concerned.

Patricia smiled as she tried to catch her breath.

"You don't know your own strength," she tried to divert the conversation. Slowly the pain eased and she straightened up.

"That's rubbish, Patty. I've hugged you tighter than that. What's going on? Are you hurt?" Bradley's voice had that protective tone; one he had every time he felt his younger sister needed help.

"It's nothing, really." Patricia lied.

Bradley looked at her and knew that she was not telling the truth, but he let the subject drop, for now.

"It's really good to see you again," she smiled and sat down on the love seat. "Especially since our last visit wasn't the greatest. It seems so strange, don't you think, without Steven. I can't believe the way Dad has totally changed his bedroom."

Bradley sat down in the chair across from his sister. He looked at his hands while he debated on whether or not to say a word about his conversation with Nicholas.

"Yes, it is," he answered and decided to wait until he had a chance to talk to Ruth. "So, how is your roommate working out?"

"Oh, fine." Patricia tensed at the sound of the words. "Fine," she nodded and avoided his eyes.

Bradley looked at his sister and knew there was something more there but it was obvious that she did not want to talk about it.

"So, when is Amanda due again?" Patricia smiled and changed the subject again.

"Oh, not for another three months. I just hope it won't be too close to Mom and Dad's anniversary. It would be a shame to miss the party."

"Keep your voice down." Patricia looked into the foyer to be sure no one heard him. "It's a secret."

"I know." Bradley whispered. "I have to admit that I am a bit worried about Amanda though. Do you think she is too thin for being six months along?"

"I don't know." Patricia shrugged her shoulders. "She could be carrying this one differently than Benji. Why?"

"She's still not eating very much and she is still throwing up. I've talked to her doctor and she is watching her weight."

"Then, don't worry, Brad." Patricia put her hand on his knee reassuringly. "The doctor knows what she's doing."

Before Bradley could say another word, the front doorbell rang out.

"I'll get it!" Ariel called as she hurried down the stairs to the front door. She swung it open and froze. Her smile faded. Before her stood a tall, thin, dark haired woman with big brown eyes. Beside her stood a tall, dark haired, young man with deep brown eyes. There was something familiar about him. Ariel forced a smile. "Hi."

"Hello," the woman nodded in return. "Is this the Wallaces' residence?" Her voice was soft and meek.

"Yes, it is," Ariel nodded.

"Is Steven home?" The woman continued.

A cold chill ran up Ariel's spine. She glanced over at Bradley who had walked over to the foyer with Patricia. He stepped forward and opened the front door wider.

"Hi, I'm Bradley, Steven's brother. Won't you come in?" He invited with a smile.

"Is something wrong?" The woman looked curiously at their faces as she stepped into the house. She held tightly to her son's hand.

"No." Bradley smiled again and tried not to frighten her. "I'll get my mother, you can wait in the parlor here if you like."

Bradley watched as the woman and young man walked into the parlor. He glanced over at Patricia and gave her a concerned look. Patricia mimicked his look back then turned and smiled at the couple as Bradley walked away.

"Go ahead and have a seat," Patricia offered the love seat. She could not help but stare at the young man. There was something strikingly familiar about him and yet she knew they had never met before. "I'm Patricia," she introduced herself.

"Hi," the woman smiled sweetly. "I'm Claudia and this is my son, Peter. It looks as though we may have come at a bad time? It appears you are getting ready for a party."

"Actually, it's my niece's wedding. She's getting married tomorrow. She was the one who answered the front door. She's expecting her fiance' any minute." Patricia looked into the foyer at Ariel. "My mother should be here right away. Excuse me." Patricia nodded to them politely and went into the foyer.

Ariel stood in the opened doorway staring out at the street.

"Don't you think you should come in and close the front door?" Patricia said more as an order than a question.

"I suppose," Ariel smiled. "I'm just so nervous. Where is he?"

"I'm sure Mark will be here any minute. Don't worry yourself."

Ruth sat at her vanity table and fluffed her short auburn hair while she struggled in her mind with how she would bring up the subject of Steven to Carl. She hated keeping secrets, first at Steven's request and now at Carl's. She longed for the days when there were no secrets. When her family was open and honest with each other as it had been when they had all lived under one roof. With a deep breath she turned around and looked at Carl.

He stood behind her drying his short graying hair with a towel. The thick hair on his chest was graying also and glistened with tiny droplets from his shower. His black slacks were zipped up but the top button was still undone. He dropped the damp towel on the dressing bench at the foot of their bed and walked over to the closet to get a shirt.

"Honey, do I have another undershirt in my drawer over there?" He asked her without looking.

"I'll see." Ruth stood up and walked over to his dresser. She opened the top drawer and took out a clean white undershirt. "Here you go." She said and handed it to him. "Carl, there is something I need to talk to you about." She began cautiously as she picked up the damp towel.

"What is it, dear?" He pulled the shirt on over his head.

"It's about this matter with Steven," she continued as she hung the towel on the rod in the bathroom.

"No!" Carl interrupted her sharply. "That matter is closed."

By the way he tucked in his shirt, Ruth could tell that he was upset, but this was important to her. She could not let it drop.

"No, Carl. The matter is not closed." Her voice was firm. "It's time we talked about this."

"I don't want to discuss it." Carl snapped back.

"Then you will listen to me." Ruth tightened her jaw and glared at him. Her heart pounded in her chest. "Steven was my son, too, and I have a say in this matter."

"Fine. You claim him, but I don't. No son of mine is a-"

"Don't you dare," Ruth interrupted him. "Steven was a kind, sensitive young man. He loved and respected both of us. If that is how he dealt with his illness, then we have to respect that. Isn't that what you said?"

"Maybe you can live with that, but I can't. He could have had the operation and he could have still been here with us today. The doctors even said so." Carl turned to the closet and withdrew a white shirt.

"Carl, we don't know that for sure. The doctors also said that kind of operation has its risks. He could have been crippled or even died on the table." Ruth tried to defend her son. "Steven wanted his last days to be happy ones, not ones filled with pain and suffering. That doesn't make him less of a man or a coward."

"Believe what you want." Carl buttoned his shirt.

"You are wrong." Ruth glared at him and walked over to the bedroom door and threw it open. "Bradley," she gasped with a start as she almost walked into him.

"Mom, there is some woman and boy downstairs. They are asking to see Steven." Bradley whispered to her.

Ruth looked over the rail into the foyer below.

"It's okay," she nodded. "I'll take care of it."

"Mom, there's something I think I should show you, first." Bradley reached into his pocket.

"Later, dear." Ruth stopped him and brushed passed him and down the stairs.

As she entered the parlor, she smiled at the sight of the slender woman. When the young boy turned around and looked at her, he took her breath away. She gasped and tried to catch her breath. The boy stood politely in front of the fireplace.

"Are you okay, ma'am?" He asked and looked at her with concern in his eyes.

Ruth stared at him and tried to catch her breath.

"Yes. Yes," she repeated. "You just remind me of someone, that's all."

"I'm sorry to bother you. Patricia told us that you were busy preparing for your granddaughter's wedding. My name is Claudia," she said as she stood up and put her arm around her son. "This is my son, Peter."

Ruth looked at Peter again.

"Peter," she said softly.

"Yes, ma'am." He nodded to her.

"I was wondering if it would be possible to see Steven?" Claudia asked. "Is he here?"

Ruth looked at Claudia and tried to focus her thoughts.

"No, he's not here, dear. Please, sit down."

Claudia and Peter sat down, still holding onto each other. Peter's heart pounded as he became anxious. Claudia tightened her grip on his shoulders. Bracing herself for what was looking like bad news.

"Claudia, when was the last time you heard from Steven?" Ruth asked.

"The last time I saw him was almost seventeen years ago. We kept in touch through letters for about five years after that. Why?" Claudia regretted her question as soon as it left her lips.

"Well, you see, dear," Ruth fumbled for the words to soften the blow. "Three months ago, Steven passed away."

"Oh my god, no." Claudia gasped and held fast to Peter. Tears filled her eyes immediately and rolled down her cheeks.

"Mom?" Peter looked at his mother in disbelief. "Dad is dead?"

"Dad?" Ruth looked at Peter and Claudia in shock. She knew it the moment she saw Peter but somehow hearing the words surprised her.

"Yes, honey." Claudia looked at her son and nodded. She looked back at Ruth. "What? How?"

Ruth took a deep breath and tried to calm her heart.

"Steven died from an aneurysm. He had a brain tumor and the doctors think that contributed to it. He died in his sleep. I'm sorry."

Claudia continued to hold her son as she tried to recover from her shock. She wiped the tears from her face.

"I'm the one who should be sorry," she tried to smile sympathetically at Ruth.

"You called Steven, dad." Ruth looked at Peter. "I'm confused." Ruth probed for an explanation.

"Yes," Claudia nodded. "It's true. Steven is Peter's father. Steven and I had been seeing each other off and on during our early college years, but nothing really serious. We were just close friends really. During our senior year a group of us got together for a party and flew to Vegas. We had been drinking a lot and having fun. I don't remember whose idea it was, but someone suggested we all go get one of those quickie marriage certificates as a souvenir. So, Steven and I went along and one thing led to another and we ended up getting married. Most of the others when they sobered up got them dissolved, but Steven thought we should give it a try. He said that he was raised to believe when a couple married, they were married for life and no one in his family had ever divorced. So, we moved out of the dorms and into an apartment. It was obvious in just a few months that we were too good at being just friends, more like brother and sister than husband and wife. So, Steven moved out here after graduation. A month later I found out that I was pregnant. Steven never knew about Peter. I didn't want to burden him with that or make him feel obligated to try to make our marriage work. We stayed friends. We never divorced. I was content being Peter's mother and being Steven's long distance wife. I wasn't looking to get into any other relationship."

As Ruth listened everything started to make sense. This must have been the secret Steven had tried to tell her that afternoon in the back yard. A feeling of relief replaced her surprise.

"What brought you out here after all these years?" Ruth could not help but to ask.

"Peter wanted to see his father." Claudia smiled. "I thought that maybe it was time for them to get to know each other. Time that Steven knew he was a father. I guess we are too late for that, now."

Ruth nodded understandingly but smiled.

"But not too late to get to know your family."

"Nonsense." Carl's voice thundered from the foyer as he stood listening to the conversation.

"Carl." Ruth gasped and looked up at her husband in surprise and anger at his tone. She quickly stood up.

"I don't know what you want, lady, but this is one sick game. I'm calling the police." Carl tightened his jaw and turned around.

"Carl Wallace, get back here." Ruth ordered.

"Dad. Stop." Bradley grabbed his arm. "It's true. Steven did get married."

Carl turned around and looked at his youngest son as they stood in the foyer by the telephone. Ruth quickly ran over to them.

"What are you talking about?"

"She is telling the truth, Dad." Bradley pulled out the paper from his pocket and unfolded it. "Steven gave this paper to Nicholas the day he died."

"Rubbish." Carl looked at the certificate and then at Claudia. "That is all this is. She knew Steven had died and now she's here to try to claim his belongings. Well, lady, he didn't have anything. Do you hear me?"

Claudia quickly stood up and put her arm protectively around Peter. Together they walked into the foyer and headed toward the door. She kept her eyes fixed on Carl.

"You are a pathetic old man. It's obvious you never knew your son. Maybe we should just go. I'm sorry to have bothered you."

"No, please, wait." Ruth grabbed her arm. "Please stay. We need to talk." She turned back to Carl. "Upstairs mister," she ordered. "Now!"

Carl threw the paper on the floor and brushed passed Bradley as he headed up the stairs. Ruth followed him closely into their bedroom. She shut the door behind them.

Carl walked over to the bed and turned around to face her.

"Don't you ever take that tone with me again," he said firmly. "I am not a child."

"Then stop acting like one." Ruth snapped. "For these last three months you have acted as though your feelings were the only ones that mattered. You stripped this house of everything that was Steven. Did you ever once stop and think about my feelings? Steven was my son too, damn you. I carried him for nine months. I gave birth to him. I'm the one who got up in the night with him, you didn't. Now, he's gone and I'm not supposed to grieve for him. I can't take this anymore." Ruth threw her hands up in the air as though giving up. "I'm leaving you." She walked over to the closet and pulled out her suitcase. "I have had enough of your self pity. Steven was more a man than you have ever been. He didn't blame other people for his trouble and he dealt with his feelings."

Carl's jaw relaxed as he watched his wife empty her dresser drawers into the suitcase. His anger melted at the thought of losing his wife.

"Ruth, stop it." He took her wrist.

"No, you stop it!" She snapped at him and jerked loose of his grasp. "We have a chance to get to know Steven's child. A part of him we never knew before and I'm not letting you throw it away. If I have to, I will leave with them. You can wallow in your pity for the rest of your life for all I care."

"Ruth, please. Stop." Carl grabbed her shoulders tightly and turned her toward him. "I'm sorry."

"You're too late." Ruth glared at him.

"No." Carl said calmly. "I love you and I'm sorry I hurt you. Please, let's try again?"

Ruth looked at her husband, her teeth still clinched in anger. She was not backing down, not just yet.

"This is it, Carl. I'm serious. If you mess this up, I am leaving. I want them in my life."

"Okay." Carl relented. "Okay, but I need you, too. Don't go."

Ruth's anger began to ebb as she looked into Carl's eyes. The same eyes that melted her heart nearly forty-five years ago. She could never stay angry with him for very long.

"Okay," she conceded.

"I'm sorry about all of this." Bradley sat down across from Claudia and Peter in the parlor. He looked at the certificate in his hands and then handed it to her. "Here, I think this is yours."

"Thank-you." Claudia smiled. "We shouldn't have come."

"No," Bradley stopped her. "You did the right thing in coming here. I'm just sorry my father has to be such a jerk. He really is a nice man. He just doesn't handle his grief like the rest of us. He lashes out a lot, but he's really a nice man, when you get to know him."

"Well, I don't know." Claudia looked at Peter.

"So, Peter, how old are you?" Bradley asked and looked at the him.

"I'm sixteen, sir," he replied.

"Please, don't call me, sir. You can call me Brad." Bradley smiled at the politeness of the young man, something lacking in most of the youth around him.

"I was noticing you don't have any pictures of Steven." Claudia asked as she looked at the mantle.

"Oh, we do." Bradley looked at the mantle with a slight frown. "Dad took them down. I guess it's just too painful for him."

"I see." Claudia nodded.

"You see, Dad and Steven were close. True, Steven kept this a secret from all of us, but other than that, they were close. When Steven died, Dad just couldn't deal with it. So, he dealt with it by not dealing with it. I guess seeing Peter and you forced him to face his grief and that scares him."

Claudia listened and understood as best she could.

"It is quite a shock all the way around."

Patricia walked into the bedroom, leaving the door slightly ajar. She sat down on her bed and watched Ariel.

Ariel stood looking out of the window at the backyard. She knew her aunt was there. She had seen her reflection in the glass. Still, she continued to stare at the darkness outside.

"So, what's on your mind?" Patricia asked.

"Just something Aunt Tamera told me," she sighed and turned around. "Does the whole family know about my Mom?"

"What about her?" Patricia shrugged.

"Just that before she and my dad were married, she got pregnant and then had an abortion." Ariel spoke thoughtfully. "I always wondered why I never had any brothers or sisters. Now, I know. I can't believe she would do such at thing."

"No. I don't think the entire family knew about that." Patricia tried to hide her surprise at the news. She had not known, not until then.

"Do you think that Grandma or Grandpa know?" She asked.

"I do now." Ruth stood in the open doorway.

Patricia and Ariel both jumped and turned around to look at her. By the tone of Ruth's voice, both knew that she was not happy.

"Mom." Patricia gasped.

Ruth turned around without another word and headed down the stairs. Patricia and Ariel looked at each other and then raced to the door. They followed Ruth down the stairs. When they reached the foyer, the front doorbell rang. Ruth ignored it and went into the parlor.

Ariel opened the front door. A smile spread across her lips as she looked into Mark's smiling face. He held a bouquet of red roses in his hand. The kissed each other briefly.

"Are you nervous?" He asked her.

"Not any more," she smiled and hugged him. "I'm so happy you are here."

"I wouldn't be any place else." He squeezed her tightly and then let go.

"Come on inside." Ariel invited. "Where are your parents?"

"Didn't your mother tell you?" Mark frowned and gave a heavy sigh that betrayed his disappointment. "They aren't coming."

"What?" Ariel looked at him. "They'll be here tomorrow won't they?"

"No." He shook his head. "Dad was called away on another business trip and Mom said her place was with him."

"I'm sorry." Ariel could see the hurt in his eyes and felt his pain. "Well, at least we will be together."

"That's right." He smiled at her again.

"Come on, you have to see the back." Ariel escorted him to the family room which was decorated with silk flower garlands and set up with folding chairs.

"It's all looks terrific." He breathed and nodded his head.

"Claudia," Ruth sat down on the edge of the coffee table. "I'm sorry for the way Carl acted."

"No," Carl spoke up from behind her. "I should apologize myself." Carl walked into the room. "Claudia, I am really sorry I acted like such a jerk. I didn't mean what I said. Losing Steven has hurt more than I ever thought it could. It's no excuse, I know, but maybe you can understand and forgive me. You were right, I am a pathetic old man, but if you will give me another chance, maybe I can be different."

"Thank you, Mr. Wallace." Claudia smiled. "I shouldn't have said that. I'm sorry, too."

"Well," Ruth smiled and stood up. "Will you stay for dinner? There are still other members of the family you haven't met. We are all together, tonight. It would be the perfect time."

Claudia looked at Peter.

"Mom, can we, please?" He asked.

"Sure." She hugged him. "We would be happy to." They stood up.

"I'm so happy." Ruth immediately reached out and hugged her. "It's like having part of Steven back, again."

"Sir," Peter looked at Carl. "Brad said you have pictures of my dad? What did he look like?"

Carl looked at the young man in front of him and tears filled his eyes.

"He looked just like you." He tried to smile. "Come, I'll show you." Carl put his arm around Peter's shoulders and led him to the closet where he had stowed all of the pictures.

Tamera walked into the parlor.

"Mom," she looked at Claudia and Ruth curiously. "I guess we're ready for the rehearsal to begin."

"Tamera," Ruth looked at her daughter and smiled. "There is someone I'd like you to meet. Claudia, this is Tamera, Steven's older sister by a year." Ruth introduced. "Tamera, this is Claudia, Steven's wife."

"Wife?" Tamera's mouth dropped open in surprise and shock.

"Yes." Ruth laughed. "Steven married when he was in college. I'll explain it to you later. There's someone else you should meet, too. Steven has a son, Peter."

"Oh, I have to sit down." Tamera gasped. "This is too much."

Claudia laughed and walked over to Tamera and took her hand.

"Steven had told me so much about you. I'm happy we finally have a chance to meet."

"Well, forgive me, but he told me nothing about you." Tamera smiled uncertainly.

Ruth and Claudia laughed.

THE ANNIVERSARY

The winter snow gently drifted down covering the leafless tree branches. The once green front lawn was now covered in a sparkling white blanket. Carl slowly turned away from the family room window and back to tending the warm fire in the fireplace. He glanced at the clock on the mantle and then turned to look at Ruth as she washed the morning's dishes in the kitchen. He smiled to himself.

Forty-five years had passed. It seemed as only a day. His heart pounded in his chest as he stood next to his father. The palms of his hands sweat with nervous anticipation. All eyes were on him as he stood in the front of the chapel facing them. Then she appeared. His heart skipped a beat and he smiled. She was so beautiful, so young. Her auburn hair was pulled back beneath her white veil. Her beautiful brown eyes sparkled with tears. She smiled and his anxiety melted.

Slowly Carl walked up behind Ruth. Her auburn hair now streaked with gray. Beneath her apron, she had not lost her slender figure after bearing five children. Gently he slipped his arms around her and gave her a gentle hug. She relaxed and leaned against him.

"I love you," he whispered into her ear.

"I love you, too." She turned her head and smiled at him. She gave him a quick kiss then pulled away. "Carl, I'm almost finished. If you don't want to get soap and water all over the kitchen, please give me a moment longer?"

Carl nodded and kissed her cheek.

Ruth turned back to her dishes and glanced out the window at the snow gently falling. Her thoughts drifting back to that day. She was so nervous and yet never more sure of anything before as she stood next to her father and held his arm.

"You okay, babe?" He smiled at her with tears in his faded blue eyes.

"Yes, Daddy." She looked at him, his round face and receding gray hair, his rosy cheeks.

Slowly she began to walk toward the open doorway of the chapel; her long white dress billowed around her. Her heart pounded as she saw the people that filled the chapel, all there to wish her a happy future. Then, as she looked up, the only one she could see was him. He looked so handsome standing beside his father. His dark brown hair was neatly combed. His black tuxedo neatly pressed. His cheeks blushed as their eyes met. She smiled at the little boy in him.

It was so long ago, so many things had happened since then. They had raised five children and were grandparents already. In just a few more months, they would have their first great-grandchild. It all happened so fast.

Ruth's smile faded as her thoughts turned to Steven. Six months had passed since his death. She could never imagine life going on without him, but it had. She closed her eyes as a single tear fell into the dishwater.

Carl nervously paced the foyer, glancing out at the building snow every once and again. He looked up at the clock. "Where are they?" He murmured to himself.

"So, there you are." Ruth walked into the foyer and startled him. "Oh," she smiled. "What are you hiding?" She said playfully as she approached him.

"Ah, nothing." Carl quickly tried to act calm and shrugged.

"Oh, I get it. We're keeping secrets from each other now, are we?" Ruth smiled and tried to pry.

"I don't know what you are talking about." Carl tried to keep from smiling at her and bit his lip.

Just then they heard a noise at the front door. The doorbell chimed and Ruth looked at Carl with a big smile.

"Is this the secret?" She raced him to the front door and beat him to the door knob.

Carl teasingly pushed at her and then with hands in the air stepped back.

"I give. Go ahead and open it."

"No, you get it." Ruth took her hands off the knob and looked at her husband.

"No," Carl smiled at her, the twinkle in her eyes. "It's for you." He folded his arms over his chest.

"You're sure of that, are you?" Ruth folded her arms over her chest.

The doorbell rang again and then a knock. Ruth wanted to continue this little game but relented and opened the door.

"Surprise!" Claudia, Peter, Bradley and Benjamin all shouted with big smiles. "Happy anniversary."

Ruth covered her mouth and smiled as she looked at her family in front of her standing on the porch.

"Can we come in, it's cold out here." Bradley asked and shivered.

"Oh, yes." Ruth stepped aside and opened the door wider. "Come in. Come in."

Bradley stepped in first and kissed his mother on her cheek.

"I love you," he greeted her. "Here, this is for you and Dad." He handed her a wrapped package. "Sorry about the wrap job. I did it myself."

"It's lovely." Ruth smiled. She realized how hard it had been for Bradley these passed couple of months being a single parent.

"Mom," Claudia hugged Ruth as she stepped into the warm foyer. "Happy anniversary."

"Here, Grandma, this is from us." Peter smiled and handed her another package.

"Thank-you, you two. You really didn't need to." Ruth accepted the gift and kissed his cheek.

"Don't close that door." Tamera called as she hurried cautiously up the front walk; stepping in the footprints made by the others so as not to get her shoes too wet. Behind her, Nicholas, Daniel and Ariel followed a bit disgusted by her slowness.

"Well, come on, honey." Ruth smiled and shook her head at her daughter. She greeted Tamera with a cheek to cheek hug. "Oh, you are so cold. You better go on into the family room and get warm."

"Happy anniversary, Mom, Dad." Daniel nodded to

his in-laws as he stepped into the foyer carrying a cake box. "I'll just put this in the kitchen."

"Here, Grandma." Nicholas started to hand her another package.

"Give it to your grandfather, dear," she smiled at him. "He's got two empty arms, and thank-you so much."

"Hi, Grandma." Ariel hugged her. "Sorry, I wasn't able to get out much. I hope you like it anyway." She handed her an envelope.

"I'm just happy you made it." Ruth kissed Ariel's forehead and smiled appreciatively.

Ariel took off her coat and hung it next to the others on the rack beside the front door then followed the rest into the family room. She paused to give Carl a hug and a kiss.

"So," Ruth closed the front door and looked at Carl. "This is the big secret," she teased.

"Not quite, but it's starting." Carl smiled.

"Well, I don't know about you." She walked toward him and turned her head playfully away from him with a smile. "I'll put these in the other room."

Bradley watched as his mother disappeared into the family room. Then he turned to his father.

"So, have you told her yet?"

"No." Carl shook his head and his smile faded.

"Dad, she's going to be here any minute. I think you should at least prepare her." Bradley pleaded.

"I know." Carl came back with almost a snap in his voice. "I don't know. This whole thing has gotten way out of hand. I understand her feelings and I don't. Maybe I'll just keep quiet and see how things go."

"I don't know if that is such a good idea, Dad."

Bradley shook his head. "You remember the blow up the last time they saw each other. They haven't talked for a month."

"Yeah." Carl nodded. "But what if she doesn't show up and I get your mother upset for nothing. It will just ruin her day."

"And if she does show up, what then?" Bradley persisted.

"Well, I guess we'll just have to deal with it then." Carl turned away from the foyer and walked into the family room.

"Morgan, look out." Bradley shook his head and looked at the front door.

Ruth busied herself in the kitchen making a fresh pot of coffee while Claudia got out the cups and saucers. It was nice to be a part of a family again, Claudia smiled to herself contentedly. Since her parents' tragic deaths in a car accident two years ago, it had only been her and Peter. Now, they had a family.

"I'm so happy you and Peter decided to move out here." Ruth smiled at her daughter-in-law.

"So, am I." Claudia nodded. "Although, I'm not sure Peter is making the adjustment very well. He's been awfully quiet and withdrawn since about a week before we left."

"Don't worry about him." Ruth reassured her. "When kids are that age, it's hard to leave friends and accept change. They are going through a hard enough time with growing into adulthood ."

"I suppose you're right." Claudia shrugged. "But, still, I can't help but feel there's something else going on."

"We mothers always worry." Ruth laughed softly.

"It's part of our job. So, how's the house coming?"

"I think it should close this week," Claudia smiled. "That is, if the weather cooperates." She glanced out the kitchen window at the building snow. "It'll be hard to go anywhere to sign the papers."

"True." Ruth nodded.

"I can't thank you and Dad enough for all of your help." Claudia turned to her mother-in-law. "I wasn't expecting anything and that is not why we came out here."

"We know. We are just happy that Steven had that insurance policy. It was rightfully yours and Peter's anyway." Ruth smiled and wiped her hands on her apron.

"Thanks. It's kind of you to say that."

"So, did you find out about getting social security for Peter?" Ruth asked as she opened a bakery box containing pastries.

"Yes." Claudia answered as she handed Ruth a plater. "He will be getting a check each month until he's eighteen or if he goes to college, until he is twenty one. It'll be a great help."

"That's fantastic." Ruth nodded. "If anything good could come from Steven's death, this must be it."

Claudia nodded without saying a word.

"So how far along are you?" Peter asked Ariel as he watched her rub her stomach.

Ariel looked up at her cousin, surprised. Since they met the day before her wedding, they had barely spoken two words to each other. She smiled at him. She liked him, although she did not know him very well, at all really.

"Three months or so," she lied since her grandfather was sitting within earshot of them.

"That's neat." Peter continued.

"Let's go in the other room." Ariel stood up from her chair. "We can talk better," she whispered.

Peter stood up and followed Ariel to the parlor. He did not know why, but he felt comfortable around Ariel. Maybe he could confide in her the things he could not say to anyone else.

"So, how do you like Washington High?" Ariel sat down on the love seat and pulled the pillow out from behind her back.

"It's okay." Peter lied. The school was fine, just the people were not.

"Are the girls all over you?" Ariel smiled. In a way, she found herself attracted to her cousin's tall, slender physique. His dark hair and piercing brown eyes were a real turn on to her; but they were still cousins and that line would never be crossed.

"No." Peter shook his head.

"You've got to be kidding." Ariel was surprised. "A stud like you. You must have broken a lot of hearts back east when you left."

Peter became uneasy with the direction of the conversation. His hands began to sweat and his pulse raced. He smiled and looked away.

"So, did you have a girl friend back there?" Ariel pressed on.

"No." Peter shook his head. "No," he repeated again and flashed her a forced smile.

"You're kidding. You've never been on a date?" Ariel was really surprised.

"No." Peter's heart pounded. He began to shake

nervously. "So, how do you like living with your in-laws in that big house of theirs? Mom drove me by the other day. It's a regular fortress."

"Actually, they are never home." Ariel smiled at his reaction to her in-laws' house. "I'm not exactly sure what kind of work Dad Jones does but he and Mom travel a lot. So, with Mark on tour in Europe, I'm alone with the maid and butler a lot. They are really nice. I like them. Although, they call me Mrs. Jones all the time. That makes me feel so old."

"It must be nice to have people wait on you." Peter smiled.

"Actually, I hate it." Ariel shrugged. "I'm not used to it and they shouldn't have to."

"It's their job. They get paid for it." Peter reminded her.

"I know, but it's still uncomfortable. I feel as though I should be waiting on them. They are older than I."

Peter laughed. His nervousness was gone.

"So, what are you two talking about?" Patricia interrupted as she removed her coat.

Ariel jumped to her feet and hurried over to her. She threw her arms around Patricia's neck and gave her a big hug. Patricia winced in pain. Ariel noticed and immediately let go.

"I'm sorry. I didn't mean to hurt you," she apologized.

"It's okay. You didn't hurt me that much." Patricia hesitantly smiled and rubbed the back of her neck.

"Let me take your coat." Ariel said as she took the coat away from Patricia and hung it on the rack. "We didn't hear you come in."

"I was trying to be quiet." Patricia said with a real smile as she looked at Peter. "It's nice to see you again, Peter."

"Same here." Peter nodded.

"Everyone is in the family room." Ariel informed Patricia as she walked back into the parlor.

"That's okay. I'll stay out here a few minutes, that is, if the two of you don't mind."

"No." Peter answered almost too quickly. Patricia smiled again.

"So, has your mother arrived?" Patricia sat down in the chair next to the fireplace and looked at Ariel.

"No. I'm nervous about how Grandma is going to take it." Ariel looked into the foyer and then back at her aunt.

"I know what you mean." Patricia shook her head. "If only we had closed that door, she would never have overheard us."

"It's not your fault." Peter offered. He had heard about the big blow up from his mother just after they had returned back East. "That is, from what I was told." He added quickly.

"It's true." Ariel added. "Mom should have told Grandma herself, years ago."

"I know, but I still can't help but feel guilty." Patricia sighed. "We all have our little secrets that we don't want anyone else to know. Not that they are harmful, it's just part of keeping our privacy. Does that make sense?"

Peter thought silently. His mind going back to his friend back East. He smiled at the thought and the warm feeling it gave him in his chest.

"Yes." He nodded without looking at either of

them.

Ariel looked at him curiously. Patricia noticed the softness in his voice.

Tamera walked into the kitchen and set her teacup down. Daniel followed her and warmed up his already warm coffee.

"Tamera, please, try to relax. You are a nervous wreck." He put his arm around her shoulders and gave her a squeeze.

"How can I?" She shook her head. "First it was that letter. Then the phone calls started. Daniel, it frightens me."

"Everything will be okay. She hasn't got a leg to stand on, not after all these years." Daniel tried to reassure her.

"I know, but that isn't what scares me. What if he finds out? What will he think of us? I can't lose him, too." Tamera's eyes began to tear.

"You wont. We wont." Daniel turned and looked her in the eyes. "Everything is going to be okay."

Tamera looked at her husband and finally nodded.

"Okay." She picked up her teacup. "What did the police say?"

Daniel scratched his head. He had tried to avoid this subject since he had talked to them three days ago.

"They can't do a thing about it unless she begins to threaten physical harm."

"I can't believe this is happening. I can't handle this anymore." Tamera sank back against the counter and put the teacup down.

"Tamera, snap out of it." Daniel said sharply while trying to keep his voice down. "We will get through this."

"I hope you are right." Tamera picked up her teacup and coldly walked back into the family room.

Ruth sat down on the couch next to Bradley. Together they watched Carl, Nicholas and Benjamin set up the electric train set.

"So, how are you doing?" Ruth asked without turning to him.

Bradley took a deep breath and sighed.

"Not so good," he answered her honestly.

"I know, it's been very hard for you." Ruth nodded and looked at her son.

"I keep thinking about how tiny she was." He cupped his hands in front of himself. "She was so light." His voice cracked a little as tears welled up in his eyes. He shook his head. "The psychiatrist said we should name her. It would help with our grieving process, she said. So, we named her Beatrice Angeline after Grandma Bea and after Amanda's grandmother."

"Grandma would have liked that." Ruth smiled sympathetically. "So, how is Amanda?"

"Oh, according to the medical doctors, she's physically fine for a person who has just been through losing a baby. However, her psychiatrist is concerned about her fixation with her weight. So that is what they are focusing on now."

"I thought she was doing better about that." Ruth looked at the boys again.

"So had I. I didn't even give it a second thought when she was still throwing up after five months. The doctor said some women have morning sickness all through their pregnancies." Bradley looked at his hands again. He fought back his tears as anger rose in his chest. "She was purging. How could I have been so stupid? If only I would have insisted the doctors do something earlier."

Ruth reached over and put her hands on his. She gently but firmly held them.

"Don't," she said sharply. "Don't do this to yourself. There was nothing you could have done. That is evidenced by the fact that she kept it a secret from all of us. Amanda is a very sick girl. What happened, as tragic as it is, happened and all the what if's in the world can't change that. Don't beat yourself up over it. It won't help."

"I know you are right. But it's hard." Bradley choked back his tears, not wanting to cry in front of everyone.

"I know, dear." Ruth put her arm around his and hugged him.

He leaned over and rested his head against hers and tried to smile.

"So, when are they sending Amanda back home?" Ruth sat up but still held fast to his arm.

"I don't know." He shook his head. "The last time I talked to them, they said they wanted to keep her there for another month or so. The treatments with her mother and step-father appear to be helping but they want to be sure she will not fall back into purging."

"Well, keep thinking positive thoughts." Ruth smiled at him.

"I will," he lied as he feigned a smile back. Inside his heart was cold at the thought of Amanda. In his mind, their marriage was over. There was no going back.

The front doorbell chimed. Carl looked up at

Bradley. His mouth dropped open. He knew who was at the door, but did not know what to do.

Bradley shrugged his shoulders.

"What?" Ruth looked at them both. "What's going on?"

Carl stood up.

"Honey," he began, but before he could say another word, Morgan and Chuck walked into the room.

Ruth looked up at her eldest daughter and immediately her mood changed to anger. She stood up from the couch.

"Hi Mom." Morgan tried to sound cheerful and smiled. She held out the gift wrapped package dotted with melting snowflakes. "Happy anniversary."

"It was." Ruth snapped and walked out of the room. "Carl, come here," she ordered.

"Why is she still angry with me?" Morgan turned around to Chuck as tears filled her eyes. "Why can't she just forgive and forget about it. It happened a lifetime ago, damn it."

Chuck held Morgan tightly as she cried into his chest. He looked around the room, finally resting his glare on Tamera and Daniel who were unaware of it.

Carl hurried after Ruth who was starting to head up the stairs to their bedroom. She stopped and turned around only two steps up.

"I can't believe you invited her here. You know how I feel about her," she snapped.

"Yes, I know." Carl set his jaw. "But like it or not, she is our daughter."

"After what she did, she is not mine." Ruth continued her anger and her ascent.

"That's bull shit!" Carl cursed for the first time in

years. "What she did happened a long time ago. If you are going to be angry with her, then you have to be angry at Amanda too."

Ruth turned around and came back down the stairs.

"It is different with Amanda. Morgan is my daughter. I raised her differently. She could have come to me. She didn't have to abort my grandchild."

"I see." Carl nodded to himself. "So this is all about you. Your daughter. Your grandchild. Ruth, it's not about you. Quit being so self-centered."

"I can't believe you said such an awful thing to me." Ruth recoiled as though she had been slapped.

"Oh, knock it off." Carl snapped indignantly. "Morgan made a mistake over twenty years ago. Don't you think she has beat herself up over it ever since? Don't you think she has thought about the child she destroyed every day since? You don't forget something like that. There is nothing we can do about it now. It is done, over, gone. You once told me that we have already lost one child and not to throw another chance away. Well, don't throw Morgan away."

Ruth looked at Carl without a word. She heard what he had said, but she could not help feeling resentment not at him but at Morgan. They had been close once. She felt that closeness was a lie. She felt betrayed. She would have understood. Why could not Morgan have just come to her? Why?

Ruth turned around and walked up the stairs to their bedroom. Carl stood at the bottom of the stairs and watched. Slowly he shook his head and turned around only to face Patricia, Ariel and Peter in the doorway of the parlor. Without a word he turned and walked back into the family room.

Morgan sat next to Chuck and dried her tears. She looked up at Carl.

"I guess she'll never forgive me."

"Give her time." Carl shrugged.

"We shouldn't have come." Chuck spoke with a bit of anger in his voice. "This was a big mistake."

"No, it wasn't." Morgan spoke up. "Even if Mom is angry with me, I still needed to be here. I wanted to be here for their forty-fifth anniversary."

"Well, I don't see what good it has done." Chuck sneered. "Mom is obviously not willing to put things behind her yet."

"I don't care. She's still my mother and I wanted to come." Morgan insisted.

Just then the telephone rang in the foyer. Chuck looked at his wristwatch.

"I'll get it." Tamera announced and hurried into the foyer.

Chuck smiled to himself as she rushed passed him.

"Hello?" He heard her answer the telephone. Silence. Daniel stood up from his chair and walked into the foyer.

Daniel looked at Tamera as she held the telephone to her ear. Her blue eyes were wide open behind her round rose-tinted glasses. Her mouth was slightly open and she began to tremble. Daniel stepped closer.

"Tamera?" He spoke softly to let her know he was there.

She looked up at him and her eyes filled with tears. She did not speak but he could tell that something was wrong.

"Who is it?" He asked, his own pulse beginning to quicken.

Tamera did not answer. She trembled and the tears began to fall.

Daniel quickly jerked the telephone receiver from her and put it to his ear.

"Who is this?" He demanded. "How did you get this number?"

There was silence, then a click. Nothing.

Daniel hung the receiver back on its hook and took Tamera in his arms. He held her while she sobbed into his chest and tried to regain her composure. He looked over at the empty parlor and slowly directed Tamera to it.

He sat her down on the love seat and continued to hold her.

"Wow. What a neat train." Peter commented as he watched Nicholas and Benjamin playing. "Where did you get that? It looks old."

"It is." Nicholas answered. "It's Grandpa's. He got it when he was a kid."

"That is really great that you kept it so nice and running." Peter turned to his grandfather. "It's got to be an antique. I mean-"

"I know what you mean." Carl laughed out loud as he sat in his chair. "I took really good care of it. It was the only toy that I can remember ever getting when I was a little boy. Your great-grandparents didn't have a lot of money for such things. So, I've been extra careful with it."

"That's really interesting." Peter sat down on the hearth. "What were they like? Great-Grandma and Great-Grandpa Wallace?"

"They were exact opposites." Carl smiled as his

mind flashed with images of his parents as he was growing up. "Your great-grandmother was warm and loving. She liked people. She would not only look after us but she never turned away a stranger that needed a cup of soup or a warm place to sleep. Your great-grandfather, well, he was a different story. He was very stern. A real stickler for working for your day's bread and butter. He was up before dawn tending the farm and if he were up, so were you. So, all of us would be out in the fields by sun-up. If you were late, you'd get a whippin'. If you didn't work as hard as he figured you were able, you didn't get your supper. So, we all worked very hard. He was also very reserved when it came to affection. I don't ever recall him hugging or kissing your great-grandmother, and he never hugged his sons. It was always a handshake. The manly thing. But, he had his moments still."

Peter listened intently as his grandfather reminisced. He loved hearing about his family history. It gave him a sense of security and yet, he wondered what life would have been like if he were born back then.

Claudia and Patricia huddled at the breakfast table. The two watched and listened to the stories Carl was telling. Claudia looked at her son's face. His smile she had not seen in a long time. The sparkle in his eyes.

"You have a really nice looking young man." Patricia commented out loud to Claudia.

"He looks a lot like my memories of his father." Claudia breathed.

"That he does." Patricia nodded in agreement. "I don't think I've ever seen him so interested in anything since you moved out here."

"I didn't think anyone but I had noticed." Claudia

was surprised by her comment. She turned and looked at Patricia. "You really think so?"

"I've noticed and I do think so." Patricia nodded. "Maybe it's just the new surroundings and as he gets used to it here, things will be better."

"That's what Mom said too." Claudia turned back to Peter. "I hope you are right, but I don't know." She sipped her coffee.

"Are you okay?" Daniel asked once Tamera had regained her composure.

"I think so." Tamera gave a heavy sigh.

"Now, will you tell me who was that on the telephone?" Daniel prodded.

"It was her. I don't know how but she got Mom and Dad's number and she called." As she heard herself say the words, her hands began to sweat and her heart became anxious. "What are we going to do?"

"Hold it." Daniel tried to calm her. "Who was on the phone again?" He had understood what she had said. He just could not believe his ears.

"It was her." Tamera repeated in all earnest. "Nick's biological mother." Tamera was trembling again. The tears were coming back.

Daniel felt his own heart pounding in his chest. His thoughts running in all directions. He tired to calm his own fears and keep Tamera from seeing that he too was scared.

"What did she say?" He heard himself ask.

"She just kept saying over and over, 'He's not your son. Your son is dead. Give me back my son.' Dan, I'm scared. You talked to the attorney who handled the adoption didn't you? She can't take him away, can she?"

"He said he'd have to get back to me. Normal adoptions are final but there was a clause in ours that we didn't catch. He's looking into it for us." Daniel looked at the floor as a sinking feeling filled his chest.

"Oh, Daniel, what are we going to do? It would kill Nick for him to find out he's adopted." Tamera looked up. "Oh my god." She froze. A chill ran up her spine. She unconsciously squeezed Daniel's hand until he jerked it way.

"What?" Daniel looked at Tamera and then turned toward the foyer. His mouth dropped open in shock. "Son?"

"No!" Nicholas shouted. "Don't call me that. You're not my father!" He turned around in a daze and ran for the front door.

"Nicholas!" Daniel shouted and sprang to his feet. Before he could get to the door, Nicholas was gone.

"Oh, god, no!" Tamera screamed and raced after them. "Nick, Dan," she cried as she stepped out onto the front porch. The snow bellowed around her but she could not feel a thing. She squinted to see through the white flurry. Daniel's voice grew fainter and fainter as he called after Nicholas.

"Tamera?" Ruth and Carl appeared in the doorway. "What is it?"

Tamera slowly turned around. Tears streamed down her red cheeks.

"He's gone, Mom," she cried and reached out for her.

"What? Who's gone?" Ruth took her in her arms and backed into the parlor.

Carl closed the front door behind them.

"Nick. He overheard Dan and I talking about his being adopted." Tamera cried. "He ran away."

"Hush." Ruth pulled Tamera away and took her face in her hands. "Tamera, Dan will bring him back and we can work this out."

"They just said on the news that we're in for the worst storm we've had in a long time." Patricia announced as she walked into the foyer. She looked at the scene curiously. "What's going on?"

"I'd best see if I can help Dan find the boy," Carl said as he grabbed his and Daniel's coats. He gave Ruth a quick kiss on the cheek as he hurried out the front door. "Don't worry, honey," He said to Tamera as he closed the front door. "We'll find him."

"Carl, be careful," Ruth called to him through the closed front door.

"What's all the commotion?" Bradley asked as he and the rest of the family gathered in the foyer.

"Nick overheard Daniel and Tamera talking and he got upset. He took off out the door and your dad and Daniel have gone looking for him." Ruth filled them all in.

"I'd best go help," Bradley said and grabbed his coat. "Patty, watch Benji for me." He did not wait for her answer but disappeared out the front door.

"You know," Chuck sneered at Tamera. "This whole thing could have been avoided if you had told the boy he was adopted in the first place."

Ruth looked at her son-in-law as she suddenly realized there was something more to this than just an accidental overhearing.

"What a minute, Chuck," Ruth interrupted before Tamera could answer. "I don't recall mentioning what

Nick overheard. I think you and I had better have a talk right now." Her voice was stern. Her temper starting to grow.

Slowly she walked over to Chuck and even though she was a head shorter than he, grabbed his arm and spun him around. Her grip was so tight on his arm that her knuckles were white. Chuck followed her obediently, not having a choice.

The two walked straight into the family room closely followed by the rest of the family. Ruth stood in the middle of the room and released her grip.

"I think you better start explaining yourself and fast." Ruth glared angrily at him. "You are messing with my family and I don't like it. Start talking."

"I don't know what you are talking about." Chuck laughed nervously as he looked at the fire in Ruth's eyes and at the faces all around him.

Ruth did not move. She did not say a word. Morgan slowly walked over to her husband and faced him. She glanced at Tamera who was standing, crying into Claudia's arms. She looked at her mother, whose glare was fixed firmly on Chuck. She turned back to her husband.

"Chuck, if you had anything to do with this, you had better speak up now," Morgan spoke softly.

Chuck looked about the room again. He looked back at Ruth. A smile spread across his lips and he smirked.

"Okay, so I had a friend write a couple of letters and make a few phone calls, so what. It was a joke," he shrugged.

"A joke." Tamera repeated through clinched teeth as she charged across the room at him. "Well, laugh at this, you bastard." Without warning she slapped him and tackled him to the floor.

Ruth and Claudia quickly grabbed Tamera off him and held her back.

"That is enough!" Ruth told Tamera sternly.

Morgan stood over her husband as he stood up. He rubbed his cheek and then clinched his fists.

"What's the matter with you people, are you all nuts! Can't you take a joke?" He scoffed.

"It's not funny, Chuck," Morgan said to him sternly. "Mom, everyone, Chuck didn't mean-"

"Oh, shut up, Morgan," Ruth snapped. "I am sick to death of your stupidity. I have nothing to say to you, Chuck. On second thought, what you did was contemptible and unforgivable. You have hurt an innocent child. Let's just hope no harm comes to him out there."

"I can't stay in the same room with him," Tamera announced and walked out of the room.

Claudia looked at Peter. He was quite shaken by all of the fighting but he managed a slight smile to his mother as though telling her he was fine. Claudia turned and followed Tamera.

"Mom," Patricia walked over to her.

Ruth turned away from Chuck and Morgan.

"What?" She said half interested.

"Shouldn't they have been back by now? I mean, how long does it take three grown men to find one boy?"

Ruth turned and looked out the family room windows. The snow was piling up and still coming down hard. She could not even see the trees in the very back of their half acre yard.

"I don't know," she said with a bit of concern in her voice.

The telephone rang and broke the silence. Ruth looked at Chuck again.

"This had better not be another one of your stunts," she said as she went into the parlor to answer it.

Chuck shrugged at her and followed Morgan into the kitchen.

Morgan poured herself a cup of coffee as Chuck leaned against the kitchen counter behind her. Her hands trembled as she tried to keep from spilling the hot steaming brew.

"Honestly, Chuck." She set the pot back on the stove and turned around to face him. "I don't understand why you would have done such a thing. It doesn't make sense."

Chuck was speechless as he stared at her cup of coffee. How could he explain his reasons to her so that she would understand? It was all so clear when he first thought of the plan on the ship. Even when they got back and the plan was set into motion, it seemed innocent enough. He just wanted to scare Tamera and Daniel, that was all. He never intended it to involve Nicholas, really.

"Tamera has been through enough hell with losing Danny and not being able to have another child. This is just mean." Morgan shook her head. "I don't understand."

"I did it for you," Chuck blurted and then just as quickly softened his tone. "I have watched the way everyone treats you. Your mother has always been cool to you. Steven just tolerated you. Tamera has never liked you. I don't know if it's jealousy or what exactly.

She's never treated you with the decency you deserve. Bradley and Patricia have never given you a chance. After all you did for them when they were children, they barely even speak to you. I did it to pay her back for hurting you. For telling your mother about the abortion and causing more trouble between you and Mom. I just meant to make them squirm. How was I to know that they would be so stupid and tell the brat."

As Morgan listened to her husband explain, a feeling of warmth filled her whole being. She looked at him and lovingly wrapped her arms around his thin waist.

"I love you for loving me," she smiled. "You are the best thing that has happened in my life."

Chuck pouted boyishly, just to keep her feeding his badly bruised ego.

"You've always looked out for me and been there for me. I should never have doubted your intentions for one moment. I'm sorry." Morgan looked into his eyes and smiled. "Do you forgive me?"

"I only tried to protect you, because I love you so very much," he smiled and then kissed her tenderly.

Ruth picked up the receiver as she stood in the foyer. Her heart pounded angrily as she anticipated who the caller might be.

"Hello," she greeted firmly.

"Hello, Mom?" The voice on the other end sounded distant.

"Amanda?" Ruth recognized the voice with surprise.

"Happy anniversary." Amanda tried to sound upbeat. "How is everyone out there?"

"Oh, we are all just fine." Ruth looked around at the empty foyer. "It's snowing something fierce right now, but we are all staying warm. How about you? How are you, dear?"

"I'm doing better. They think I should be out of here soon. I can't wait to get back home. To see little Benji and Bradley. By the way, how is Bradley? I haven't heard from him in two weeks, is everything okay?"

"They are both doing fine." Ruth tried to hide her surprise. "He's been working a lot, I know," she tried to cover for him but made a mental note to ask him about it later.

"Are they there right now? Can I speak to Bradley?"

"I'm sorry, dear, Bradley isn't here just yet. I do expect him back very soon. Shall I have him call?" Ruth paced the floor a bit. This was all she needed to hear at the moment. Another one of her children having troubles.

"I guess that would be okay. Have him call real soon, they don't let us have calls after dinner." Amanda's voice sounded so different, so childlike. It worried and frightened Ruth at the same time.

"Okay, dear. I love you. Get well so you can come back to us real soon."

"I will, Mom," Amanda agreed. "Give Dad my love and tell everyone hello for me."

"I will," Ruth breathed and listened as the line went dead. Slowly she hung up the receiver.

Tamera stood on the front porch straining to see through the falling snow. The cold winter wind swirled around her, stinging her tear streaked cheeks. She pulled her sweater closed and folded her arms over her chest to shield herself from the biting cold.

"Oh, Nick," she shivered and cried. "Not you, too. Please, don't leave me. Come home. I promise, everything will be all right."

In the distance she spotted shadows coming closer. Her heart leapt with hope. She smiled and began to run toward them.

"You've found him!" She screamed. "Nick." She ran with open arms. Suddenly, she stopped as she looked at the three sullen faces of her brother, husband and father. Their expressions said everything.

"No," she whimpered. "You have to find him. Where could he have gone?" She fell to her knees and cried.

"Tamera, honey," Daniel reached down to her to lift her out of the snow. "We couldn't find him but he will come home when he gets cold enough."

"No," Tamera's voice was near panic. "No, you have to keep looking for him. You have to bring him back to me, Dan." Tamera cried hysterically and pushed Daniel away.

"Tamera Irene Lynch!" Carl grabbed her arm and spun her around. "Listen to me. We have combed the neighborhood. We couldn't find any sign of him. He has to be around here somewhere. He's probably hiding from us not wanting to be found, so there is no point in our being out here. Daniel is right, when he gets cold enough, he will come back."

Tamera shook her head not wanting to listen to her father. Fear had gripped her and she it, she was not going to give up. She began to shiver in the cold.

"Let's get you inside, where it's warm." Daniel put his coat over her shoulders and held her close to him as they headed back toward the house.

The family room was uncomfortably quiet. Claudia sat on the couch and watched Peter and Benjamin across the room. Peter sat holding Benjamin on his lap as they looked out the window watching the snow fall. Occasionally Peter would point out a snowflake and Benjamin would giggle in excitement. Claudia wondered what Peter thought about the things that were happening. In all his sixteen years, she had never exposed him to such yelling and fighting. She worried that maybe she had made a mistake insisting they move out here leaving Virginia and their former lives.

"Welcome to the family, Claudia," Patricia sighed sarcastically as she sat down next to her on the couch. "I'm really sorry about all of this."

"No need to apologize." Claudia shrugged. "I'm more worried about how all of this is affecting Peter. He's been so quiet since our move out here. That's not normal for him. He was so talkative and alive back in Virginia, but out here it's completely different."

"He'll be fine," Patricia tried to reassure her again.

"Maybe so," she nodded. "But I don't understand it. Steven told me about your family and growing up here. He made it sound so different. He never mentioned the fighting and always some crisis happening."

"It wasn't like this," Patricia nodded to herself and smiled as she remembered fondly her older brother and best friend. "Not when Steven was alive." She shook her head. "Steven had a very special affect on the family. When he was around, he acted like a buffer, a counselor. We all went to him with our problems and he'd make us laugh and somehow they didn't seem so big. He took them on his shoulders and carried them for us. He wouldn't admit it to anyone, but I know he worried about us all." Tears began to fill Patricia's eyes and she turned away. "I sure wish he were here now."

Claudia listened quietly. She wondered if Steven were there, would she have been? She wondered how he would have taken the news about Peter? Would he have been angry with her or would he have forgiven her for keeping this secret? She liked to think that he would have. That the two of them would have continued to be close friends and that he and Peter would have been close as well, father and son. That could never happen now.

"Mom, look at the snow." Peter turned to his mother. "It's really coming down now. The flakes are so big." Peter turned back to the window.

Claudia sat forward on the edge of the couch.

"Oh, that poor boy," she moaned softly to herself as she thought about Nicholas being outside in the cold.

The sound of the front door opening brought everyone to their feet. They turned around as Carl walked into the room and hugged Ruth then stood by the fireplace to get warm.

Ruth looked around as Daniel entered the room with Tamera under his arm. She turned to Carl.

"I take it he's still out there."

"Didn't you find him?" Patricia asked Bradley as he entered the room.

"No," Tamera answered and began to cry. She reached out for Ruth.

"It's okay." Ruth held her and stroked her wet blonde hair. "He'll come back."

"I don't understand it. He couldn't have gone far. It's just too cold and the snow was blowing around. We tried to follow what we thought were his tracks but nothing." Bradley reported. "Tamera, he's just upset now. He'll be back. We just have to wait."

"They just said on the radio that the telephone lines are out in most of the city." Morgan reported as she and Chuck entered the room. She looked at all of their sad faces and knew they had not found Nicholas. "They said," she continued. "A tree fell over the lines causing a pole to come down. The weatherman said we are in for near blizzard conditions for the next few days," she talked faster. "Oh, god, you didn't find him did you?" She suddenly realized and truly felt regret and concern. "I'm really sorry."

"Sorry?" Daniel repeated and looked over at her and Chuck. "For what?"

"Daniel." Chuck stepped forward. He looked sheepishly at his hands and braced himself for Daniel's reaction to what he was about to say. "I wrote those letters and am responsible for the phone calls."

"You wrote those letters?" Daniel repeated as he tried to understand. "Not Nicholas' birth mother?

"Yes." Chuck nodded. "But I never-"

"I don't understand." Daniel shook his head. "Have I done something to you to make you mad at us? I thought we were friends?"

"I'm sorry. I was just angry at Tamera for telling Ruth about Morgan's abortion. I wasn't thinking."

"Chuck, Tamera didn't tell Mom. I did." Patricia turned to Chuck.

Daniel's temper rose fast. His jaw tightened. His fists were clinched.

"Why you-" Daniel lunged at Chuck. Bradley and Morgan quickly stood between them and held them apart. "Sorry!" Daniel shouted. "My son is out there hurting because of you. You dirty son of a-" Daniel struggled to get closer to Chuck. To get his hands around his neck.

"Dan!" Carl's firm voice thundered throughout the room. "That will be enough! I know you are angry but I will not have you brawling in my house. Besides, hitting Chuck isn't going to bring Nicholas home."

"No, but it will sure make me feel better," Daniel said through clinched teeth.

"Well, cool it!" Carl ordered. "You know deep down that isn't true anyway."

Daniel quit struggling and relaxed as his temper ebbed.

"You're right," he nodded. "I've got to get out there and find my son."

Cautiously Bradley released his hold on Daniel and stepped back. Daniel looked about the room then turned around and started for the door.

"Dan," Chuck spoke up. "I'll help you, if you want?"

"You've done enough already," Daniel said without turning around. He continued out the front door.

The family room became uncomfortably silent after Daniel left the room. Everyone looked at each other without saying a word. Peter and Benjamin returned to watching the snow fall. Ruth and Tamera sat down on the couch next to Claudia. Slowly Bradley walked over to Carl.

"So, what about our reservations at the Tower?" He reminded his father.

"Oh!" Carl jumped as he remembered. He looked at his watch and then out at the snow. "Well, I guess from the looks of things I best call and cancel. The weather looks too bad out."

"That's what I was thinking," Bradley nodded in agreement. "I'll go make the call."

"Thanks, son," Carl smiled at him as he walked into the foyer.

"Where's Bradley going?" Ruth asked Carl curiously. She had observed their hushed conversation.

"Well, I guess I might as well let you all know. Due to the weather outside, we're going to have to cancel our dinner reservations at the Towers."

Ruth's mouth dropped open. She was surprised and saddened at the same time. She had wanted to go there for years but never had the chance. The Towers was the most popular, nicest dinner theater in town. She loved the theater ever since she saw her first play back in high school. Having a leisurely dinner and watching a performance was her idea of the ultimate experience, but it was one that would have to wait.

Bradley returned to the family room. His brow pinched with concern and confusion.

"The telephone is dead," he announced.

"What?" Carl heard what his son had said but was surprised. He walked out of the room and seconds later came back. "Well, things are looking a bit serious. Hope you all don't mind spending the night here. Looks as though we are in for a good storm."

Tamera jumped to her feet. Without a word she left the room. Moments later, the front door closed with a loud bang.

"Do you think you and Bradley should go back out

and look for Nicholas some more?" Ruth looked at Carl and shook her head. "We women can start getting dinner and the beds ready."

"Sure," Carl smiled. He kissed Ruth's cheek and then turned around to head outside. "Come on, Brad." He called as he left the room.

Bradley obediently followed.

"Patty, would you go downstairs and get the candles, just in case, please," Ruth instructed. "As for you two, Claudia and Ariel, would you two be dears and get the spare blankets and sheets out of the closet upstairs. We'll need enough for the couch in the den, parlor and in here."

"Sure, Mom," Claudia smiled and followed Ariel.

"What can we do to help?" Morgan asked as she and Chuck sat at the breakfast table.

Ruth looked at her daughter for a moment. Still angry about her secret and Chuck's behavior; yet, somehow, a softening.

"I could use a hand in the kitchen. Chuck, we could use some wood for the fire."

"I'd be happy to get it, Mom." Chuck quickly left the room. He truly meant what he had said. Her asking him to get the wood was a sign that he was forgiven, at least a little.

Ruth busied herself at the sink washing the potatoes as Morgan tied on an apron. She was not so much angry with Morgan, as she was hurt. Hurt because she had thought their relationship was closer than it appeared it was. She looked up. They were alone in the kitchen. Peter kept Benjamin busy in the family room. She looked at Morgan and then began to peel the potatoes.

"Let me help you with that," Morgan offered and took a potato and began peeling it.

Ruth took a deep breath.

"Why didn't you come to me?" She asked.

Morgan instantly knew what Ruth was talking about. It was so long ago. She was so young and yet the feelings all came flooding back.

"I was afraid," she answered plainly.

"Afraid? Of what?" Ruth paused without looking at her.

"Afraid that you would be disappointed with me and even worse, angry with Chuck. You always seemed to favor the other kids. All my life I've been second to them. While they got the best of everything, the attention, the love and affection, the praise; I got the critical looks, the you could do better's, the cold glares. Nothing I ever did was good enough."

"Morgan, that's not true." Ruth shook her head.

"Mom," Morgan tried to control her emotions. "It is true. It seemed the more I tried, the harder I worked, nothing was ever good enough. When was the last time you told me you were proud of me? That I did something right for once? You told Steven and Patricia that many times. Why couldn't you tell me?"

Ruth listened. She tried to think of an instance when she had praised Morgan. It was hard. So many years ago and so much had happened since.

"You and Dad never thanked me for all the times I stayed home and baby sat, made dinner, or cleaned up after them. Whenever I did try to come to you, you were always too busy with your charity work. You always told me, 'Not now.'"

"Morgan, I'm sorry," Ruth apologized. She had

not realized how different their views were of the past. She was not going to deny or justify something she could not remember. She did feel sincere regret that Morgan felt the way she did.

"When I found out that I was pregnant, I was excited and then I panicked. I wanted to tell you right then, but I was afraid, afraid of disappointing you again. So, Chuck and I made the wrong choice and I have paid for it every day of my life since. You never knew that they messed me up? That I was told I could never have another child. Many times I wanted to tell you and have you make the pain and the guilt go away, but I couldn't. I used to cry myself to sleep every night for years afterwards. Then after we were married and I became pregnant, I felt I was forgiven. Ariel is my little miracle." Tears fell from Morgan's eyes.

Ruth was shocked. She turned to Morgan for the first time. All her hurt left and was replaced with genuine concern for Morgan.

"I had no idea. I'm so sorry," she apologized again.

"I had wanted to tell you for years," Morgan sighed. "But one year passed and and then another and another and then I figured I couldn't tell you. Too much time had gone by."

Ruth reached out to Morgan and hugged her close to her heart. Morgan held her mother tightly as tears silently streamed down her cheeks.

"Morgan, I am proud of you," Ruth whispered into her ear. "I've been so foolish and I'm sorry."

The two held each other for a few more moments. Morgan closed her eyes and remembered the little girl that used to sit on her mother's lap as they read a book, the little girl that used to laugh and bring a smile to her mother's face. So long ago, and yet just yesterday.

The basement was cold and dark. The snow outside had piled up against the windows and blocked out the little light that was outside. Carefully, Patricia felt the wall for the light switch. With a sigh, she found it and the basement lit up. Without further delay, she walked down the stairs and over to the storage closet.

She had not been in the basement in years. It smelled a little musty and damp, probably from being winter. She looked around the open room at the old bedroom lamps and bed from Steven's room. His desk was covered with dust and sat among the many boxes of books and memories that once defined her big brother. A tear came to her eye as she remembered him. How she used to talk to him about her problems. She needed to talk to him now. She turned away and opened the closet.

The box of white tapers sat right in front of her. She quickly picked them up and shut the door. She froze as something caught her eye. Slowly she opened up the door again. There it was sitting on a shelf all by itself. She had forgotten all about it. She smiled to herself and picked up the tattered and love-worn teddy bear. She hugged it and closed her eyes as she remembered the confused teenaged girl that used to cry herself to sleep at night. She opened her eyes and sat the bear back on the shelf and closed the door.

Tamera paced the front porch, pausing occasionally for a second to peer out at the darkening street. She did not feel the cold air against her cheeks. Her hands were numb. Still, she paced.

Off in the distance the sound of footsteps crunching through the snow touched her ears. She turned around, her heart leapt with hopeful anticipation. She took two steps from the porch and stood in the snow, wanting to catch her glimpse of her son.

Slowly the three figures came closer. Once again Tamera's hopes were crushed as she could see her father, brother, and husband returning, alone. Tears fell uncontrollably from her eyes.

"Tamera," Daniel walked up to her. "We have to stop and get warm for a moment. We'll go back out. We haven't given up."

Tamera did not say a word. She returned to the porch and leaned against the pillar. She stared out at the street.

"Come inside with us," Daniel pleaded and put his arm around her. "You're freezing."

"No. I have to stay out here." Tamera shook her head. "You go on inside. I'll be all right."

Daniel looked at Carl and shrugged helplessly. Carl motioned for him and Bradley to go inside. They silently obeyed.

"Tamera, honey," Carl walked over to his daughter and rubbed her back. "Please come inside for a few minutes."

"I can't." She shook her head again as the tears continued to fall silently. "I should be out here looking for my son." Her body jerked as if stung by the sound of that word. She smirked to herself. "My son," she repeated. "I was such a fool to ever believe that he was really mine. I should have told him the truth years ago, but when would have been the right time? When he was two? Five? I guess I didn't want to tell him, because I would have had to admit to myself that I could never have another child of my own. I'm still not ready to admit that to myself. Oh, Daddy, what have I done?" She turned to him and hugged him as she cried into his chest.

"You haven't done anything wrong." Carl took her by her shoulders and looked into her blue eyes. "You did the best you knew how and I am proud of you."

"Did I really, Daddy?" Tamera turned back to the pillar. "Then why is he out there freezing in the cold, lost and confused. His whole world has been destroyed, turned upside down. Face it, I'm a lousy mother. I couldn't even keep my own son from dying and now I may have killed someone else's . If anything happens to Nick, I will never forgive myself."

"Stop that kind of talk right now." Carl took her in his arms again and held her tightly. "You know you don't believe that. What happened to Danny was out of everyone's control. Even if you or the best doctors in the world were standing right there, there was nothing anyone could have done to save him. S.I.D.S. just happens. As for Nick, don't sell yourself so short. You've done a wonderful job of raising him. You may not have given birth to him, but he is your son and you are his mother."

Tamera listened as she held her father tightly. She stared out at her car and suddenly noticed it's fogged up windows.

"Everything is going to be all right." Carl kissed the top of her head. "Just give him time."

"Okay." Tamera nodded and continued to be transfixed by her car.

"Come inside, now," Carl coaxed.

Tamera stepped away and leaned against the pillar again.

"I will, in a few more minutes. I promise." She looked at him and smiled.

"Okay." Carl nodded and then disappeared into the warmth of the house.

Ariel and Claudia dropped the blankets and sheets into a pile on the couch in the family room. They looked around at the room.

"So, where is everyone going to sleep?" Ariel asked anyone who was listening.

Claudia shrugged, deferring the answer to Ruth.

"Well," Ruth wiped her hands on her apron as she walked over to them. "I was figuring that Peter, Nicholas and Benjamin could sleep on the floor in here with Bradley. You two and Patricia could sleep in the den. Your parents could have the parlor and Tamera and Daniel could take the guest room. Unless someone has a better idea, that is."

Ariel and Claudia looked at each other and nodded. "Sounds good to us."

"Good," Ruth sighed. "Dinner will be ready in about an hour. Why don't you get started making up the rooms for me?"

"Sure." Claudia smiled and the two picked up the bundle and headed off to the den.

Tamera turned her collar up against the cold wind that began to blow. Slowly she walked down the front walk toward her car. The street lamps flickered and then came on casting a yellow glow across the snow covered street and sidewalks. There was an eerie silence up and down the street.

She looked at the snow on the top of her car as she neared. The familiar crack around the passenger door was all she needed to see. Her heart pounded in her chest as she tried to figure out what to do next. Slowly she walked up to the driver's door and opened it. Without looking in the back seat, she sat down behind the steering wheel.

"Oh, Nick, where are you?" She sighed out loud.

Slowly the blanket in the backseat began to stir. Nicholas poked his head out from beneath the blanket and sat up. He listened and watched as Tamera cried into her hands. Slowly he reached out and touched her shoulder.

"I'm sorry," he spoke softly.

Immediately Tamera twisted around to see her son.

"Oh, Nick, my baby," she cried real tears, this time of joy. "You are okay?" She hugged him over the back of the seat. "You had me so worried. Please, don't ever run away again. I love you so much."

"I love you, too." He hugged her and smiled uncertainly and then let go. Slowly he climbed into the front seat and sat beside her, facing her. He looked at his hands and then nervously back at her. "I have to know, is it true? Am I adopted?"

Tamera bit her lip and turned away from him so he would not see her cry again. She wiped the tears from her face and looked back at the young boy that sat next to her.

"Oh, Nick, there's something I want to tell you before I answer your question. I never told you this before because I never talked about it much. After Dan and I got married, we had a baby. He was a beautiful creature. Soft blonde hair and big blue eyes. We named him after Dan, but we called him Danny. One morning when he was only four months old, he was up late at night. He couldn't sleep and I was so tired. I put him to bed and he looked up at me with his beautiful eyes and smiled. I couldn't stay awake, so I lay down on the bed next to his crib. I woke up only a couple hours later. I hadn't really slept that long. I looked at my baby, he just stared up at the ceiling. His eyes unmoving. His rosy cheeks were blue and cold. He was gone." Tamera choked back her tears as she tried to continue. "Sudden Infant Death Syndrome, the doctors told us. After that, Dan and I tried to have another child. I miscarried three times and then I couldn't get pregnant. So, after months of testing, the doctors told me I could never have another child of my own. I was crushed. I felt as though I were being punished for sleeping when Danny needed me. I wanted to die.

"Then, Dan convinced me we should adopt a child. I wasn't sure I could but he desperately wanted to. So, I agreed. We saw a lawyer and he arranged for us to see you. You were so beautiful, tiny and helpless. I instantly knew you were my son." Tamera smiled through her tears and touched his cheek. "So, yes, honey, you were adopted. Dan and I aren't your birth parents, but we couldn't love you more even if we were."

Nicholas turned and looked at the snow covered windshield in front of him. The words rang in his ears. He nodded to himself as though telling himself it was okay. Then slowly he found his voice.

"So, what about my real parents? Do you know who they are?"

"We never met them," Tamera bit her lip as she tried to see his face, to be able to read his expression. "But from what we were told, your birth mother was only fifteen when she had you. Her parents couldn't afford to take care of a child, so they thought it was best to give you to someone who could. We don't know anything about your birth father."

Nicholas continued to stare at the windshield. He did not really hear what Tamera had said. Inside his thoughts and emotions were at war. Flashes of growing up, the family gatherings, the trips all came flooding back.

"Nick," Tamera tried hard not to cry again. "Nick," she spoke softly. "If you want me to, I will do what I can to find your birth parents for you."

Nicholas looked at her with tears in his eyes.

"Would you like that?" Tamera looked at him and feared his answer.

"No," he cried and hugged her. "No, I want to go back to the way things were before. I want you to be my mom and Dad to be my dad again."

Tamera hugged him tightly and stroked his hair.

"We are, honey. We are." She kissed the top of his head as her tears of relief began to fall.

Daniel stood at the back door and looked out the window at the darkening night. The snow had begun to ease up a bit, gently falling in slow feather-like drifts. His thoughts turned to Danny and the morning when he was awakened by Tamera's screams. He sprang from their bed and raced to the nursery. Tamera stood over the crib and held their little baby close to her chest. He looked at Danny's hands so blue and lifeless. His heart raced and his throat tightened causing him to gasp for air as he realized what it all meant. Tears flooded his eyes until they fell freely. He quickly grabbed Danny and ordered Tamera to call the ambulance. Immediately he tried to revive Danny, but his little body wasn't responding. No. This can't be happening. Daniel thought to himself. No. Not Danny. Not my son. How can I go on without him?

Daniel's thoughts turned back to the day when he and Tamera received the news. Their son was waiting for them. A beautiful, healthy baby boy. The first time he looked into Nicholas' eyes, all the pain of losing Danny was eased. Replaced by the joy of the little bundle in his arms. He could not have been more proud if Nicholas were his own flesh and blood. To him, Nicholas was.

Now, the pain was back. The tightening in his chest. The helpless feeling. All of it had returned. Not for Danny, for Nicholas. Tears fell from his eyes.

"Dad?" A voice came from behind him.

Daniel slowly turned around.

"Dad." Nicholas repeated seeing the tears in his father's eyes. He ran across the room to him with opened arms.

"Nick!" Daniel choked and the tears began to stream down his cheeks. "Nick," he repeated as he held his son tightly in his arms. "You've come back to us. Don't ever leave us again."

"I'm sorry, Dad. I'm sorry," Nicholas cried with him as they stood in the family room unaware of the family around them.

"I love you so much, son." Daniel closed his eyes tightly and said a silent thank-you to his unseen helper.

Ruth and Carl walked over to Tamera and hugged her.

"He's home." Ruth smiled at her.

"Dinner's ready." Morgan announced and smiled at the sight of Nicholas back where he belonged.

The house was quiet as Ruth slowly walked toward the stairs. She paused by the guest bedroom and listened to the sound of Tamera, Daniel and Nicholas sleeping peacefully at last. She smiled to herself as she descended the stairs. The parlor was dark but Ruth could tell that Morgan and Chuck were sound asleep. A warm feeling rose in her chest as she remembered their conversation earlier that day. She had no idea of what Morgan had been through all those years ago. Such a heavy secret to have kept. Ruth turned toward the family room and a dim light caught her eye from the dining room. Curiously she made her way toward it.

Bradley set at the table cradling a warm cup of milk in his hands as he stared at the photograph of his wedding day. Things looked so bright and hopeful then. His chest ached as he thought about it. He turned the photograph face down on the table.

Ruth looked lovingly at her son. She could tell that he was troubled. Slowly she walked into the room.

"Couldn't sleep either?" She said softly and sat down in the chair next to him at the end of the table.

"No. Not really," he sighed without looking at her.

"With everything that happened today, I forgot to tell you that Amanda called before the phones went out." Ruth tried to look into his eyes but he kept his head down.

"That's okay," he sighed. "I suppose she told you

that I haven't been calling her."

"She did mention it." Ruth admitted. "Why, may I ask?"

Bradley looked up at the ceiling and took a deep labored breath as he collected his thoughts.

"I just can't," he said. His throat tightened as he fought to keep his feelings in check.

Ruth watched her son and felt his anxiety. She gently stroked his short dark brown hair.

"Part of me wants to hold her and tell her everything will be okay; but the other part of me wants to tear her apart for all the pain and anger I feel." Tears filled his eyes as he voiced the tug of war that raged in his heart. "I don't know what to do."

"I know it's hard, dear, losing a child no matter when is never easy. Right now is you have to be strong, for her." Ruth tried to be sympathetic.

"Strong for her?" Bradley shook his head. "What about me? I'm supposed to swallow my feelings, my anguish as if nothing has happened. I can't and I won't. She's to blame for losing this child. She was the one in control. She knew what she was doing all along. She let me believe that we were actually going to have another child when all along she was killing it. Starving it to death. I can't."

Ruth put her arm around her son. Shocked but understanding what he was going through.

"You're right, dear. You can't ignore your pain and feelings, but you have to remember, Amanda is a sick girl. We don't fully understand why she did the things she did, but I have to believe that she didn't do this intentionally."

"Believe what you will, Mom, but it's over. I

can't be there for her any more. I can't." Bradley wiped the tears from his cheek.

Ruth took her arm away from around him and picked up the photograph and turned it up so they both could see it.

"You remember when this was taken?" She asked him.

"Of course, I do," Bradley sighed.

"When you stood up there in front of all of us and looked Amanda in the eyes, you promised her, each other, that you would be there in good times and bad. Well, you owe it to her and yourself to see this through, together. Don't abandon her or give up on her because things aren't going as smoothly as you would have liked. Marriage takes hard work and at times it's down right painful, but in the end it brings so much joy."

Bradley listened to his mother without looking at her. He had hoped she would have been supportive of him. That he had made a right decision. He never expected to hear such harsh words. Somewhere, deep down, he still had love for Amanda but he wondered if it would be enough.

"I don't know, what to do. I'm so confused," he finally said softly.

Ruth smiled at his honesty and kissed his cheek.

"Think about what I've said, honey. We are here for you. Everything will be all right, you'll see if you give it time."

Quietly she stood up and left the room. Bradley sipped his warm milk and set the glass down. He slowly picked up the photograph and stared at the images of Amanda and himself.

"I can't," he said outloud to himself and turned the

photograph face down on the table.

The bedroom was dark except for the soft glow that reflected off the snow outside through the window. Ruth listened to the silence as she lay next to Carl. She felt her wedding ring and smiled to herself. Forty five years of joy, laughter, sorrow and pain; it all happened so fast and yet unnoticed at the time.

Carl slowly reached up and took her hand. She looked at him and he smiled.

"Happy?"

"Yes." Ruth smiled back to him.

He kissed her softly and they fell asleep in each others arms.

THE SHOWER

Tiny green buds dotted the branches of the tall oak trees in the back yard. The sounds of birds chirping and the fresh sweet scent of flowers filled the air and announced the arrival of spring.

Ruth smiled to herself as she looked up at the clear blue afternoon sky. A perfect day for a baby shower, she thought to herself as she carried the tray of punch glasses out to the picnic table. She glanced at her watch then hurried back into the house.

"Carl," she called as she entered the kitchen. "I need a hand in here." Quickly she removed the tray of hors d'oeuvres from the oven.

"Here I am. What can I do?" Carl smiled as he walked into the kitchen. He could tell that Ruth was enjoying herself. She had always loved having people over for a party, something he did not care that much about. It seemed the older he grew, the more he liked his quiet space.

Ruth glanced at him.

"The girls are going to be here any minute. Would you be a dear and take the punch bowl out to the table for me. Be sure to leave it covered, there seems to be a lot of bees out this afternoon. Also, could you light the repellent torches for me."

The back screen door slammed shut as Carl carried out his assignment. Ruth quickly and carefully slid the tiny pastry hors d'oeuvres onto a platter then turned her attention to the cake on the counter. She carefully added the finishing touches to the icing and then smiled to herself. Everything was coming together nicely. Ariel will be pleased.

Ruth picked up the cake and started for the back door just as the front door bell chimed. Frantically she looked around for a place to set the cake. Finding none, she returned it to the kitchen counter and hurried off to answer the front door.

"Coming," she called ahead of herself as the door bell chimed again.

"Hi, Mom," Tamera greeted as Ruth opened the front door. "Are we early?"

"As a matter of fact, yes." Ruth smiled and stepped aside to let Tamera and Nicholas enter. "That's quite all right, though, I could use the help. The guests will be arriving soon and I still have a few things to do."

"Great," Tamera smiled. "I hope it's all right that I brought Nick. I thought that maybe he could keep Dad busy while the party is going on."

"That's fine." Ruth smiled at her grandson. It was hard to believe he was now fifteen. It had seemed as only yesterday he was a baby. "Claudia is bringing Peter, too. So between the two of them, they should be able to handle your father. Come on. The kitchen awaits."

Ruth shut the front door and started back to the kitchen.

"Nick," Tamera said as she turned to her son. "Be a good boy and watch the front door. When the guests arrive, have them meet us out back."

"Sure, Mom." Nicholas smiled even though he hated being called a boy. He was not a boy anymore. He was a young man, almost an adult.

"Tamera?" Ruth called from the kitchen.

"Coming, Mother." Tamera hurried off to the kitchen.

"Would you get the door?" Ruth motioned toward the back door with her head as she picked up the cake.

"Oh, Mom, the cake is beautiful," Tamera said as she held the back door open.

Slowly Tamera followed Ruth out to the long table covered with a pale yellow cloth. Festive balloons of pastel pinks and blues hung in the mid-air, tethered by matching ribbons. Streamers twisted from the tree branches above the table to the poles near the swimming pool, forming a open canopy. Tamera smiled as she remembered the baby shower Ruth had thrown for her when she brought Nicholas home from the hospital. Time had flown by.

The back door opened and Bradley stepped out carrying a wrapped gift. Ruth looked up at her son and a smile spread across her lips.

"Bradley." She went to him and gave him a hug and a kiss.

"I just thought I should stop by and drop off this for Ariel," he sighed.

"That's so sweet of you." Ruth took the gift.

"How is Amanda?"

"She seems to be doing better," he shrugged. "The doctor's say that her relapse was to be expected but she seems to be improving steadily."

"Did they say when she'll be able to come home?" Ruth took his arm as they walked over to the gift table.

"No," he sighed heavily. "Maybe in a month or two."

"Well, it will take time, honey." Ruth squeezed his arm. "In the meantime, how are you and Benjamin holding up?"

"He really misses his mom." Bradley avoided answering the whole question. "But, I think he understands as best a three year old can."

"Kids are stronger than we give them credit for," Ruth assured him.

"Well, I think if it's all right I'll just hang out in the house for awhile." Bradley looked back at the house. •

"That would be fine, dear." Ruth looked at her son concerned. He seemed quiet; somewhat depressed. "There's some fresh coffee on the stove. Help yourself."

"Thanks, Mom." Bradley kissed her cheek and disappeared into the house.

Tamera slowly walked over to her, still staring at the back door where Bradley had entered.

"He sure seems quiet. Is everything okay? This is so unlike him."

"I don't know," Ruth sighed heavily. Then she shook her head as though shaking the thoughts from her mind and back to the party. "Well, looks like we are almost ready for the party to begin."

Nicholas opened the front door and stepped aside to let the small group enter.

"Hi, Nick." Claudia smiled as she entered.

"Hi, Aunt Claudia." Nicholas smiled at her and then his smile faded as he looked at Peter. He did not say a word.

"Hi, Nick." Peter smiled at him, ignoring the cold expression in Nicholas' eyes.

Nicholas did not answer.

"Mom says for everyone to go out back." Nicholas closed the front door and followed the group.

"Claudia!" Ruth smiled and gave her daughter-in-law a hug as she entered the kitchen. "I'm so happy that you made it. I know you are still busy getting settled into your new house and all. How do you like it?"

"I love it." Claudia smiled proudly. "Peter seems to like it too. Although, he has been having a rough time adjusting at school. It was so nice of Nick to offer to show him around. Can I give you a hand with those?" Claudia looked at the trays of hors'doeuvres on the counter behind Ruth.

"That would be wonderful." Ruth smiled and handed her a tray.

Claudia followed Ruth out the back door and over to the refreshment table. A bee buzzed by her head and she ducked, nearly dropping the tray.

"Oh, my," she gasped as she looked around at the handful of bees that were buzzing over the table. "Mom, look at the bees."

Ruth turned around from setting her tray on a nearby table.

"Oh dear," she gasped as she noticed the bees. She glanced over at the lit torches that did not seem to be helping. "Just leave them alone. We should be okay. Here, grab that torch over there and I'll get the other one. We can put them at either end of the table. That should keep them away."

Claudia and Ruth pulled up the torches and stuck them into the ground at either end of the table. The bees flew off quickly. Ruth smiled to herself, it had worked.

"Hi, Brad." Patricia greeted as she walked into the dining room.

Bradley did not look up from his coffee cup as he sat alone at the table. His thoughts were far off. He stared blankly at the picture that hung on the wall in front of him.

"Is everything all right, Brad?" Patricia sat down next to him.

Bradley did not look at her. He had heard her when she first spoke.

"Today, my precious little girl would have been three months old," he said softly.

Patricia looked at her folded hands on the table. She knew that Bradley had taken it hard, losing the baby. She had practiced over and again what she would say to him, should the opportunity come. Now that it had, she was speechless.

"I'm sorry."

"I'm the one who is sorry." Bradley smirked and then sipped his coffee. "I shouldn't burden you with that."

"No," Patricia reached out and put her hand on his

shoulder. "That's what family is for. It's not a burden."

Bradley fought back the tears and looked into his coffee cup.

"You know what the hardest thing is? It's not so much losing the baby, but it's how. Damn it, why wouldn't she eat? If only she would have stopped all that nonsense about her weight. If only she would have thought about the baby and not herself."

"Brad," Patricia spoke softly yet with a firmness in her voice. "You can't blame her."

"The hell I can't!" He snapped back and looked at her. "She killed our baby. She starved it to death." The tears began to fall and he took a deep breath. "Promise me you wont tell anyone."

"Tell anyone what?" Patricia looked at her brother curiously.

"Promise?" He repeated and looked at his coffee again.

"Ok, I promise." Patricia shrugged to herself.

"I've filed for a divorce a month ago." He breathed in a labored breath. "I don't want her to come back here. She can stay with her mother. I'll raise Benji by myself. She not only killed our child but she also killed any love I had for her."

The words hit Patricia like a brick. She sat back in her chair in stunned silence. She looked at the wall in front of her and then back at her brother.

"A month ago?"

"Yes," he answered matter-of-factly.

"What does Amanda say about it?"

"She's upset but frankly I don't care. There is no judge in this state that will give her custody of Benji, not now that she has been committed."

"Oh, Bradley, I am so sorry." Patricia shook her head and gave her brother a hug.

Bradley sat motionless in her grasp.

The backyard was a buzz with the chatter and laughter of the crowd of women. In the center of it all was Ariel. She sat at the table of gifts, rubbing her round stomach. Her long blonde hair was pulled back in a pony-tail by a sheer pink scarf. She smiled at all of the attention she was getting.

"So, when is Mark coming home?" One of the girls asked as she sipped her punch.

Ariel looked up at her and her eyes sparkled.

"Tomorrow. I can't wait. It's been really lonely in that big empty house."

"Tamera?" Morgan walked over to her sister.

"What?" Tamera looked coldly at her.

"Can I talk to you for a moment, alone, please?" Morgan asked sheepishly.

"Fine." Tamera glared at her sister. Only three months had passed since the incident, yet it was still fresh in her mind.

The two walked away from the gathering to a quiet corner of the yard. Their departure did not go unnoticed. Claudia nudged Ruth and motioned with her head in their direction. Ruth gave a motherly look at the two, although they had not seen her.

"What do you want, Morgan?" Tamera's tone was curt.

"I just want to apologize again. I know what Chuck did was wrong. He shouldn't have done it," Morgan spoke softly.

"He shouldn't have done a lot of things!" Tamera snapped at her. "He may be your husband, but I don't have to like him and I don't have to like you either." Tamera turned around and headed back toward the tables.

"Tamera," Morgan called after her. "You are not being fair."

Tamera froze and turned around slowly.

"Fair," she repeated and walked back toward her sister. "Fair," she said louder. "You and that good-for-nothing husband of yours nearly destroyed my family and you say, I'm not being fair?"

"Well, what about you telling Ariel about my abortion?"

"Just be thankful I did or we wouldn't be here today." Tamera tried to keep her temper under control.

"What are you talking about?" Morgan looked at her confused and suddenly without anger.

Tamera looked smugly at her sister.

"Ariel wanted to get an abortion herself. She told me so the day before her wedding. That is way I told her. I did you a favor, Grandma," Tamera said flatly then turned and walked away without another word.

Morgan stood in dumbfounded silence.

"Hey, Nick." Peter walked into the family room and looked at his cousin.

Nicholas did not look up from the television. He tried to ignore Peter.

"Nick, where's Grandpa?" Peter asked and tried to catch Nicholas' eyes.

"He's out in the garage tinkering with the lawn mower," Nicholas answered and turned his head away.

"Do you want to go out front and shoot hoops?"

"No," Nicholas answered flatly.

Peter sighed. He had figured that since his mother had bought a house close to theirs and they attended the same school, even though being two years apart, they could be friends. At least it started out that way, but something happened and he did not understand what it was.

"Do you want to play catch?"

Nicholas muted the television and then turned to face Peter.

"Don't you get it. I don't want to play anything with you. Leave me alone." He turned back to the television and unmuted it.

Peter looked at Nicholas for a moment and tried not to let his hurt feelings show. Without another word he turned around and walked out of the room.

"Faggot." Nicholas glared at the doorway and muttered under his breath.

The roar of laughter rose from the backyard as Ariel opened her gifts, holding up each gift for their approval. Wrapping paper littered the ground around her feet while the bows were piled up next to her opened gifts.

"Who is that one from?" Ruth asked as she wrote down the gift into the baby book.

"It's from Aunt Patty." Ariel smiled. "Thank-you, very much." She smiled at her aunt.

Tamera smiled as she turned away from the group and headed over to the punch bowl to get another cup. She was lost in her thoughts and not paying attention to the buzzing around her ears. Unconsciously she swatted at the sound.

Suddenly there was a sharp pain on her neck behind her ear. She screamed and spun around, falling into the table and knocking over one of the torches. The torch splattered it's hot oil across the lawn and ignited the table cloth.

"Oh my god," Ruth gasped and grabbed the table cloth off the empty table nearby. Quickly she ran to the burning table and began swatting the flames. "Morgan, get a bucket of water, now." She called over her shoulder.

Morgan quickly emptied the pitcher of lemonade and drew water from the swimming pool. She quickly doused the fire and extinguished it.

"Boy, that was a scare," Ruth said out of breath as she shook her head. She turned around and looked at the shocked faces of her guests "It's okay. It's over," she smiled but then it faded as she looked at their frozen expressions.

"Mom, Tamera!" Morgan gasped and dropped the pitcher. It shattered as it hit the concrete surrounding the pool.

Ruth looked beside her at her daughter lying on the ground.

"Morgan, get your father out here, now!" Ruth ordered as she knelt down beside her daughter and checked her neck for a pulse. "Ohmygod," she gasped as she felt the swollen knot behind Tamera's ear. "Morgan get Tamera's purse, on the double!" She screamed. "Tamera! Tamera!" Ruth repeated and shook her daughter to try to bring her to. No use.

"Ariel, take everyone into the house and get your grandfather out here, now," Ruth ordered.

Quickly everyone rushed into the house. Morgan

returned Tamera's purse and handed it to Ruth. Ruth grabbed it and emptied it onto the ground next to her.

"There it is," she said out loud but more to herself as she grabbed the bee sting kit. She quickly opened it and took out the syringe. At first she was uncomfortable about giving her daughter a shot. However, after having done it several times over the years as Tamera had grown up, she had become quite used to it. Slowly she pushed the contents of the syringe into Tamera's arm. She withdrew the needle and sat back.

Carl ran up to them just as Tamera opened her eyes. He glanced at the burnt table cloth and broken pitcher.

"What happened?"

Ruth sat holding Tamera's head in her lap.

"Tamera got stung by another bee," she sighed. "Behind her ear. Her breathing is becoming normal again, but I think you should take her to the emergency room and have her looked at, just to be sure. She may have hit her head when she collapsed."

"Sure thing." Carl turned to Morgan. "Get Bradley out here to help me."

Morgan hurried off to the house just as Nicholas ran out the back door.

"Mom!" He shouted as Ruth and Carl helped her to her feet.

"She's okay, Nick," Ruth assured him. "She was just stung by a bee. She'll be fine."

Nicholas looked at his mother. Tiny beads of sweat dotted her forehead and her eyes were a bit glossy. His heart pounded in his chest. He had seen her before when she had been stung, but this time she looked different, not all there inside.

"Mom?"

"I'm okay, baby," Tamera nodded to him still groggy. Her mouth felt dry and her tongue felt thick.

Bradley ran over to them and took Tamera's arm from Ruth.

"Help your father get her into the car. He's going to take her to the emergency room to have her checked out." Ruth instructed Bradley.

"I'm going, too," Nicholas demanded.

"No, you're not," Ruth said firmly and grabbed his arm. "She will be fine. Besides, there isn't anything you can do there that you can't do here."

Morgan opened the back door for them as the five made their way into the house.

"I called the emergency room and they will be waiting for you."

Ruth, Nicholas and Morgan followed the three out the front door and watched as Carl and Bradley put Tamera into the car. Morgan shook her head.

"Boy, I never realized that Tamera was so allergic to bees. It seems to have gotten worse as she as gotten older."

"That it has," Ruth agreed as the car pulled out of the driveway and started down the street.

"Is she going to be okay?" Claudia asked as she walked up to Ruth's side.

"Yes," Ruth nodded. "We've been though this several times over the years. It's almost a yearly occurrence."

"Wow," Claudia sighed. She had never known anyone who was allergic to bees and this was definitely unsettling.

Nicholas pulled loose of Ruth's grasp and walked

out onto the front lawn.

"Well, I better get back to the guests," Morgan excused herself and disappeared into the house.

Peter walked over to him with the basketball tucked under his arm. He watched the car turn the corner and then put his hand on Nicholas' shoulder.

"I'm sorry about your mom. She'll be fine." He tried to assure Nicholas.

"Get your hands off me, you queer!" Nicholas snapped and pushed Peter away.

"Hey. What did you call me?" Peter's anger blazed instantly. He shoved Nicholas back.

"You heard me, faggot." Nicholas doubled up his fist and punched Peter in the jaw.

Peter instinctively fought back grabbing Nicholas and tumbling to the ground.

"Boys!" Ruth screamed and ran over to them with Patricia and Claudia. "Stop it!" Ruth demanded as the other two women pulled them apart. Nicholas took one last swing at Peter, connecting with his mouth. A ribbon of blood seeped from the corner of his lips.

"I said that is enough!" Ruth glared at Nicholas. "Now, what started this?"

"He did." Nicholas hissed and looked at Peter.

"No, I didn't." Peter glared back at Nicholas.

"Go ahead and tell them, Peter. Tell them about the rumors at school," Nicholas egged on.

Peter clinched his jaw and looked around at the faces of his mother, aunt and grandmother. Without a word he turned around and ran off down the street.

"Peter!" Claudia called and started to go after him. Ruth grabbed her arm.

"Suppose you tell us what this is all about?" Ruth

looked angrily at her grandson.

"Well, there's this rumor going around school that Peter is a fag."

The words hit Claudia so hard it took her breath away. Instantly she understood why Peter never talked about school and avoided the subject. Her heart ached for his pain.

"I better go after him."

"No, Claudia," Patricia stopped her. "Let me. Maybe he will talk to a stranger."

Claudia looked at Patricia and reluctantly nodded. Patricia hurried off to catch up to Peter.

"As for you, Nicholas," Ruth spoke forcefully. "I don't ever want to hear those words in my house ever again. Is that understood."

"Yes, ma'am." Nicholas answered as he looked at grandmother and realized she was not kidding around.

"Now, get in the house and get cleaned up," Ruth ordered.

Nicholas obeyed.

"Claudia," Ruth turned to her daughter-in-law. "Don't worry, boys go through this name calling thing. It's part of growing up. Peter will be fine."

"Yeah." Claudia nodded but deep down she knew there was something more here. She had heard these same type of rumors from the last school Peter had attended back East. She thought that it would pass, but now she was not so sure.

Slowly Ruth and Claudia walked back into the house.

The family room was filled with the noisy chatter of the guests. The gifts had been moved inside and were stacked on the coffee table in the center of the room as the party continued.   Ruth quickly poured fresh bowls of chips and cookies.

"I hope you don't mind, Mrs. Wallace, that we moved the party inside," one of the girls sheepishly said.

"No, that's quite all right, dear." Ruth smiled and handed her the bowl of chips. "With the bees outside, I think it was a good idea. Pass those around and I'll fix us some more punch."

"Peter," Patricia called as she ran after him. "Wait up."

Peter kept running, heading for the park just around the corner, three blocks from the house. It was the only place he could think of to run to. Never had he felt so alone as he did at that moment. Tears streamed down his cheeks, stinging the tiny cut on the corner of his mouth. He did not care. Finally he stopped and leaned against a tree. He could not run any longer. Slowly he slide down the trunk until he sat on the ground. He buried his face in his crossed arms and cried.

Patricia stopped running after him when she entered the park and saw that he was sitting on the ground. Slowly she walked over to him trying to catch her breath. She stopped and stood beside him for a moment before she spoke.

"Do you mind if I sit down?" She asked.

Peter did not answer her. He kept his head down.

Patricia sat down beside him nonetheless. She stared across the park at a man walking his dog and two children playing on the swings with their mother close by.

"Do you want to talk about it?"

"No." Peter said flatly.

Patricia nodded to herself and continued to stare out at the trees.

"You wouldn't understand," Peter continued much to Patricia's surprise.

"Probably not, but you never know," she said without emotion.

"You don't know what it's like to grow up without a father." Peter looked up and stared straight ahead. "There was this guy, Matthew, at school when I was a freshman back East. He was a year ahead of me and really nice. At first he would look out for me when the other kids teased me about my absent father. I liked him and we would talk after school. Sometimes we would go on a walk or just hang out in the gym, he liked basketball. Mom liked him, too. She thought it was nice that I had another guy to talk to, since I didn't have my father around. Well, one day some kids beat me up and I hid out in the gym under the bleachers. Matthew heard about it and he found me. He took me over to the locker room and helped me get cleaned up. One thing led to another and before I knew what was happening, he was undressed in the shower with me. We, well you know the rest or can guess what happened."

"Did you tell your mother?" Patricia tried to hide the surprise in her voice.

"No." Peter came back quickly almost in panic. "I couldn't."

"That's understandable." Patricia nodded. "Did he threaten you?"

"You don't understand." Peter shook his head. "I didn't want to. She would have been angry and he

would have been in trouble. I couldn't do that to him.
I was in love with him."

Patricia was silent. She did understand more than
he realized, but she listened.

"I guess I've always known that I was attracted to
men." Peter continued. "Since I was in the fifth grade,
really. There was this guy in my class; all the girls had
a crush on him, and so did I. When we were in the
locker room after P.E., sometimes I'd glance over at
him while he showered. He had a great body, for a fifth
grader. So, you see, Aunt Patty, I am gay; but I can't
tell my mother. I don't want to disappoint her."

"Why do you think it would disappoint her?"
Patricia turned and looked at Peter. "Has she ever said
anything to that effect?"

"No," Peter shrugged. "But wouldn't any parent be
disappointed if their son turned out queer?"

Patricia looked away. She realized at that moment
that what he said was true. Any parent would be upset
if their son or their daughter for that matter, turned out
to be gay.

"You know, Peter," she spoke reassuringly. "The
main thing you have to do is be true to yourself. Be
honest. You should tell your mother how you feel and
if she has a problem with that, then that is her problem,
not yours. You can not live your life to be someone
everyone else expects you to be. You will be miserable
and your life will be empty. Okay?"

Patricia heard a faint voice inside her head answer,
"Okay."

Peter looked up at his aunt and tried to smile.

"Thank-you." He nodded. "I'll try."

Patricia looked at Peter's bruised cheek and swollen

lip.

"Looks like we better get back to the house and get some ice on that." She smiled. "Come on."

Patricia stood up and dusted the dirt from the seat of her blue denim jeans and then held out a hand to Peter. He grasped it tightly and pulled himself to his feet.

"Wow," he smiled. "You're pretty strong for a girl," he teased.

"Well, don't mess with me," she teased right back.

Ariel laughed out loud as she picked up another package.

"Let me guess," she said as she squeezed the sides. "I bet I know what this is." She looked around at the girls gathered about her. With a sharp tug, she ripped open the package. "They're baby bottles!" She screamed and laughed as she showed them to everyone and then set them beside the other two packages. The whole room roared with laughter.

The clock on the wall chimed four. As though on cue, three of the members of the party rose at once. They made their apologies and then their good-byes. Ruth stood up to escort them to the front door. They stopped briefly to thank Ruth again for her hospitality and then disappeared out the front door.

Ruth turned around to head back to the party when a knock came at the front door. She smiled to herself.

"Okay, what did you forget?" She said as she swung open the front door.

"Oh," she said with a start. "I'm sorry. I thought you were someone else. Can I help you?"

"Is Patty here?" The woman in a flannel shirt and denim jeans demanded more than asked.

"No," Ruth answered quite puzzled by the woman's roughness.

"Liar!" The woman snapped and then pushed her way into the foyer. "Patricia get your butt out here now!" She yelled into the house.

Ruth took a deep breath and tightened her jaw.

"Now, see here, young lady." She reached up and grabbed the woman's arm.

"Patricia!" The woman jerked away from Ruth's grasp and ignored her. "I know you are here, get out here," she yelled up at the second floor.

Claudia and Morgan came into the foyer. They looked at Ruth in puzzlement. Ruth shrugged and then forcefully grabbed the woman's arm and spun her around. With her jaw firmly set she glared at the woman.

"Look, I don't know who you are, but you have no right to come into my house and -"

Just then the front door opened and Patricia walked into the house followed by Peter. Patricia froze as her eyes met with the woman's. A wave of panic swept over her and her hands began to sweat.

"There you are, you bitch," the woman cursed and lunged at Patricia. Her hands closed around Patricia's throat and the force of her lunge sent them crashing backwards into the front door. Patricia's head hit with a loud thud.

"You aren't going to leave me." The woman tightened her grip as Patricia struggled unsuccessfully to break free.

Ruth's temper flared, mixed with fear. In one swift movement she grabbed the woman by the hair and jerked her backwards, catching her off balance and sending her crashing to the floor.

"Get out of my house!" Ruth demanded.

Morgan quickly ran to Patricia and helped her toward the parlor. Patricia coughed as she tried to catch her breath, unable to speak. Peter watched in wide-eyed shock at the scene.

The woman instantly sprang to her feet and threw Ruth to the floor.

"I'm not leaving without Patricia!" She lunged again at Patricia.

Morgan protectively stepped in front of her and pushed the woman back. Morgan's heart pounded as adrenalin coursed through her veins. She was almost surprised by her reaction to protect her sister and yet, it gave her satisfaction to know she would.

The woman glared hard at Morgan. She clinched her teeth.

"Okay, bitch," she hissed.

"Hold it right there!" Claudia shouted as she lowered her pistol at the woman.

Suddenly the hostility in the woman's eyes was replaced by fear. She stepped back as Claudia cocked the hammer.

"I don't know who you are, but you are not welcome here," Claudia said in a firm voice.

"Mom?" Peter looked at his mother in surprise.

"Claudia, no." Patricia found her voice. "It's okay. Please, don't."

Claudia kept her aim and her eye on the woman.

Slowly Ruth stood up. She was shocked at the sight of a gun in her house. Never before had such a thing been brought in; not even when the boys were young had she allowed even a toy gun around. Yet, at that moment, she was glad that it was there. Ruth looked at the woman and then at Patricia.

"Patty, what is going on here?" She demanded.

Patricia looked at the woman, then slowly at each of the faces around her, Morgan, Peter, Claudia, then finally her mother.

"Please, Claudia, put the gun down," Patricia almost begged. "Mom, this is Jo, my ex-roommate." She glared at Jo.

"Your lover, don't you mean?" Jo blurted out.

Ruth looked at the woman again in shock. She could not believe what she had just heard. What did she mean by that remark? What was she implying? She looked at Patricia confused.

Morgan shook her head as though disagreeing. This woman could not possibly be meaning what she said. Not Patricia. Obviously she is out of her mind or on drugs.

"Go ahead, tell them." Jo spoke directly to Patricia.

Patricia stood in stunned silence, her mouth open as though she were about to speak only the words would not come out.

"Aunt Patty?" Peter looked at his aunt.

Patricia's eyes filled with tears as she looked at Peter and then at her mother. She took a deep breath.

"Not any more."

"I've had enough of this." Ruth shook her head in disbelief. "Get out of my house, now!" She pointed directly at the front door. Her heart breaking, her throat tightening, her eyes filling with tears. "Get out!"

Jo backed away, toward the front door. She opened it and slipped out without a further word.

Patricia looked at her mother. Tears fell from her eyes.

"Mom, I'm sorry," she cried.

"Get out of my house," Ruth said through her tears.

"Mom, please, let me explain." Patricia pleaded.

"I've heard enough, already. Go." Ruth turned around and left the room.

Patricia looked around the foyer at the stunned faces, then bolted for the front door.

"Aunt Patty," Peter called to her and followed her outside.

Patricia stopped on the front walk and turned around to her nephew. Tears dampening her cheeks. She tried to smile, to reassure him.

"You see, Peter. I do understand, but I was wrong."

With that she turned around and headed for her car.

"No, you weren't wrong." Peter called to her and wiped the tear from his eyes.

Ruth walked across the back yard. Her head still reeling from what had just occurred in the house. Her thoughts going in all directions. Slowly she began to pick up the torn wrapping paper and ribbons.

Claudia slowly walked around the swimming pool. She watched as Ruth stuffed the trash into a plastic garbage bag. She wrung her hands nervously as she mustered up the courage to speak.

"Mom," her voice was soft. "I'm sorry. I should have told you about the gun."

"Yes, you should have," Ruth answered flatly without looking at her.

"I have carried it for years. Ever since I was mugged shortly after Steven moved back out here. I just forgot that it was there, in my purse," Claudia explained. "I'm sorry."

Ruth looked at Claudia. Her mind frozen on the word mugged. Her anger melted and was replaced with empathy.

"I'm the one who should be sorry. I didn't know."

"I never told anyone before." Claudia smiled faintly. "I guess we all have our little secrets that we keep to ourselves. It's safer that way, sometimes."

Ruth nodded and continued to pick up the napkins and paper plates that litter the lawn. She tried not to think about Patricia but she could not stop.

"Mom," Claudia again spoke softly. "You need to talk to Patty. You can't let her leave here, not like this."

Ruth looked up at Claudia, confused by her own conflicting emotions. She knew Claudia was right, but she could not give in. It went against every part of her being; every part of her moral upbringing. It was so unnatural. No. She did not have to discuss it. Ruth returned to her cleaning.

"Mom, give Patty a chance to explain," Claudia pleaded. "You wouldn't want to lose her, too."

Ruth froze. Slowly she turned around, her heart aching, tears filling her eyes.

"I don't know what to do. I don't if I can. What do I say?" She searched for answers in the tree branches and in the flower beds that lined the fence. "I don't know how to deal with this."

"You are not alone, Mom." Claudia walked over to her mother-in-law and put her arm around her. "We are all here. We can handle this together. We need to give Patty a chance."

Ruth nodded and turned to hug Claudia as she cried.

Ariel closed the front door and leaned against it.

"They are all gone," she sighed as Morgan placed the telephone receiver back on its rest. "What a day. Who was that on the phone?"

"It was your grandfather," she answered. "He and your Aunt Tamera are on their way home. She's fine. Where's Nick?"

Ariel thought for a moment.

"I think I saw him last in the dining room."

"Thanks." Morgan smiled and headed for the dining room.

Ariel shook her head. Despite everything that had happened she still enjoyed her party. She could not wait to show Mark all the things she had received for the baby. Unconsciously she rubbed her round stomach as she headed back into the family room.

Peter stood by the window. His arms folded over this chest. He quietly stared out at his mother and grandmother in the backyard. His thoughts kept going over his conversation with Patricia and the events that unfolded in the foyer. He could not help but remember the look on his grandmother's, mother's, and aunt's faces as Patricia revealed her secret. No, he could not live with that. He turned around just as Ariel walked into the room.

"Hi, Peter." She smiled at him.

"Hi," he replied and avoided eye contact as he quickly left the room. He was not in the mood to talk to anyone. He headed into the foyer.

Ariel watched him curiously and then heard the front door shut. She did not give him another thought but busied herself picking up the baby's gifts and packing them into an empty box.

Peter walked over to a quiet corner in the front yard and sat down under the tall oak tree. Tears filled his eyes as he thought about his friend Matthew back East. If only he had put up more of a fight to stay back there, but how he could disappoint his mother. She thought it was important for him to be with his family.

Tears began to roll down his cheeks. His heart ached as he thought about his afternoons with Matthew. Matthew's strong arms wrapped around him, giving him a feeling of peace and security. The smell of Matthew's after shave mixed with his sweat. The feel of his soft lips as they kissed. Peter missed him so much. How could he have left his best friend? The only one who understood him. The only one with whom he could truly be himself.

Peter looked at the pistol in his hands. He fumbled with the tumbler as he thought about his life without Matthew. He did not want to go on alone and he could not face disappointing his mother. Slowly he brought the barrel up to his lips. The metal was cold and hard against his tongue.

Claudia opened the back door and stepped into the family room, followed closely by Ruth. They set the punch bowl and platters down on the counter in the kitchen without a word.

"Ariel," Ruth turned to her granddaughter. "Where's your mother?"

"She's in the dining room talking to Nicholas, I think. Grandpa and Aunt Tamera are on their way home right now." Ariel replied and continued to fold the baby clothes she had received.

Ruth looked at Claudia and the two of them hurried off to the dining room.

"Morgan, can I see you in the parlor, please?" Ruth interrupted as she walked through the dining room. "Now."

Morgan obediently stood up from the table and followed Claudia into the parlor. They both sat down and waited for Ruth to speak.

Ruth walked over to the fireplace and thoughtfully touched Patricia's photograph. She did love her daughter, that was never in question. She just did not know what to do. What to say. What to think. Slowly she turned around and faced the two women.

"I know I've never been one to keep secrets from any of you, and especially your father," she began. "However, I do not want anyone to tell him about what went on here this afternoon. I need to talk to Patty, first. So, please, do not say a word."

Morgan readily nodded her consent.

"Shall I try to call Patty for you?" Claudia offered.

"No." Ruth looked back at the photograph. "I need to do it, myself."

Claudia nodded silently and smiled. She was glad that Ruth was not going to leave things the way she had. She liked Patricia, liked being her friend, her sister-in-law, no matter what. She looked at the coffee table and noticed her purse laying opened. She did not remember leaving it there. Curiously she picked it up. Immediately she noticed it was lighter. Her heart pounded. She began to breath faster as her feeling of panic grew.

"Mom, Morgan, who was into my purse?" She asked.

"I didn't see anyone, why?" Morgan shrugged.

Ruth turned around sharply. She knew why.

"Ohmygod, Claudia." Her tone was almost a chastisement.

Claudia turned around and walked into the foyer.

"Peter, Nicholas, Ariel," she called out in a loud voice.

Immediately Ariel and Nicholas rushed into the foyer. They could tell by the tone in Claudia's voice that something was wrong.

"Were either of you two in my purse?" She asked sharply.

Ariel shook her head.

"No." Nicholas answered. "Why?"

Just then a shot rang out in the front yard. Everyone jumped and stepped back. Then Ruth ran to the front door followed closely by Claudia. Together they stepped onto the front porch and froze.

"Peter!" Claudia screamed as she looked at her son leaning against the oak tree facing away from them.

"Oh, god, no." She ran over to him and knelt down.

Peter did not move.

Claudia grabbed him up in her arms only to let go when he pulled away.

"Peter!" She grabbed his arm and turned him around to face her. Her anger replacing her fear. "What is the matter with you?"

Peter looked at her but not really seeing her.

"Nothing!" He snapped and looked away.

"Where is it?" She demanded.

"Where's what?" He asked her calmly.

"Don't play games with me. That gun is not a toy." Claudia shook him.

"I don't have it." He pulled away again. "What's going on?"

"Then what was that shot I heard?"

Peter laughed out loud as he thought quickly.

"That wasn't a gun shot. That was a car back firing."

Claudia looked at her son and felt so foolish, yet still angry with him for scaring her so. Slowly she stood up and walked back to the house, leaving him sitting under the tree.

Peter listened as the front door closed behind them. He glanced over his shoulder just to make sure they were gone. He smiled contentedly to himself. She had believed his lie. Slowly he stood up and walked across the street. Cautiously he stooped down and picked up the pistol from the bushes where it had landed. Quickly he stashed it into the front of his jeans and covered it with his shirt.

"Aunt Claudia, we've looked everywhere and still can't find it," Ariel reported as she walked into the parlor. She sat down in the chair by the doorway and rubbed her round stomach.

Ruth wrung her hands as she stood by the fireplace.

"I guess we have to conclude that one of the guests took it," she sighed.

"I suppose you're right; although I can't imagine who it would have been," Claudia conceded. She rubbed her slender neck, massaging her tense muscles.

"Are you going to file a police report?" Morgan asked, more concerned about her reputation with her women friends than for the missing gun.

"I know I should," Claudia thought out loud. "But I can't. I'm actually relieved it's gone. You hear those awful stories about children getting their hands on their parents' gun. I was always worried about Peter. Now I don't have to worry."

"But what if something should happen to the person who took it?" Ruth spoke up. "I really think you should reconsider. Afterall, you could be opening yourself up to a lot of unnecessary trouble."

Claudia thought for a moment. She knew Ruth was right. On the other hand, she knew if she were to report it missing, then she would be the one in trouble for not having a permit to carry it.

"I'll think about it," she nodded.

The front door opened and Carl helped Tamera into the foyer. A large white gauze bandage was taped to her neck over the bee sting. She smiled at her mother and her sisters.

"Hi. I'm sorry that I messed up the party," she apologized in a tired voice.

"Nonsense." Ruth rushed over to her and gave her daughter a hug. "You didn't ruin a thing. If you don't believe me, just ask Ariel."

"No, Aunt Tamera, you didn't. I'm glad you are okay." Ariel gave her aunt a hug and kissed her cheek.

"Mom!" Nicholas shouted and ran into the foyer. "Mom, you're okay." He threw his arms around her and hugged her tightly.

"Oh, my," she gasped. "I'm fine, honey." She kissed the top of his head.

"So, what did the doctor say?" Ruth turned to Carl.

"The same old thing, keep that bee sting kit close

and be careful." Carl took a deep breath and sighed.

"That's comforting," Ruth smirked. "Doesn't he realize it's Spring and the bees are everywhere?" She asked rhetorically. "Okay," she sighed.

"Well, Mom, I think it's time I took Ariel home. Then I need to be getting home, myself. I still have to make dinner for Chuck." Morgan spoke up as she looked at her watch.

"Okay, dear." Ruth smiled and gave them each a hug and a kiss. "Thank-you for your help this afternoon. I really appreciate it."

"Nick, could you help me out with my things?" Ariel asked her cousin.

Nicholas looked at his mother, still holding fast to her waist. Tamera nodded at him to go as she pried his arms loose.

"I think it's time for us to get going, too," Tamera announced. "It's been quite a day and I'm a little tired."

"I don't think you should be driving just yet," Ruth spoke up. "Carl, would you please take her home for me? With everything that has happened today, I don't need any more worries. You can have Dan pick up your car tomorrow," she added.

"Sure, honey." Carl kissed Ruth's cheek a bit puzzled by her comment.

"Thank-you," she smiled, a bit relieved.

Claudia watched as everyone gathered their belongings and headed for the front door.

"Shall I stay and give you a hand with the dishes?" she asked Ruth.

"No. I think I can handle it." Ruth smiled. "Why don't you go on, too. It'll be nice to have some quiet time."

Just then Peter walked in the front door. He looked around as one by one his aunts and cousins filed out the door in front of him.

"So, is everyone leaving?" He asked and looked at his mother.

"Yes," Claudia nodded. "Get your jacket."

"Mom, can I spend the night here, if it's okay with Grandma, please?" Peter looked at his grandmother and then back at his mother.

Ruth looked at her grandson and smiled. She could not help but see Steven when he was that age. Peter's eyes were just like his. He was so much his father's son.

"It's okay with me." She heard herself say.

"If you are sure he wont be a bother." Claudia smiled approvingly.

"No bother," Ruth smiled.

"Gee, thanks, Mom." Peter kissed his mother's cheek and then gave Ruth a hug. "I really appreciate it, Grandma."

"Well, I guess I'll be on my way." Claudia picked up her purse and took out her car keys. "You be good," she said as she walked out the front door.

Ruth closed the door behind her and then turned around and looked at her grandson.

"You can sleep in the guest bedroom. Why don't you go wash up and I'll fix us a snack before dinner."

"Okay." Peter smiled and started up the stairs.

Ruth watched him disappear into the bedroom at the top of the stairs then quietly walked over to the telephone and lifted the receiver. She dialed quickly and then listened to the phone ring once. Twice. Three times. A click and the answering machine turned on.

Ruth sighed as she listened to the voice of her daughter and then the beep. She hesitated for a moment, trying to find the right words to say.

"Patty, this is your Mom. Please come back home. We need to talk. I need to talk to you. Please, come. I love you. I'm sorry." She hung the receiver back on its hook and then walked into the kitchen.

Peter cautiously walked over to the rail and looked down at the telephone. He folded his arms and rubbed his shoulder, deep in thought. Slowly he turned back to the bedroom and closed the door behind himself.

He took the pistol from his waistband as he sat down on the bed. He replayed what he had just overheard over and again in his head. Now he was more confused than ever. He looked at the pistol and then shoved it between the mattresses.

Ruth held the garbage can lid while Peter lifted the sacks of trash into the can. They closed the garbage can and Ruth put her arm around his shoulders.

"Let's sit out here for a moment," she invited him and walked over to the bench.

Peter felt a little nervous anxiety, not knowing what she wanted. Yet, he went along with her.

They sat down on the bench and stared up at the setting sun.

"Thanks for letting me stay." Peter tried to control the conversation. Keeping it on a safe topic.

"Anytime you want to stay over, you can." Ruth slipped her arm around his and hugged him. "I want you to feel comfortable here."

Peter smiled at the words. He was not comfortable anywhere, except in Matthew's arms, but he could not tell her that.

"Peter," Ruth continued. He noticed that her tone had changed and his heart began to pound nervously. "I heard what Nick said this afternoon."

"Yeah," Peter nodded trying to break her line of thought.

"Do the kids at school really tease you?" She asked trying to hear both sides.

Peter rubbed his hands on his knees. His mouth was dry and he felt sure she could hear his heart pounding in his chest.

"Yeah," he nodded. "But they tease a lot of us new guys."

Ruth knew that was not true. She looked at him and he, her.

"I hope it isn't true," she nodded.

Peter nodded back to her and then looked away. She stood up and walked silently back into the house. He sat there and stared up at the sky. "Why didn't I just stay with you?" He said quietly to Matthew.

The fire in the fireplace crackled and filled the family room with a warm glow. It was not really cold out, it was more for the relaxing feeling it gave Ruth as she sat in her chair and looked at the flames. The house was quiet. Peter had gone to bed hours ago. Carl had been up and down twice to ask when she was coming to bed. She told him she could not sleep and she would be up later. She just wanted to think. Think about Patricia.

How could she have been so foolish. Patricia is her daughter. How could she have ordered her out of her house like a total stranger.

Feelings of guilt overwhelmed her and tears filled her eyes. Could Claudia have been right? Did she lose Patricia, too? Why would not Patricia return her calls? Ruth looked away from the fire for a moment as she wiped her tears from her eyes.

Slowly the front door opened. Patricia quietly stepped into the foyer and closed the door behind herself then tucked her house key back into the pocket of her jacket. The flickering glow of the fire in the family room told her where to go. Slowly she walked over to the doorway.

In the glow of the fire, she could see her mother sitting in her chair. She hesitated to speak. Maybe this was not such a good idea afterall. The look on her mother's face, in her eyes, was indelibly etched into her memory. The feelings she had, the loneliness, welled up in her chest again at the thought. She turned around to leave.

Ruth looked up from the fire and caught a glimpse of Patricia as she walked back into the foyer. Her heart leapt and she jumped to her feet.

"Patty?" She spoke softly so as not to wake the others.

Patricia stopped and turned around to look at her mother.

"You phoned," she said nervously.

"Yes. I did." Ruth smiled. "Please, can we talk?"

"I guess." Patricia shrugged her shoulders.

Ruth invited her back into the family room.

"Would you like some hot tea?"

"Sure." Patricia followed her into the kitchen.

Ruth quickly poured the hot water into two cups and dropped a tea bag into each. She motioned toward the dinette table where there were sugar and cream already set out.

The two women sat down.

Patricia played with the tea bag, dunking it several times not really paying attention to it. She looked up at her mother.

"Mom, I'm sorry you had to find out the way you did," she began.

"No. I'm the one who should be sorry." Ruth quickly countered.

"Please, let me finish." Patricia removed the tea bag and set it on the saucer. "Ever since I was a young girl, I always felt different inside. Never really knowing where I fit in. I liked boys, you remember, but I also had strong feelings for some of the girls too. I was confused. I didn't know what was the matter with me.

"When I went away to college, I met a woman, Jo. She introduced me to other women who felt the same way I did. We would talk about things I couldn't with anyone else. They understood. Then, when Jo broke up with her lover and had no place to turn, I felt I owed her. So, I let her live with me. We were just friends, that was all, but then one day we crossed that line. I was more curious really. Until then I had never experienced being with anyone before.

"Anyway, things were going okay, I guess. That was until I met this cameraman named Roger at work. He changed my whole thinking. I found myself thinking about raising a family and the two of us living happily ever after. I wanted to spend more time with him than with Jo. So, about a year ago, I told her to move out. That is when she became violent. Possessive. She started following me. When I came home from work, she would meet me at my front door and demand to know why I was late. I thought about getting help from the police but if word got out it would ruin my career. So, I kept quiet and hoped it would pass. Then Roger was transferred to Seattle about three months ago. I hadn't heard from him until today. He wants me to move up there. I told him I would."

Ruth listened quietly. She did not know what to think or what to say.

"I am not really gay. I was just going through a phase of finding myself." Patricia shrugged. "I know that I want to be married and have a family and all of this." She motioned toward the house. "And I want to take a chance and see if Roger is the one for me."

Ruth smiled disbelievingly at herself. How could she have been so blind to all that was going on in her daughter's life?

"I'm sorry," she spoke gently and touched Patricia's hand. "I had no idea. I wish I could have been more of a help to you instead of acting as I had."

"It's okay." Patricia smiled. "It's over now. I spent the afternoon at the police station. I filed a report with them."

"But what about your career?" Ruth looked surprised. "Aren't you afraid it'll ruin it?"

"There's more important things in life than work." Patricia smiled. "Family."

"That's right." Ruth smiled and hugged her daughter. "That's right."

THE GATHERING

The warm mid-July sun shone brightly across the rolling hillside. Except for the occasional caw from a crow in the tall trees, a peaceful quiet filled the air. Below, stone images of angels stood guard over the bright and colorful flowers that dotted the hillside. Urns and marble slabs stood proudly in rows as remembrances of lives gone by.

In the distance, the gentle hum of an automobile engine drew closer. The dark navy blue Bonneville slowed to a gentle stop at the crest of the hill. The engine shut off and the quiet once again returned. Ruth slowly stepped out from the passenger's side. She held in her hands a bouquet of colorful summer flowers. She stood quietly staring out at the lovely view that only the visitors could see.

It seemed as though it were only yesterday when she and Carl stood on that very spot and chose this view for Steven. He would have liked it. She smiled at the thought.

Carl walked up beside Ruth and slipped his hand into hers. He smiled softly at her as though he could read her thoughts. He wondered if she could tell how frightened he was. Not of the cemetery, of himself. It had been a whole year since he had come out there. He could not bring himself to do it, to face the pain, to face the memories not even the joyful ones. His heart pounded and his throat tightened. He looked at Ruth. She smiled understandingly at him.

"Are you ready?" She asked as she looked into his tearing brown eyes. "I'd like us to have a few moments alone before the rest of the family arrives."

Carl tried to smile. He drew a deep quivering breath. His hands were sweating. Silently he nodded and they took a step onto the grassy hillside.

Quietly they walked passed stone after stone. Carl glanced at each one seeing the names and the dates but not really reading them. Ruth stopped beside a gray marble stone and released Carl's hand. Slowly she walked around and faced it. She bent down and gently traced the letters of the inscription. Softly she whispered, "Steven Peter Wallace." She looked at the words below. "Remember me with joy and laughter."

Carl's heart pounded in his chest. He dug his hands deeper into his pockets and turned his head away and remembered. He remembered the small boy that caught his first fish. He remembered the sparkle in Steven's eyes and the smile that lit up his face as he looked in surprise at his first bicycle. He remembered that morning a year ago how he and Steven splashed about in the swimming pool. They did have fun. A smile found Carl's lips even as the tears fell from his eyes. It was not so painful to remember afterall.

Ruth slowly laid the flowers on the ground at the base of the headstone. As she looked up at the dates on the stone. She remembered the day she had brought Steven home from the hospital. So tiny. So helpless. Her first son. Slowly she stood up and took Carl's arm.

"It's hard to believe a year has already gone by," she sighed.

"Yeah," Carl nodded and held her hand in his. "It has gone by so quickly. I remember thinking I couldn't imagine life without him, how I could go on, and yet, here we are." He took a deep breath and smiled at Ruth.

"Yes," she nodded.

The sound of an approaching car caused them to look up. Slowly they started back up the hillside. They smiled as they watched the tan sedan slow to a stop behind their car on the edge of the narrow road.

"We made it." Tamera stepped from the car and bit her lip as her parents approached. "I don't know if I can do this, Mom, but I'm going to try." She gave a nervous smile.

"You'll be fine." Ruth hugged her daughter and understood.

Daniel and Nicholas walked around the car and stood by Carl. Nicholas held the single white rose he had picked from the rose bush he had planted in their backyard in memory of his uncle. The first bloom of the year. White roses were Steven's favorite, at least that is what his mother had told him. He looked down the hillside at the gray headstone and then up at the sky. Slowly he took a deep, unsteady breath.

"So, how are you, Dad?" Daniel shook Carl's hand and smiled.

"I'm actually doing better than I had thought I

would." Carl smiled. "I'd be lying if I said it didn't hurt but it's getting better."

"Time," Daniel breathed. "The healer of all wounds."

"Yeah," Carl nodded.

Another car pulled to a stop followed by another and still another. The family had arrived. Ruth looked up and greeted Morgan with a kiss on the cheek.

"I'm so glad you made it." Ruth grasped Chuck's hand and smiled. "It's very nice of you."

"I wouldn't miss it. Although Steven and I weren't close, we were still brothers." Chuck smiled. He looked over at Daniel and his smile faded. It had been three months since the big blow up. They had not spoken since. Chuck looked away.

"Tamera," Morgan walked over to her and held out her hands.

Tamera hesitated for a moment and then smiled. She hugged Morgan. Again Morgan whispered an apology into her ear.

"I know." Tamera smiled and held onto her tightly. "It's okay, really."

Morgan looked over at Nicholas as she and Tamera let go of their hug. She noticed the white rose in his hands. Nicholas smiled at her but did not say a word. She turned around and rejoined Chuck.

Ariel and Mark slowly walked over to Ruth and the family. Mark carried the tiny blue bundle in one arm as he held Ariel's hand. Smiling and beaming, ever the proud papa, he showed Ruth his sleeping baby.

"Oh, he's so beautiful," Ruth cooed.

"He is, isn't he." Mark beamed. "Wake up, Kevin." He softly stroked Kevin's soft cheek.

Kevin grimaced and continued to sleep.

"Honey, let him sleep," Ariel playfully said as she stood with her arms around them both.

Ruth looked passed them at Bradley and Benjamin as they slowly approached. Her heart ached at the lost look in their faces. His filing for a divorce had not brought the relief he had thought it would. Ruth walked over to them and hugged Bradley.

"Hello, son." She kissed his cheek. "How are you two getting along?" She asked as a reflex already knowing the answer.

"As well as could be expected, I guess," Bradley frowned. "It's not easy. I miss her still. I guess I always will, but-"

"I know," Ruth interrupted and nodded. She looked down at Benjamin and then crouched down to his height. "My, that's a pretty white rose." She playfully smiled. "Is that for me?"

"No." Benjamin turned away so that Ruth could not see the flower. "It's for Uncle Stebben."

Ruth smiled at how he was beginning to talk in sentences. It also warmed her heart that he was being taught about who his uncle was. She touched his cheek and stood up.

"So, do you think that Patricia will make it?" Bradley asked as they walked over to join the others.

"I don't know." Ruth sighed. "I tried calling her apartment and calling Roger's, but no answer. I don't know."

"Since she moved to Seattle, it's a wonder if anyone ever hears from her." Bradley shook his head. "What does anyone know of this guy she's seeing anyway?"

"Only that he was a cameraman when he worked down here. Patty seemed smitten by him but she didn't say much else," Ruth answered and looked back as she heard another car approaching. "Excuse me." She patted Bradley on the shoulder, gently nudging him to continue toward the others.

Claudia stepped from between the parked cars. She looked tall in her black dress and large brimmed black hat. In her hands she carried three white roses. Slowly she walked over to Ruth. Her heart pounded nervously. She had been avoiding coming here ever since she and Peter had moved to town. Somehow, she could not bring herself to face the reality of Steven being gone. To her, he was just away as he had always been in the past.

Peter closed the car door and stood looking out at the hillside filled with headstones. He put his hands into the pockets of his dress slacks. He had refused to wear his suit. It was too hot he had complained. Actually, he was never comfortable wearing it. He felt the envelope in his pocket and gave a heavy, quivering sigh. He looked over at Nicholas and then looked away. Nicholas did the same.

Ruth gave Claudia a polite cheek to cheek hug.

"I'm so happy you made it," she smiled at her daughter-in-law.

"We almost didn't.," Claudia admitted. "I don't know," she breathed. "I've been kidding myself all this time. Thinking Steven is just on a trip or away. I've gotten used to that idea. Coming here meant that I had to face that he's gone and not coming back. I guess it's time to face reality."

Ruth nodded and smiled.

"We all eventually will have to. When we're ready." She glanced over at Peter. He still stood alone by the car, staring down the hill at the headstones. "How is Peter doing?" She asked without looking at Claudia.

"I don't know." Claudia turned and looked over her shoulder at Peter. "He's changed so much since we moved out here. After school ended, he's gotten to be so quiet. He keeps to himself a lot more. Something is bothering him and I don't know what it is or how to approach him about it," she sighed. "He received a letter the other day from someone back East. I think it was from his friend named Matthew. It was the first time in a long time I've seen him smile, but that didn't last long. I wish I knew what was troubling him."

Slowly Peter began to walk down the hillside. He looked at each of the headstones, reading the names, searching for the one that bore his namesake's. Ruth and Claudia watched silently as he neared Steven's grave.

Peter stopped sharply as he found the one he had been looking for. His heart pounded in his chest as he traced the engraved name. He crouched down and looked at the ground beneath his feet. A tear came to his eyes for a man he never met. He looked up at the headstone.

"I know you can't hear me," he spoke softly into the air. "You died before we could ever meet; but I wish we had, maybe we could have been friends and I would have someone I could talk to." He looked down at the ground again and a tear fell from his eyes and ran down his cheek. "I know that Mom loves me, but I can't tell her the things I'm feeling. I'm so confused. I don't know where to turn." He looked at the stone, then bowed his head and began to cry.

Ruth looked around at her family. She looked over her shoulder, hoping that she would catch a glimpse of an approaching car carrying Patricia. She had wanted the family all to be present. Steven would have wanted it that way. She reluctantly turned back to her family and slowly started over to them.

She smiled as she approached them. They all huddled closer and then slowly made their way down to the grave site. Ruth held Carl's hand. It was not sweating anymore. She smiled to herself.

Mark carefully guided Ariel down the hillside behind Morgan and Chuck. Tamera and Nicholas held hands as they followed. Bradley picked up Benjamin and carried him as he walked with Daniel. Claudia walked over to Peter and put her arm around him as they all stood around the grave.

One by one they placed their flowers at the base of the headstone.

When it was her turn, Ariel knelt down with Kevin in her arms. She touched the cold headstone and a tear came to her eyes.

"Uncle Steven," she whispered softly. "I wish you were here to meet your great-nephew, Kevin. You would have loved him as you did us and as I will always, you." She kissed her fingers and pressed them against the stone.

Mark gently helped Ariel to her feet and they stepped back.

Bradley and Benjamin stepped forward.

"I miss you, big brother," Bradley whispered. "I could sure use your kind ear."

He motioned to Benjamin to place the flower next

to the others. At first he did not want to, but then he dropped the rose and quickly reached up to his father. Bradley scooped him up and hugged him close to his chest.

They all stood silent for a few more moments. Then slowly, one by one, they made their way back up the hillside.

The sound of a car approaching caused everyone to look up. A taxi slowed and Patricia stepped out, followed by a tall, slender, brown haired man. Patricia straightened her black skirt, then took the man's arm. She smiled as she walked over to the family.

"Hi, Mom, Dad," she greeted them with a kiss and quick hug. "I'm sorry we're late. It was hard catching a flight at the last minute and then the taxi." She glanced over her shoulder as the taxi drove away. "But, we made it."

"I'm happy you did." Ruth smiled and looked at the man beside her daughter and held out her hand. "You must be Roger."

"I'm sorry," Patricia gasped. "Where are my manners. Mom, Dad, this is Roger Ferguson. Roger, this is my mother Ruth and my father Carl," she introduced.

"Pleased to meet you," Roger said in a deep voice as he shook their hands.

"Well, the family has already placed their flowers and shared a quiet moment. If you want to go ahead, we can wait?" Carl invited.

Patricia looked at Roger and nodded encouragingly. Roger gave in and the two slowly walked down the hillside together. Patricia glanced over at Peter and smiled a silent hello to him.

Peter strained to smile back. He did not know how he felt seeing her with Roger. Not really jealous. A little betrayed. She said she understood, but had she really? He turned away and a feeling of loneliness filled him. He walked back to their car and sat down.

Tamera walked over to Ruth while looking down at Patricia and Roger.

"So, late as usual," she said with a slight irritation in her voice.

"At least she's here," Ruth said with a relieved tone in her voice.

The drive back to the house was a quiet one. Tamera stared out of the window at the passing scenery. She did not know why it bothered her, but seeing Patricia with that man did. It was not jealousy. It was something else. She shifted in her seat and looked over at Daniel. He smiled at her unaware of her thoughts.

Ruth had already busied herself in the kitchen with preparing lunch for the family. The scent of freshly brewed coffee and warm bread filled the house. Carefully she took the hot bread pans from the oven and set them on the cooling racks on the counter.

Morgan quickly tied an apron around her waist and closed the oven door.

"That smells wonderful." She breathed deeply.

Ruth smiled. She loved baking for an appreciative audience.

"Thank-you, dear," she nodded. "Grab the lunch meat platter out of the refrigerator, please."

Morgan did as she was asked without hesitation. She struggled with her thoughts as she set the tray on the counter and removed the cellophane wrap. She

looked at her mother and tried to organize her thoughts
carefully. She had to choose just the right words or else
she could jeopardize their renewed relationship.

"Mom," she began cautiously. "Have you talked to
Bradley since he started this divorce thing?"

Ruth continued to slice an already cooled loaf of
bread.

"I've tried to but he hasn't been much for
conversation," she sighed.

"Do you know if he's been drinking again?"
Morgan asked trying to be coy.

Ruth paused for a moment. She had noticed
alcohol on his breath over the last couple of months
come to think of it. She mentally kicked herself for not
realizing the significance at the time. She sighed and
shook her head.

"Oh, no. Not again."

"I noticed this morning out at the cemetery,"
Morgan said as she turned around and faced her mother.
"His breath smelled of whiskey."

Ruth gave a concerned look as her thoughts raced.
She had talked to him this morning, had she not? Why
did she not notice that about him?

"I'll talk to him later this afternoon," she told
herself out loud.

Morgan nodded and returned to her chores. She
realized her mother's comment was her way of ending
the conversation, so she did not pursue it.

Patricia and Roger stood in the foyer in each other's
arms. They smiled at each other and occasionally gave
each other a playful kiss. Patricia looked at the
handsome man in her arms. She could not believe he

was really there. With his short dark brown hair, mustache and goatee and blue eyes he was everything she ever wished for. She kissed him again.

Tamera froze as she opened the front door and stepped inside.

"That is disgusting!" She quipped then walked passed them into the family room.

Patricia and Roger looked at each other and laughed like to love struck teenagers.

"Hi, Aunt Patty," Nicholas greeted and hurried after his mother. He really did not want to watch their public display of affection.

Daniel closed the door behind them. He smiled at them as he passed by but did not say a word.

"What's wrong with them?" Roger gave a curious look in their direction.

Patricia glanced over her shoulder and then back at Roger.

"Who cares?" She kissed him again.

"Well, do you think we should tell them the news?" He looked at her and smiled.

Patricia released her hold on him and looked away. She was anxious to let the family in on their secret and yet, she was not sure if it was the right time. Afterall, it was the anniversary of Steven's death. She looked back at him.

"I think we should wait," she frowned. "Maybe after you get to know them a little better this afternoon, we can?"

"Sure." Roger smiled. He really did not care whether he knew her family better or not. He was in love with her and that was all that mattered. He took her hand and the two of them joined the others in the family room.

Claudia opened the front door and stuck her head inside.

"We're here," she announced as a formality. Even though they were family, she still was not used to the idea of just walking in. She removed her hat and set it on the table next to the telephone as Peter closed the front door behind them.

Claudia turned to Peter and studied his sullen expression. Slowly she walked over to him and put her arm around his shoulders.

"Are you okay?"

Peter looked up at her and nodded.

"Yeah." He lied. His thoughts kept going back to the letter in his pocket. He had been so excited when he had read it. Matthew had graduated and was coming to see him. He had something important to tell him. However, with each passing day and no further word, Peter's excitement gave way to depression.

The sound of laughter and loud talking touched their ears. Peter looked at the family room doorway and then pulled away from his mother's arm.

"I think I'll just stay in the parlor for a few minutes. I'd like to be alone."

Claudia nodded to her son.

"Okay." She reluctantly gave in to his wishes again. She kissed his forehead and then joined the family.

Peter sighed heavily and disappeared into the parlor.

A crowd gathered around the kitchen counter they all helped themselves to the lunch spread out before them. Ruth smiled as she sipped her cup of coffee and stood back. That was her family, a bunch of hungry animals. She looked over at Roger who stood back politely waiting for an opening.

"Don't be shy, Roger, or there will be nothing left," Ruth laughed.

Morgan looked at the faces around the counter. Someone was missing. Bradley. She picked up a plate and hurriedly made a sandwich for him. She grabbed a soda from the refrigerator, pausing momentarily as she noticed a bottle of beer. She closed the door and turned to Ruth.

"I'm going to go find Bradley. Would you make sure someone gets Benji something to eat?" She asked.

Ruth nodded to her daughter. She was pleased that Morgan had taken an interest in the family. Things were changing. They were all growing up.

Morgan paused as she looked at Bradley as he sat at the dining room table, alone. Slowly she walked over to him and set the plate down before him.

"I thought you might be hungry," she spoke softly.

Bradley looked at the sandwich plate. He smiled to himself. She had remembered how he liked his sandwiches after all these years, dry, no mayo and lots of lettuce.

"Thanks, sis," he nodded. "But I can't eat."

Morgan sat down at the table across from him. She looked around and sighed.

"Boy, this brings back memories." She looked at her brother again. "We always sat across from each other when we were kids, and look at us now."

Bradley did not look up. He looked at the melting ice in his glass and sipped on the water.

Morgan looked around the room for a moment to collect her thoughts. She was nervous about bringing up the subject, not knowing how he would react. She looked at her hands and then back at Bradley.

"You've been awfully depressed since you started this divorce," she began. "How are you doing?"

"How do you think?" He answered back sarcastically. "I am so confused. I don't know what to think, what to feel, what to do. Have you ever done something totally stupid and wish you could go back and change it?"

The image of Luke's young face flashed in her mind. She nodded quietly in response.

"I think I made a big mistake." Bradley continued.

"What did you do?" Morgan urged him to go on.

"I should never have filed for this divorced. I should have stuck it out with Amanda."

Morgan was surprised by his answer. She had thought of a lot of other possibilities, but not this.

"I still think about her constantly. Everywhere I turn in that house, she's there. I've taken down pictures, rearranged the furniture, even repainted some of the rooms, but she's still there. Why doesn't she put up more of a fight about the divorce?"

Morgan reached out and touched her brother's hand.

"Maybe she wants it too? Maybe she wants to put all of this behind her. You should try to, too."

"I can't," Bradley sighed. "I still love her."

"Have you told her?"

"Don't be ridiculous. I can't tell her that now. Afterall, I'm the one who filed for the divorce," Bradley smirked.

"Then maybe it's time you moved on. I mean, sell

the house and get a place for you and Benji to start over," Morgan suggested cautiously.

"I don't know, maybe you are right." He looked across the table at the soda can. "Do you have anything stronger than that?" He motioned at the can with his head.

Morgan looked at the soda and then back at him.

"You don't need to start drinking again. You've done so well for so long, don't go back."

Bradley's jaw tightened.

"I will do what I want," he snapped. "If I want a drink, I'll have one. I can handle it."

Morgan recoiled at the harshness of his words.

"Well, we don't have anything," she snapped back at him. "I was only trying to help. You know what happened the last time you started drinking. Think about it." She stood up and left him alone again with his thoughts.

The front doorbell chimed, giving Peter a start as he sat quietly alone in the parlor, lost in his thoughts. He watched to see if someone would answer it. When it chimed the second time, he decided to go himself.

Just as he entered the foyer, Tamera also entered.

"I'll get it, Aunt Tamera," he told her.

She nodded but stayed to see who it was.

Peter opened the door and gasped with a smile.

"What?" He could not believe his eyes. "How?"

Tamera stretched her neck to see passed Peter. Standing on the front porch was a tall, muscular, blonde haired and blue eyed young man. She did not recognize him, in fact, she had never seen him before. Obviously, Peter had. She thought to herself.

"Well, aren't you going to say, 'Hi?'" The young man asked and held out his arms.

Without thinking about Tamera, Peter hugged the young man and kissed his cheek.

"I can't believe you actually came. I've missed you so much," Peter gushed softly into his ear.

Tamera's mouth dropped open in shock. She stepped closer so as to been seen. The young man sheepishly released his hold when their eyes met.

"Peter?" Tamera spoke.

Peter quickly let go of the young man and turned around to face his aunt. His face blushed in shock at having being seen. He looked back at the young man.

"Ah, Matthew, I'd like you to meet my Aunt Tamera." He looked at Tamera. "Matthew is a friend from back east. We practically grew up together." He tried to explain away her suspicions.

Tamera nodded disapprovingly, yet politely.

"Nice to meet you," she said coldly.

"Same here." Matthew smiled not being fooled for a moment. "Say, can we go for a walk?" He asked Peter.

"Sure," Peter agreed eagerly. "Tell my mom," he called back to Tamera as he closed the front door behind them.

Tamera nodded to herself as she reviewed in her mind what she had just witnessed. She began to think about how Peter had been so depressed and how when he saw Matthew, his mood changed immediately. She thought about the kiss. Even though it was on the cheek, it still seemed an odd thing for a boy of his age to do. Without reaching a conclusion, she turned around and returned to the family room.

Ruth poured Claudia and Patricia another cup of coffee then set the pot down on the warming plate in the center of the breakfast nook table. She sat down across from Claudia and sighed.

"It feels good to sit down, at last," she smiled at her daughters.

"So, what do you think of him?" Patricia asked and looked over at Roger. He stood talking with Chuck and Carl by the fireplace. Every now and again, he would glance over at her and wink.

Ruth looked over at Roger and shrugged.

"He appears to be nice. I really haven't had a chance to talk to him." She was teasingly indifferent.

Claudia did not say a word. She glanced over in his general direction but did not focus long enough to see anything. Her thoughts were on Peter.

Patricia did not notice that Claudia had not said a word. She looked at her mother and could not help but smile.

"I think he's the one."

"Oh?" Ruth sipped her coffee and continued her little game. "That's nice, dear. The one for what?"

Patricia cocked her head and swatted at her mother. "Mom. You know," she feigned disgust. "The one I want to marry."

"Oh," Ruth nodded with raised eyebrows. "Has he asked you yet?"

Patricia's smile faded. She did not expect that question.

"Ah," she hesitated to answer. "Well, we've talked about it." She avoided a direct answer.

"Well, you let us know when he has and we'll have

our little mother-daughter talk," Ruth continued to tease and patted Patricia's hand.

"Mother," Patricia sighed. "I'm trying to be serious here."

"I know," Ruth smiled and nodded. "I just can't help teasing you. You know, this is the first boy you've brought home to meet the family in a long time."

Patricia recoiled at her mother's observation although she tried not to show it. What did she mean by that comment? Was she trying to bring up the subject of Jo? Patricia suddenly became uneasy. She looked over at Claudia.

"Well, you are sure quiet this afternoon." Patricia changed the focus of the conversation.

Claudia looked over at Patricia and then Ruth.

"I'm sorry. I'm just concerned about Peter. That's all."

"How's he doing? I haven't really had a chance to talk to him since I moved away. Did he finally come out of the closet?" Patricia asked carelessly.

Claudia looked at Patricia with wide, shocked eyes.

"What?"

Immediately Patricia realized she had made a terrible mistake.

"Oh, me and my big mouth," she chastised herself. "Forget I said that."

Claudia put her coffee cup back on the saucer and reached over and grabbed hold of Patricia's hand and squeezed it tightly.

"No, you tell me what's going on," she said through clinched teeth.

Patricia looked to Ruth for help. It was not going

to come. She looked back at Claudia and continued to try to pull free.

"Okay," she gave in.

Claudia released her hold.

"You remember three months ago at the shower when he and Nick were fighting. Well, I went after Peter and we had a talk. He told me that he is gay. He's known it for years but was afraid to tell us, you, for fear of being rejected," Patricia spoke softly.

Claudia listened but did not know what to say. She looked around the room but could not form a thought.

"He met a boy at school and fell in love. He didn't want to move out here but he wanted you to be happy. He knew how important it was to you," Patricia finished.

Claudia looked at her.

"I had no idea." She finally spoke in shock. "That explains why he's been so depressed. Oh how could I have been so blind?" She looked down at the table.

Ruth's mind was a spin. Her thoughts conflicting with her sense of morals. She struggled to suppress her feelings of repulsion and let the love she felt for Peter and Claudia surface instead.

"It's okay," she heard herself say to Claudia. "You can't know everything. Children do keep their secrets from us."

"The one fear he has," Patricia spoke to both of them. "He's afraid that if you knew, he would lose your love and you would be ashamed of him."

"Oh, that would never happen." Claudia was near tears feeling his isolation and loneliness. "He's still my son and I want him to be happy, no matter what. If he's gay, then he's gay. I will always love him."

"Then let him know," Patricia urged gently. "He needs to know that."

Claudia stared at Patricia for a moment. She nodded silently to herself.

The park was nearly empty as Matthew and Peter walked shoulder to shoulder. The warm summer breeze gently stoked their faces and tussled their hair as it blew. They walked over to a picnic table in a secluded part of the park, away from view. Matthew sat down on the table and faced Peter. He thought about the things he came to say as he looked at the young man and remembered all the special moments they had shared. He still loved Peter and that made it all the more difficult for him.

Peter smiled at Matthew. He could not believe that after nearly nine months he was sitting in front of him. All those lonely days were gone, erased from his memory. Matthew was here and everything was going to be all right again. He sighed contentedly to himself and put his hands on Matthew's knees.

"So, how long are you going to stay?" Peter started the conversation.

"A couple of days," Matthew shrugged. "My sister lives not too far from here and I'll be staying with her. She wants me to move out here, but I can't."

"I wish you could. I've missed you so much." Peter looked lovingly into Matthew's blue eyes. "I'm so happy you are here."

Matthew smiled and looked down. He struggled with what he had come to say. Part of him wanted to take Peter in his arms and run away; yet, the other part of him knew what he had to do. Matthew looked up at

Peter.

"Pete," he spoke softly in his deep manly voice. He hesitated. "Thank-you for the graduation gift. You didn't need to get me anything, you know."

"I know," Peter nodded. "But, I wanted to."

Matthew took Peter's hands in his and stood up. He needed to talk to him and he could not do it, not like this. He faced Peter and held his hands in his.

"Peter, I came all the way here because we need to talk."

Peter's heart began to sink. His mind raced in every direction trying to anticipate what Matthew would say next. His smile quivered.

"What? What is it?" He asked and could not help but be frightened by what he might hear.

Matthew could sense Peter's anxiety. He felt it himself.

"Pete, when you left, I did a lot of thinking. What we had between us was wrong."

Peter could not believe his ears. His throat tightened and he could not catch his breath. This could not be happening. This had to be a bad dream.

"No," he managed to choke.

"Yes." Matthew continued. "Yes, it is wrong and God can help you to stop."

Peter jerked his hands free and turned around, taking two steps away before tears filled his eyes.

"Me stop? What about you? I can't believe you came clear out here, just to tell me this." Tears began to stream down his pale cheeks.

Matthew sighed and looked at his hands.

"No. I didn't. There's something else."

Peter did not turn around. He looked up at the clear

blue sky. His heart being crushed.

"After you left, I met someone. At first we were just friends, but," Matthew stepped closer to Peter. He tried to see his face, but Peter kept turning away. "But, we're in love. We're getting married next month."

"Married?" Peter repeated confused.

"She said she would kill herself if I didn't. I have to," Matthew announced.

"She?" Peter spun around. He looked at Matthew and tried to focus through his tears. "You?" Peter could not think, his heart ached and his head was spinning. Tears streamed down his cheeks. "Get away from me," he choked. "Leave me alone." Peter took a step away from Matthew.

"Pete, I'm sorry." Matthew felt his own throat tighten as he choked back his tears. "I still love you."

"Don't." Peter held up a halting hand. "Don't say that to me again," he said firmly though his voice trembled from his heart breaking..

"But, it's true," Matthew pleaded.

"No." Peter cocked his head and looked away. "You love her. That's what you said. Leave me alone. Please."

Peter turned around and began to run. Matthew watched for a moment. His own heart now confused. He did love Peter. That was true. How did things get so complicated? Matthew began to run after Peter.

"Pete, please, wait!" He called as he ran.

Tears blurred Peter's vision so that he could not see where he was running. Suddenly he tripped on something and hit the ground hard. He lay there sobbing heavily, as much for the pain in his right knee as in his heart.

Matthew stopped and gently turned Peter over. He wrapped his strong arms around Peter and held him tightly to his chest as Peter continued to cry.

"I'm so sorry," Matthew repeated over and over again.

Peter hugged Matthew tightly. This was not happening. Any moment he would wake up.

"Let's get you back to your grandparents," Matthew said as he lifted Peter to his feet. "I've got to get back home, myself."

This was not a dream. It was real. Peter gave in without a word and the two started back to the house. When they arrived at the front door, Matthew turned Peter around to face him.

"Are you going to be all right?" He asked.

Peter just looked at him. The tears had stopped and he could see clearly again.

"What does it matter, anymore," he said flatly. "My memories of you and my love for you were all that had kept me going. It's over now. She won."

Matthew looked at Peter. His heart still confused. He loved Peter, that much he knew for sure; but he could not say that of Diana.

"It isn't a matter of winning. I have no choice. Besides, if my parents and family ever found out about us they would disown me."

"What does that matter? My aunt once told me, if they can't deal with it, that is their problem, not yours."

Matthew looked at Peter.

"You're a better man than I, Pete. I can't do that." Without another word, Matthew turned around and walked back to his car.

Peter watched as Matthew drove off down the street.

Slowly he turned around and walked into the house. As he closed the front door the sounds of laughter and chatter emerged from the family room. He looked up at the guest bedroom door and started up the stairs.

"So, what do you do?" Carl asked Roger as they stood by the fireplace in the family room.

"Well, I do freelance work for the local news in Seattle. Whenever they need a spare cameraman, they call me or I go out and film footage of news items and they use what they want," Roger shrugged as he explained.

"Sounds interesting," Chuck raised his eyebrow and smiled. "Is there much money in that?"

Roger smiled. He had expected this interrogation. He did not mind. It was fun, in a weird sort of way.

"It brings in enough to get by. Not necessarily rich, but enough. The main thing is that I enjoy what I do. Not many people can say that about their nine to fives."

"True," Carl agreed with a nod and a sip of his coffee.

"So, how have you managed to stay single all these years." Chuck probed.

Carl cast a surprised look at him. He had been trying to figure out a way to tactfully bring up the subject. Carl looked at Roger.

"Who said I had?" Roger sipped his coffee.

Carl took the cue to let Roger off the hook.

"Well, how do you like Seattle?"

The conversation drifted into generalities. Talking about Seattle and trivial matters. Roger was thankful the interrogation was over. He did not know what to think of Chuck. Was he just being protective of Patricia or was there something else that motivated him? He liked Carl although he could not pin point just why.

Patricia slowly walked over to the couch where Tamera sat. She sat down next to her sister and watched Roger and Carl talking.

"So, what do you think of him?" Patricia asked aware that Tamera did not approve.

"Don't ask." Tamera tried to avoid the issue. She also tried to avoid looking at Patricia.

"No," Patricia nudged her playfully. "I really want to know."

"All right," Tamera said coldly. "You could do better."

"What?" Patricia laughed out of shock. She did not expect such a blunt answer. "Fine. Why do you say that?"

"He's hiding something," Tamera said and looked at Roger. "That's why. I've seen his type before. You would be better off to dump him."

Patricia struggled to keep from becoming irritated at her sister.

"Well, what type is that?" She persisted. Perhaps in her answer, Patricia could show Tamera how wrong she was about Roger.

"Oh, they're clever." Tamera said with a sneer. "They give a good first impression. Very smooth. Say just the right things. All hugs and kisses. Then the ax falls and their true colors show. I haven't figured out yet what he's hiding, but I will."

"So, is this how Dan is?" Patricia jabbed back.

"Hey," Tamera became very defensive. "You asked

me, remember."

Patricia smiled to herself at Tamera's reaction.

"Oh, my I hit a nerve," she laughed. "Think what you want, but all I have to say is, you are barking up the wrong tree. Roger has no secrets."

"Patty, we all have our secrets, even you," Tamera continued with her speculation.

Patricia could feel her jaw tighten at her sister's unrelenting stubbornness.

"From the sounds of it, I'm not the only one." She stood up and stormed out of the room.

Tamera glanced at her and shrugged to herself. She was more than ever determined to find out what Roger was hiding. Why? She really did not know herself, but something was not right.

Claudia walked into the parlor and looked around. She sighed and wrung her hands as she walked back into the foyer. She looked up and noticed Ariel coming down the stairs.

"Have you seen Peter?" She asked and walked over to the staircase.

"No, Aunt Claudia," Ariel shook her head. "Why? Is something wrong?" She noticed how nervous her aunt was.

"No," Claudia smiled. "I just wanted to talk to him, that is all." She turned around and started back to the family room.

Ariel watched her curiously. Carefully she stepped off the stairs and held her stomach, still sore from delivering Kevin only a month ago.

The front doorbell chimed behind her. She turned around and opened the door. Standing on the front steps were two uniformed policemen. They removed their hats when they saw her.

"Good afternoon, ma'am, my name is Officer Tom Bead." the middle-aged, rough looking officer greeted her.

"Hello, can I help you?" She smiled politely.

"Is there a Mark Jones here?" He asked.

"Why do you ask?" She said not thinking. Her mind racing in every direction trying to guess what two policemen would want with her husband.

Tom smiled at her, realizing her shock. "It's okay, ma'am. We just need to talk to him."

"Certainly," Ariel's voice cracked nervously. "Please, come in." She stepped aside and held the door as the two men entered. "I'll get him. You can wait in the parlor." She motioned toward the empty room.

"Thank-you," Tom nodded and the two walked into the room.

Immediately the quiet one began to look over the photographs on the mantle. He paused when he saw the one of Mark and Ariel's wedding. He picked it up and turned around to the other.

"Hey, Tom, take a look at this." He said and handed the framed photograph to his partner.

"What do you know, Martin," Tom nodded and handed it back. "Mrs. Jones."

Ruth and Carl walked into the parlor just behind Mark and Ariel.

"These are my grandparents," Ariel introduced them. "They own this house."

The policemen did not acknowledge them. They looked directly at Mark.

"I think it would be best if you both sat down,

Mrs. Jones, Mr. Jones." Tom instructed.

Ariel did as he suggested while Mark stood his ground.

"Why? What's this all about?" He insisted to know.

Tom looked at his hat in his hands and then at Ruth and Carl before turning back to Mark.

"I regret to inform you, sir, but there has been a plane crash," he spoke softly.

Mark dropped to the love seat next to Ariel and held her hands. He did not say a word. He just listened.

"Your parents' small plane went down just after take off in Columbia. There were no survivors. I'm sorry."

The words hit Mark like a blow to the ribs. He gasped for air and held fast to Ariel's hand. She put her arm around him and he put his head on her chest. No tears. Just shock. He sat up as he caught his breath and looked at the policemen.

"There is more," Tom continued. "Aboard the plane was discovered a large package containing cocaine. Were you aware that your parents were involved in drug trafficking?"

Mark did not say a word. His mind was a total blank. No thoughts. No emotion. Nothing.

Ariel held fast to her husband. A feeling of hostility toward the policemen grew as their words sank in. Her in-laws were good people. How dare they say such an awful thing.

"Officers." Ruth stepped forward. "Is it possible to continue this at a later time? This is quite a shock." She looked at Mark and Ariel with sympathetic eyes.

"Certainly, ma'am," Tom nodded to her politely.

"Just give me a few minutes," Mark spoke up in

an unsteady voice as he sat up. "I'll answer your questions. I don't mind."

Ariel drew back and looked at her husband. Her anger toward them was replaced by confusion.

"Mark?" She said as though asking what was going on.

He looked at her and nodded.

Suddenly she understood what the policemen were saying about his parents was true and he had known all along. Immediately she began to wonder about him. How deeply was he involved in all of this? She looked up at her grandparents. What would they think of her now? She thought about her son and panic set in. What would become of them now.

"Okay," Tom nodded.

"In that case, can I get you some coffee?" Ruth offered. She tried not to show her surprise at the news of the drugs. Carefully she avoided eye contact with Ariel, even though she could feel Ariel was looking at her.

"That would be nice.," Martin spoke up and took a step toward her.

Ruth smiled and left the room. She was grateful for this moment to get out of the room.

As she entered the kitchen, she motioned to Morgan and Chuck. The two of them walked over to her. She quietly relayed the news to them and they immediately left to be with their daughter and son-in-law.

Peter sat quietly on the bed in the guest bedroom. Images of Matthew flashed in his mind. Their many walks. Their nights together. Then Matthew's words echoed in his ears. Tears began to fill his eyes again.

Slowly he stood up and knelt down beside the bed. Carefully he reached between the mattresses until his hand found the hard metal object. He sat back down on the bed and looked at the pistol. He ran his finger down the barrel.

The front doorbell chimed again. Carl excused himself and went to answer it. Claudia rushed into the parlor just as Carl opened the front door.

"Hi," Matthew smiled nervously at Carl. "Is Peter here?"

Carl turned and looked at Claudia. Claudia rushed to the door.

"Matthew?" She looked at him with a smile and yet confused. "What a surprise. Does Peter know you're here?"

Matthew hugged Claudia politely. His hands sweat as he tried to put up a calm front for her.

"Yes," he nodded. "We had a talk a few minutes ago and he was quite upset when I left."

"I'll leave you two." Carl excused himself and returned to the parlor.

Claudia looked at Matthew. In light of the things she had just learned about her son, she put two and two together. She smiled at Matthew.

"Why would he be upset?"

Matthew could feel his heart beat faster as he became nervous. He thought about whether or not to tell her and then decided to just say it.

"Can we talk privately?" Matthew invited her outside.

"Sure." Claudia stepped out and closed the door behind herself.

The two walked silently over to the bench and sat down. Matthew looked at his hands.

"Matthew," Claudia spoke softly. "I already know about you and Peter." She patted his nervous hands.

Matthew turned and looked at her in surprise.

"You do?"

"Yes," she smiled.

"How long have you known?" Matthew began thinking about his parents and family again. If she had known, possibly they did too.

"I just found out," she admitted. "It's okay."

"Pete told you," Matthew concluded and looked at the ground. "Then he also told you that I'm getting married, at least I thought I was. Oh, Mrs. Wallace, I've made such a mess of things." Matthew began to open up.

Claudia tried not to act surprised at what she was hearing.

"Perhaps you should tell me your side of the matter," she urged.

"I wish my parents were as understanding as you, but they are not. My father and mother have this great plan for me. I should be married and settle down and have lots of grand-children for them and take over the family business. So, they introduced me to this girl named Diana, she's the daughter of a business associate of my father. I was told that I was to take her out." Matthew sighed. "So, we went out for a couple months but I realized that I could never love her as much as I love Pete. When I tried to break up with her, she freaked out. She said if I didn't marry her, she'd kill herself. I couldn't live with that guilt, so I agreed."

"Oh, Matthew," Claudia sighed as she felt his

anxiety.

"So, I came out here to get away and I told Pete, it was over between us. He was pretty upset. After I left, I did some thinking. I can't marry her. If she can't handle it, as Pete says, that's her problem, not mine. I love your son, Mrs. Wallace. I want to be with him, I mean."

"That makes two of us." Claudia smiled at Matthew. "Being gay or straight doesn't matter to me, I just want him to be happy and I know with you, he is. I want to tell him that, that is, as soon as I can find him."

Suddenly the crack of a gunshot rang out from inside the house. Claudia jumped to her feet as did Matthew. Without thinking they both ran into the house. The two officers stood in the parlor looking up at the second floor with their guns drawn. Claudia's heart pounded in her chest. A wave of panic swept over her.

"Peter!" She screamed and lunged for the stairs.

One of the officers held her back.

Matthew fell back against the threshold of the front door. A sinking feeling drained him of all his strength as he thought about Peter.

"Please, God, no," he said softly to himself as tears filled his eyes.

Claudia began to cry hysterically as Tom crept up the stairs and slowly opened the bedroom door. He lowered his pistol as he looked inside the room. Quickly he turned back to the rail.

"Martin, get an ambulance. Now!" He ordered his partner and then disappeared into the room.

"Peter, no!" Claudia screamed and collapsed on the

floor. Ruth quickly rushed to her and held her tightly. She glanced over at Carl as he dialed the telephone.

Martin quickly scaled the stairs and disappeared into the bedroom. Moments later he stepped out holding the missing pistol with a pen.

The parlor filled with the silent shocked faces of the family. All staring up at the open bedroom door.

Carl walked over to Ruth and helped her and Claudia to their feet.

"The ambulance is on its way," he assured them and looked up at the bedroom door as Tom reappeared.

"Do you have any clean rags or bandages?" He asked with an urgent tone in his voice.

"Yes," Ruth answered quickly and turned Claudia over to Carl. She hurried up the stairs to the linen closet and pulled out a brand new, white sheet. "Will this do?" She asked him.

"Yes," Tom nodded and grabbed the sheet. In one swift movement, he tore it in half. "I could use some help. Can you stomach the sight of blood?" He asked but did not wait for an answer.

Without thinking about what lay beyond the door, Ruth rushed into the bedroom. Her heart skipped a beat as she gasped at the sight of Peter laying on his back across the bed. Blood splattered his face and soaked the bedspread around his head and left shoulder. She covered her mouth with her hand and fought back the tears that flooded her eyes.

"Is he?" She asked and feared the answer.

"No. The bullet appears to have grazed the side of his head," Tom answered as he placed a folded piece of the sheet over the wound and applied pressure to try to stop the bleeding. "The bullet lodged in the wall near the ceiling. Here, hold this tightly but not too tight, we don't know if his skull was fractured."

Ruth moved quickly to do as she was instructed.

"Oh, Peter," she breathed as she looked at his pale face.

Tom busied himself tearing to pieces the rest of the sheet.

"Where did he get that gun?" He asked very businesslike.

"It's his mother's," Ruth answered. "He must have taken it from her purse months ago and hidden it."

"Is there any reason why he would want to kill himself?" Tom continued to question her.

Ruth looked up at him surprised by his comment. She looked back at Peter.

"What makes you think he tried to kill himself?"

Tom stepped back over Peter and moved Ruth's hands away. He applied a fresh bandage to the wound and wrapped it tightly with a long strip he had torn from the sheet.

"I've seen it a dozen times but usually they aren't so lucky."

Ruth stepped back as both of the officers gently lifted and turned Peter onto the bed. As Tom began taking Peter's pulse, Ruth looked at her hands. Blood reddened her palms but she did not care.

The sound of clanking and voices downstairs brought Ruth to the rail. The paramedics were bringing a back board up the stairs. The gurney was set up in the foyer, waiting to carry Peter to the ambulance and hospital.

Claudia and Matthew followed close behind the paramedics. Ruth hugged Claudia tightly as she reached to top of the stairs.

"He's still alive," she whispered into her ear.

Matthew pushed into the bedroom just as the policemen lifted Peter onto the back board. He covered his mouth and bit his lip as tears filled his eyes. The sight of Peter unconscious, and the blood was more than he could take. Tears began to stream down his cheeks.

"Please." He pushed his way to Peter's side. "I have to tell him something."

One of the paramedics, the woman, looked at Matthew and reached across Peter to touch Matthew's arm.

"We have to get him to the hospital."

"I just want him to know that I love him." Matthew looked at her and cliched his teeth. "He has to know that I love him. I don't want him to die. I need him."

The woman released Matthew's arm, not sure what was going on and not really caring. Without further delay, they lifted Peter and carried him out of the room.

Matthew slowly followed them out, tears blurring his vision. He stopped beside Claudia and watched as they placed Peter on the gurney.

"This is all my fault," Matthew said out loud.

Ruth looked at the young man for the first time. She was confused by his comment but did not say a word.

"No, Matthew." Claudia took his arm and hugged him. "No. This is not your fault."

Still confused, Ruth ushered the two of them down the stairs.

"We best be getting to the hospital," she urged.

Carl grabbed the car keys from the table next to the

telephone and rushed to the front door.

"I'll drive," he said.

The two policemen slowly walked back into the foyer. They paused and looked at Mark and Ariel. Tom gave them a sympathetic smile.

"We'll talk later. Don't leave town."

"I'm not going anywhere." Mark nodded and watched them walk out the front door.

"Oh my god." Patricia said as she rested her face against Roger's chest. "Poor Peter."

Tamera looked at Patricia.

"Crazy faggots." She shook her head.

Patricia straightened up and looked angrily at Tamera.

"You don't know what in the hell you're talking about, you bitch," she hissed.

Tamera recoiled as if slapped. Her mouth opened in shock at her sister using such language.

"I saw them kissing," she said disgustedly. "What further need of we for witnesses. They are queers."

Without thinking Patricia slapped Tamera across the face. Tamera responded by gripping her fists and glaring back at her sister.

"Don't you ever say that about him again." Patricia commanded through clinched teeth. "You are not so perfect yourself."

Not willing to back down, Tamera pointed her finger at Patricia's face.

"I'll let this one go, but don't ever slap me again, or it'll be the last thing you do." She turned around, grabbed her purse and stormed out the front door. "Nick, Daniel. We're leaving!" She yelled over her shoulder.

Daniel and Nicholas quickly followed without a word.

Roger stepped over to Patricia and put his arm around her protectively.

"What was that all about?" He asked as he looked out the opened front door.

"She has just been a bitch today." Patricia answered with a lingering hostility. She turned around and walked back into the kitchen.

Roger looked at the others and shrugged before following her.

Morgan gently handed a sleeping Kevin to Ariel.

"Here, honey. I should go up and clean up the bedroom before they get back. We can talk later, okay?" She gently touched both Mark's and Ariel's cheeks and smiled a sympathetic smile.

Ariel nodded. Her head was spinning with everything that had occurred. She was overwhelmed and could not focus her thoughts. She turned around and walked back into the parlor.

Mark closed the front door. Still in shock over the news that his parents were dead. Still numb and unable to cry. Then there was the news about the drugs. He thought about Ariel, poor innocent girl. She had no clue as to the family she had married into. What would she think of him now? Slowly he walked into the parlor.

Ariel sat on the love seat and gently rocked Kevin. She did not look up at her husband. She kept looking at the peaceful, sleeping face of her baby.

Bradley slowly stepped into the doorway of the bedroom. He stood silently and watched as Morgan stripped the blood dampened sheets from the bed. Aside from that and the hole in the wall, the bedroom did not look any different than before. He watched as Morgan tried to bundle up the soiled linens.

"Could you use a hand?" He gently spoke up.

Morgan looked up at her brother and nodded.

"Sure, Brad," she smiled.

The two of them finished bundling up the linen and then turned back to the bed. The blood had not reached the mattress, but it had the pillow. Morgan threw it next to the bundle.

"Can you get a clean set of sheets and the spare pillow out of the closet?" She asked and pointed down the hall.

"Sure," Bradley answered and disappeared only to reappear a few seconds later with the items she had requested.

"What a day," Bradley commented as he assisted Morgan with making the bed.

"Tell me about it." Morgan shook her head. "First Mark's parents are killed in a plane crash and now this. I don't know about this family sometimes."

"I know what you mean," Bradley answered her. "I haven't been much help either, with my moping around and all. I can't help but wish that Steven were still here. I could talk to him and he always knew what to say. In a way, like you did earlier."

Morgan looked up at him. She could not remember what she had said earlier. With everything else that had happened, she could not think clearly. She smiled uncertainly.

"You are right. I should just get on with my life and find a new home for Benji and me." Bradley reflected. "A place where we could start over and don't worry, no booze."

"Good." Morgan smiled at the thought. "If you need help, I'm here. Now, grab that pillow case for me."

Bradley smiled and handed her the pillow case. Now that he had made up his mind, it felt like a large weight had been lifted from his shoulders. Everything was going to be all right for Benjamin and himself.

Mark sat down next to Ariel and looked about the room. At the mantle with its many pictures of the family. The wing backed chairs and crystal floor lamp. He had never really noticed how nicely the room was decorated before. How warm and safe it felt.

He looked at Ariel and Kevin and thought about his own childhood. His parents' home was never this comforting. Never this safe. It always seemed so cold with its marble tiles and stark white walls. Even in his bedroom, the one room that was totally his, it was cold.

Gently he put his arm around Ariel as he realized the reason why there were no tears for his parents. It was because they were really strangers. As far back as he could remember, they were always gone on business, so they would say. As a child, he never questioned it, not even when the police would search the house in the middle of the night.

"They're just checking for monsters, so you can sleep safely." That is what his nanny always told him.

Now everything was so clear. How could he have been so blind? He took a deep breath and kissed Ariel's cheek. She let him.

"Everything is going to be okay," he assured her in

a whisper.

Ariel looked at him.

"Is it?" She asked disbelievingly. "What is going on, Mark? What did those policemen mean when they said Mom and Dad were trafficking drugs?"

"I guess, it's true." Mark shrugged and admitted. "Ariel, I had no idea and I was never involved in it. But suddenly things that happened when I was growing up finally make sense."

"It's true?" Ariel was shocked. Her thoughts raced in every direction. "What are we going to do? What about Kevin? Mark, where are we going to live? You know the police are going to seize all the property."

Mark nodded and tried to calm Ariel's fears.

"I know, Ariel. We will find someplace else to live. Everything will be all right. I'll tell the police what I know and we'll be okay."

"Oh, Mark, I'm scared." Ariel laid her head on his shoulder.

Mark took a deep breath. He was frightened too, but he could not let her know. He kissed her forehead and hugged her close.

The Wedding

A warm September breeze blew through the trees in the front yard as Daniel parked the car next to the curb. Tamera tightened her lips as she looked out at her parents' house. Two white, paper-mesh bells hung on the front door. White and pink streamers, draped along the walk on lawn stakes, gently lifted and waved in the air. Tamera turned her head away from the house.

"Tamera, just let it go," Daniel said sternly and took her hand in his.

"I can't," Tamera hissed and jerked her hand away from him. "How can I just forget what I found out about Roger."

"There was nothing proven. He was never under any suspicion. It was a freak accident. It could have happened to anyone," Daniel pleaded.

"That's exactly why I can't let it go. What if Patty were next?" Tamera continued to tighten her jaw.

"Mom, look who's just walking in," Nicholas interrupted.

Tamera looked out her window again. Claudia just entered the front door and walking behind her were Matthew and Peter. Matthew held Peter's arm as he helped him up the walk. It was obvious that Peter was still having difficulties as a result of his suicide attempt.

"Oh great," Tamera shrugged. "What's a wedding without a couple of fags?"

"Tamera!" Daniel snapped at her. "What in the hell has gotten into you? I will tell you this right now, if you so much as say one word out of line today, we are finished. I'm leaving. You have been nothing but a bitch for the last six months and it has got to stop."

Tamera continued to look out her window, unfazed by his threat.

"Tamera, do you hear me?"

"Yes. I heard you!" She hissed.

"I'm not kidding this time," Daniel said and opened his car door. "I'll be inside." He shut the car door behind him and walked alone into the house.

"Dad isn't going to leave us." Nicholas patted Tamera on her shoulder.

"I know," Tamera sighed. "He just doesn't understand. That's all."

"Are we going to go inside?" Nicholas looked out the window as more guests arrived.

"Yes." Tamera heaved a heavy sigh and opened her car door.

The family room was a buzz with excited chatter as the guests signed the guest book and made their way into the backyard. Ruth looked up from directing the flow of guests out the back door and smiled as she saw Claudia, Matthew and Peter walk into the room. She quickly hurried over to them.

"Oh, I am so happy that you all made it." She hugged and kissed Claudia on the cheek.

"You look wonderful, Mom," Claudia smiled and complimented Ruth.

Ruth looked down at her white dress studded with silver rhinestone sequins. She was not sure about how the dress looked when she tried it on at the store; however, at the insistence of the saleswoman and her shortness of time, she agreed to the purchase. With Claudia's compliment, Ruth felt more at ease about her decision.

"Thank-you," she smiled. "Well, we had better get you up those stairs and changed if you are going to be the matron-of-honor."

Ruth turned and looked at Peter and Matthew.

"My don't the two of you look nice," Ruth smiled.

"Thank-you, Grandma." Peter returned her smile. "Matthew picked out my suit." He said as he looked down at his lightweight, grey-blue suit. The color matched Matthew's suit with just a enough difference in style that they did not look identical.

"Well, you sure do have good taste in clothes, Matthew." Ruth nodded at him. "I'm so happy you made it too and I know your aunt Patty will be happy to see you." She smiled at Peter and placed a gentle hand against his cheek. The scar from the bullet was very noticeable near his temple. "How are you feeling, dear?"

"I'm doing okay, Grandma." Peter nodded and smiled at her despite his being lightheaded and weak. "Mom and Matthew are helping me a lot." He looked up at Matthew lovingly.

"That's wonderful." Ruth looked at Matthew and smiled. "I truly mean that. Thank-you for helping Peter."

"I'd do anything for him, Mrs. Wallace." Matthew smiled and his blue eyes sparkled. "He's means the world to me."

"I know," Ruth nodded. Despite her trying to be open-minded, she still felt a little repulsed by the thought of the two boys being together. "Right now, why don't you boys go out back and find yourselves a seat . I need to get your mother upstairs on the double!"

"Okay, Grandma," Peter nodded and continued to hold tightly to Matthew's arm.

Claudia watched the boys through the back door until she was sure they were safely seated.

"Still worried about him aren't you?" Ruth put her arm around Claudia's shoulders.

Claudia flashed a concerned smile.

"Yes. I am." She sighed. "I guess I have to be more patient about things, but I'm worried. He still gets really terrible headaches and has been so dizzy lately. Also, as you can see, he is still having trouble walking."

"What have the doctor's said?"

"They say it's normal for this type of injury and it takes time for the body to heal itself. I guess I should be happy that it wasn't more serious." Claudia shook her head. "I just can't help but worry. I came so close to losing him, too. Did you know the police wanted to have him locked up in a mental ward perminately? They heard what Matthew said up there that day and figured Peter needed more help than he was getting at home."

"I heard rumors to that effect." Ruth nodded. "Don't let that bother you. Peter is and will be just fine. The police don't know everything."

"Thank-you, Mom."

"For what?" Ruth smiled.

"For staying by us. I know this isn't easy for you. I remember our conversation about six months ago out back." Claudia patted Ruth's hand as it rested on her shoulder.

"It's true. I don't understand or profess to agree with his lifestyle, but I do love him very much and have to respect him for who he is." Ruth gave Claudia a gentle hug. "Now, enough of this. We have to get you up those stairs and changed or Patty will be a nervous wreck."

Matthew sat silently next to Peter, still holding onto his arm as he watched the rows of chairs fill up in front of them and behind them. He could not help but notice that as one of the ushers escorted a couple to the empty chairs next to them, as soon as their eyes met his, the man leaned over and whispered something to the usher. The usher turned around and showed them to seats in another row behind them. Matthew looked over at Peter, hoping that he had not seen what had happened. By the look in Peter's eyes, he could see that he had.

"Maybe I shouldn't have come," Peter sighed near tears.

"Nonsense." Matthew put his arm around Peter and hugged him. "Remember, we are here for Patty. To hell with everyone else."

"But this is my family," Peter protested. "I could take it from strangers, but it's different when it's family."

Matthew nodded understandingly and hugged Peter even tighter.

Daniel stood in line at the back door and watched as one by one the ushers escorted the guests to their seats, avoiding the empty chairs next to Peter and Matthew. His heart ached for the obvious shunning they were receiving from people who should be supportive. Even Morgan and Chuck were escorted to seats three rows away from them. Intentional or not, they could have chosen to sit with the boys. Daniel watched as the usher approached him.

"Are you with the bride's family or the groom's?" The thin, dark haired, young man in a black tuxedo asked.

"The bride's," Daniel replied. "There are actually three of us. My wife and son will be out here in a few minutes."

"Fine, sir. Right this way."

Daniel began to follow the usher up the make-shift center aisle between the rows of folding chairs. He watched as the usher directed him to a row in front of Morgan and Chuck. The row was already crowded with only three chairs left unoccupied in the middle. Daniel stopped next to Matthew and put his hand on Matthew's shoulder. Speaking directly to the usher, Daniel said in a voice loud enough to be heard by many of the guests.

"How about these seats? My family and I will sit here with my nephews."

The usher's mouth dropped and his face blushed with embarrassment. He quickly joined Daniel and pretended to show him to the seats.

Matthew looked up at Daniel and smiled.

Daniel winked and smiled back at Matthew as he scooted by in front of them.

Tamera looked around at the back yard as she stood at the door. The swimming pool had been cleaned and bouquets of red roses and daisies surrounded by greenery floated gently on the top of the water. The sturdy wooden bridge Carl had made turned out quite nicely and divided the swimming pool in half. Garlands of greenery and roses were draped along the rails. Just beyond the bridge, rows of white folding chairs were set up, leaving a center aisle that lead to a large gazebo. Tamera noticed that one of the large trees had been cut down to make room for the new gazebo. Everything looked wonderful.

She glanced to the tables next to her on the deck. The four tier wedding cake towered in the center of the big table, flanked by tapered candles. Slowly Tamera walked over to the table. She picked up the champagne glass with the word Groom etched onto it. She was tempted to spit in it, but then thought better. She set it back down and turned around just as Roger stepped through the back door.

Roger looked over at Tamera and smiled.

"Nice to see you, again." He tried to be polite. "How have you been?"

Tamera met his smile with a intense glare. She walked over to him slowly like a cat about to pounce on a rat.

"I know all about your little secret," she whispered when she stood face to face with him.

Roger pulled his head back.

"Oh, you do, do you?" He said smugly. "And just

what do you think you know?"

"I know about your wife, that's what," Tamera hissed.

"So." Roger shrugged unconcerned.

"I know you killed her," Tamera continued. "And if you think for one minute that I am going to just sit back and let you marry and then murder my sister, you've got another think coming!"

Roger clinched his jaw tightly.

"I did not kill my wife, Tamera."

"Is that so?" Tamera smiled to herself seeing his reaction.

"Yes. That is so," Roger said firmly. "You can think whatever the hell you want to about me, but I love your sister and would never to anything to harm her. If you love her as much as you profess to then you will keep your fat mouth shut and let her be happy for once in her life."

Roger turned around before Tamera could reply and headed toward the gazebo.

Tamera watched him as he greeted the guests along his way. Her anger was still raging inside her when she saw him stop and shake Peter's hand. Suddenly she caught sight of Daniel seated next to Peter and her mind went blank.

"That son-of-a-." She stopped herself from finishing her curse. "Nicholas, come on," she demanded as she marched up the aisle, not waiting for the ushers.

Tamera stopped beside Matthew and glared at Daniel. Daniel looked up at his wife. The color of her reddened cheeks clashed with the deep purple and blue flowers on her lightweight summer dress. He smiled pretending innocence, knowing he had pushed her buttons.

"Daniel, I am not sitting next to these faggots," she cursed through her clinched teeth.

Daniel smiled and tightened his jaw.

"You will sit where I tell you to sit. Now get your ass over her and sit down and keep your mouth shut. And that goes for you too Nicholas, march."

"Do I have to, Mom?" Nicholas protested.

Daniel stood up and grabbed his son's arm tightly.

"When I tell you to do something,young man, you will do it. Do you understand me?"

Nicholas looked up at his father and did not say a word.

"That's okay, Uncle Dan, we're leaving." Peter tried not to cry in front of his aunt. "It's obvious that no one wants us here. Matthew, please help me."

"Peter, no. Don't go," Daniel pleaded.

Matthew stood up causing Daniel to release his hold on Nicholas. Slowly he helped Peter to his feet.

"I appreciate everything you have tried to do for us, Uncle Dan." Peter tried to smile as a tear fell from his eye. "But I think it would be better for Aunt Patty if we left."

Just as Matthew helped Peter into the aisle, Ruth walked up quickly.

"What's going on here?" She asked in a hushed voice. She had witnessed the commotion from the family room window.

"Matthew and Peter are leaving, Mom," Daniel answered his mother-in-law.

"Why? Is something wrong?" Ruth looked at Peter. Her protective instinct kicked in when she saw his tears. Immediately she took his face in her hands.

"Are you feeling okay?" She asked him directly.

"Yes." Peter drew a deep, shaky breath. "I just think that everyone would have a better time if we left."

"Matthew, please help Peter back to his seat." Ruth looked up at Tamera and glared. "You two are not going anywhere," she said sternly, not taking her eyes off Tamera. "As for you, get in the house, now! I want a word with you."

Ruth turned around without letting Tamera respond and headed back into the house.

Tamera felt a wave a panic come over her. Suddenly she felt like a child again about to be disciplined by her mother. Her anger was gone. She looked at Daniel as though asking for help. He turned his face away from her, still incensed by this intolerant side of her that he had never known before. Tamera nudged Nicholas toward his father and followed obediently after Ruth.

Nicholas walked down the row of seats and sat in the one furthest away from Peter and Matthew. He looked straight ahead with his teeth clinched. He loathed Peter and Matthew and yet, he did not really know that much about either of them.

Daniel sat down next to Peter and took his hand into his.

"Don't let people like your Aunt Tamera win," he smiled and spoke softly. "Don't give your power away. They are not worth it."

"Thank-you." Peter looked up at his uncle and smiled.

Daniel nodded and gave Peter a hug. He honestly liked Peter. His gentleness. His loving concern and care for everyone around him. Peter reminded Daniel of someone he had not thought about in years. If only things had been different back then maybe he would not be just a memory. Daniel turned his attention back to the gazebo where Roger and the ushers were talking quietly with the Justice of the Peace.

Tamera closed the back door quietly behind her. The family room was empty and quiet, except for Ruth, who stood off to the side.

Ruth drew a deep breath and exhaled with a firm sigh.

"Just what is your problem? You have done nothing but berate Peter and make him feel unwanted ever since you found out that he is gay."

Tamera tightened her jaw as she felt her anger grow again. She did not care that this was her mother in front of her. She was ready to do battle.

"I don't like him and I don't want my son subjected to their perverted ways," Tamera said smugly.

"What?" Ruth looked at Tamera confused by her comment.

"I don't want my son to be molested by them. There, is that blunt enough?"

"Oh, I don't believe your ignorance and stupidity," Ruth scoffed. "First of all, being gay does not make you a child molester. In fact, most child molesters are so called straight people. And secondly, Peter is part of this family like it or not."

"Well, I don't have to like him because you say so!" Tamera snapped back at her mother.

Ruth felt her anger grow in her chest. She could not believe how bigoted Tamera had become since she was a child. At that moment everything in her being wanted to slap that smug look off Tamera's puffy, round face. Slowly she walked over to her daughter and struggled hard to maintain some decorum.

'It is true. I can't force you to like anyone, but I can tell you this. This is my house and in my house all of my family is to be made to feel welcome. That includes Peter and his friend, Matthew. And if you don't like it, you know where the door is. Is that clear, Missy?"

Tamera drew a deep breath and looked into her mother's brown eyes. She could see Ruth's anger boiling deep inside her. At the same time her own stubbornness was not about to give in.

"Yes," she retorted.

"The choice is yours. Either stay and keep your mouth shut, and act like a human being, or get out and don't come back until you can," Ruth snapped back and then left the room.

Tamera stood by herself in the empty room as she weighed her options. She looked out the window at the gathering in the backyard. She would stay. She had further business, more important, to tend to.

Ruth opened the bedroom door and stepped inside. She smiled proudly to herself as she looked at her baby girl standing before her in her wedding dress. Patricia was so beautiful. Her auburn hair was pulled up and away from her face and neck. The low neckline of the lace-appliqued bodice made her neck appear long and striking. The full length skirt and long train draped around her thin waist made her look tall and statuesque. Slowly Ruth walked over to her and gave her a gentle hug.

"You look so beautiful," Ruth breathed into Patricia's ear.

"Thank-you, Mom." Patricia smiled through tear filled eyes.

"I have something for you," Ruth said as she opened her hand to reveal a string of pearls. "I wore these the day I married your father. I want you to have them."

"Oh, Mama, they are so beautiful," Patricia gasped as she looked at the dainty necklace. "Would you help me put them on?"

"Of course," Ruth smiled.

Patricia turned her back to her mother as the pearls were draped around her neck and then fastened securely. Patricia took a deep breath and put her hand to her stomach. She could not shake the strange feeling deep inside her. She tried to tell herself it was just her being nervous, but the feeling did not go away.

Ruth noticed the sudden change in Patricia's expression in the mirror. She rested her hands on Patricia's shoulders.

"What's the matter, dear?"

"I don't know, Mom," Patricia answered and looked at their reflections in the mirror. "I just have a strange feeling that something is going to go wrong."

"Everything is going to be fine," Ruth smiled.

"I hope so." Patricia smiled and then paused. "When you married Daddy, how did you feel?"

"Oh, I felt excited and nervous. I knew I couldn't live without him and that was all I needed to know," Ruth reminisced. "That is what got me down that aisle."

"Mama, I don't think I love Roger," Patricia blurted out.

"What?" Ruth could not believe what she was hearing.

"I mean, I do love him very much." Patricia tried to sort out her thoughts. "I'm just not in love with him. I don't feel those feelings you had. I'm so confused."

"It's okay." Ruth smiled at her daughter and gave her a little reassuring hug. "You are feeling what they call cold feet, that's all. It's a big step getting married. 'Until death do you part.' they say. You will be fine. Roger is a good man. He loves you without any doubts. Everything will be fine."

"I hope you are right." Patricia smiled an uncertain smile.

"I am and you will see that too."

A knock at the door interrupted their conversation. Ruth turned around.

"Yes?"

The bedroom door opened and Carl stepped into the room. Ruth smiled at her husband. He looked so handsome in his black tuxedo and white shirt.

"Well, it looks like everyone has shown up down there and we're about ready to start."

"In that case, I best be getting down there." Ruth leaned forward and gave Patricia a soft kiss on the cheek. "I love you, dear. I'm so proud of you."

"I love you too, Mama." Patricia smiled and fought back the tears in her eyes. "Thank-you for everything."

With that, Ruth left the room and hurried down the stairs. As she reached the foyer she glanced over toward the parlor and froze. A smiled spread across her lips and she rushed into the room.

"Amanda." She reached out and hugged her former daughter-in-law. "I'm so happy to see you. How are you?"

Amanda hugged Ruth tightly not wanting to let go.

"I'm fine," she answered as Ruth pulled away.

"Honest?"

"Yes, Mom. Honest." Amanda nodded. "I see you still have Brad's and my wedding picture on the mantle." She glanced over her shoulder at the family pictures.

"Yes," Ruth sighed. "I guess I'm still hopeful that you and Bradley will get back together."

Amanda looked at the floor and then back up at Ruth.

"So am I. I miss my family so much."

"We miss you, too," Ruth said and hugged Amanda again. Ruth could tell that Amanda had in fact put on a few pounds since that day nearly a year ago. No longer was she just skin and bones. Ruth was happy about that. It meant things were better.

"So, have you seen Brad?" Amanda asked as she straightened her dress.

"He and Benji are out back already."

"Is he with someone?" Amanda asked fearing the answer.

"No. To be honest with you, he hasn't seen anyone since your divorce. He couldn't even bring himself to sell the house you three shared. It's just sitting there empty. He and Benji are renting an apartment on the other side of town."

The sound of the bedroom door opening upstairs touched Ruth's ears and snapped her back to the wedding at hand.

"I've got to get out there, now," Ruth apologized.

"Are you here for the wedding?" She held out her hand to Amanda.

"Yes," Amanda nodded. "Patty sent me an invitation." She showed Ruth the envelope.

"Wonderful." Ruth took her hand. "Come on."

The two hurried out the back door and followed the usher over the bridge and up the aisle.

Amanda searched the guests looking for Bradley and Benjamin. She stopped when her eyes met those of her son. She smiled and bit her lip. He no longer looked like a baby. In his little suit he looked so grown up to her even though he was only four years old.

"Mama!" Benjamin called out to her from his seat.

Bradley looked first at his son next to him and then up at Amanda. He smiled reflexively and then stopped. He stood up and faced his ex-wife.

"Hi," he greeted her nervously. Deep down he wanted to take her in his arms and kiss her right then and there. He had missed her terribly this passed year being apart. Try as he might, he could not stop loving her. His anger and pain from losing their daughter had eased and he felt awful about what he had put her through.

"Hi, Brad." Amanda smiled sheepishly at him. "You look great."

"Thanks." He smiled and looked at his gray suit, the same one he had worn to their wedding over four years earlier. He was surprised that it still fit, but he had lost weight himself since the divorce.

"Are you here with someone?" Bradley looked around nervously.

"No," Amanda assured him.

"Then, would you like to sit here with us?"

Bradley stuttered as he motioned toward the empty chair next to Benjamin.

"I'd love to." Amanda smiled and scooted by them to her seat. When she passed in front of Bradley, she intentionally brushed against his arm with the back of her hand. It felt good to touch him, she sighed to herself. She took her seat and Bradley resumed his. Benjamin leaned over and wrapped his arms around her neck and gave her a tight hug and a kiss on the cheek.

Claudia, dressed in her pastel pink, tea length bride's maid dress with matching pumps, handed Patricia her bouquet of roses and baby's breath. She smiled at her sister-in-law and could not help but feel a bit envious. If she could have married Steven properly, she would have wanted it just like this, surrounded by family and friends.

"Well, this is it, Patty." She kissed her cheek. "Be happy. You deserve it."

"Thank-you, Claudia," Patricia smiled. "I just wish Steven could have been here to see it."

"Me too." Claudia smiled back her tears. "But he is in a way. He's in our hearts."

"I know," Patricia sighed as tears fell from her eyes. "I just miss him so much."

"I do too." Claudia took a deep breath and tried not to cry. "We better stop this or we both will be in a puddle. Now, chin up. Shoulders back. Stand straight and tall."

Patricia did as she was told and flashed a brief nervous smile at Claudia.

"You look perfect."

"Thank-you for everything you have done,"

Patricia said as Carl walked back into the bedroom.

"Well, ladies, they are waiting for us downstairs. Let's go." Carl held out his arm to his daughter.

Claudia hurried out of the bedroom and down the stairs to wait with the other two bride's maids by the back door.

"You doing okay?" Carl whispered to his daughter as they approached the top of the stairs.

"I think so," she answered in a quivering voice and took his arm.

"Hold it." A voice came from the bottom of the stairs.

Patricia looked up just as the flash from the photographer's camera went off momentarily blinding her. She stumbled and nearly dropped her bouquet. Carl caught her.

"Easy does it," he coached her. "You okay?"

"Sorry about the flash, Miss Wallace," the photographer apologized realizing what he had done. "When you get to the middle of the stairs, I'd like to take another picture of the two of you. So, maybe stop and look this way. Try not to look at the flash."

"Ok." Carl nodded to the young man. The two proceeded down the stairs and then stopped for the picture. One more stop at the foot of the stairs for a picture and they were on the main floor and ready to go.

Outside the recorded music began to play. The theme from the old movie Love Story, Patricia's favorite, gently touched the ears of the guests and everyone turned their heads toward the house. One by one, the bride's maids slowly walked out onto the deck and then down the steps toward the bridge.

Ruth smiled through her tear filled eyes as she

watched for her daughter. She glanced over at Morgan and Chuck. Morgan held tightly to Chuck as tears streamed down her cheeks. Ruth smiled to herself. Morgan did love Patricia, more than she would admit.

As the first bride's maid finished crossing the bridge, she took the arm of an usher and continued up the aisle toward the gazebo. Then came Ariel, the second bride's maid. As she took the arm of the usher, she glanced over at Mark and smiled. He smiled back at her and winked, holding up four month old Kevin to see his mother.

As Claudia and the best man reached the gazebo, they turned to face the gathering. The music ended and a new song began to play. The back door opened and Carl stepped out and held out his arm to Patricia.

Patricia held tight to her father's arm as the two descended the steps toward the bridge. Her heart beat nervously in her chest as she looked about at all the faces of her family and friends. As her eyes met Peter's, she smiled and winked at him. He smiled and shyly looked down. With a deep breath, she looked up at Roger. Her nervousness faded and a feeling of warmth filled her completely. It felt right, her marrying him. It felt as though it was meant to be, natural. She smiled broadly at him.

Roger stood up straight and rigid. Every muscle tensed as he watched Patricia walking toward him. He could not help but smile at his lovely wife-to-be. She was so beautiful. So caring. There was no doubt in his mind that she was the one for him.

As Patricia passed by Matthew and Peter's row, she glanced over at Tamera. Her smile vanished momentarily as their eyes met. A feeling of panic swept through her. She did not trust the disapproving look in Tamera's eyes. She quickly looked back at Roger and the feeling vanished.

Roger glanced over at Tamera. When their eyes met, he glared at her, almost threatening her to keep her mouth shut. Tamera noticed and defiantly glared back.

Daniel noticed the exchange of glares between them and put his hand on Tamera's and gave it a firm squeeze. Tamera looked at him trying to look innocent.

"Don't you dare say a word," he whispered firmly to her then turned his attention back to the wedding.

Carl kissed Patricia on her cheek and whispered, "I love you." into her ear. He took her hand and placed it in Roger's. With a smile he left them to sit next to Ruth. Roger and Patricia entered the gazebo together and stood before the justice of the peace.

The music faded away and the Justice of the Peace opened with a few words of greeting to the congregated family and friends and then to Patricia and Roger. Patricia kept looking into Roger's brown eyes. She could not help smiling. She did not hear a single word that was being spoken. Instead she kept repeating over in her mind, "Mrs. Roger Allen Ferguson."

"Is there anyone here present that knows of some reason why these two should not be united, let them speak now or forever hold their peace." The Justice looked about the faces of the gathering.

Roger held his breath, knowing that Tamera was behind him staring at him. The silence seemed to drag on for an eternity. His heart pounded. His hands began to sweat. Tiny beads of sweat formed on his brow and he wiped them away. As he looked at Patricia and he smiled.

"Well, then," the Justice of the Peace broke the silence. "Let us continue."

Roger heaved a heavy sigh of relief and smiled again at Patricia.

"I'm sorry. I can't let this happen." A voice from behind them shouted.

Patricia suddenly snapped back to the present. She was confused. Had she really heard what she thought? She turned around and looked at the faces of her family and friends. There standing in the middle of them was Tamera. Daniel had a hold of her arm and was pulling at her to sit back down.

"No. Let go," Tamera whispered harshly at him.

"Tamera, you are making a fool of yourself," Daniel said sternly. "Have you no feelings for your sister?"

"Yes, I do. Now let go." Tamera pulled free from his grasp. "I do have an objection," she stated firmly to the gathering.

Patricia looked at Ruth in shock and disbelief. How could this be happening? Ruth saw the hurt in Patricia's eyes and she felt her pain and embarrassment. As she turned her head to look at Tamera her anger grew inside her.

"Family and friends," the Justice of the Peace spoke up. "Please remain calm. I've been marrying people for years and never has there been a wedding actually called off. Please, stay in your seats." Turning his attention to Tamera. "Miss, please meet me in the house and tell me what this is all about. Patricia, Roger, please come with me."

"I hope you are satisfied," Daniel sneered as Tamera pushed passed him.

Tamera did not respond and continued into the house.

Patricia handed her bouquet to Claudia and quickly gathered her train, her hands shaking, partly from embarrassment and partly from anger. She could not believe that Tamera was doing this to her. She took Roger's arm again and followed the Justice of the Peace back down the aisle.

Ruth and Carl quickly stood up and followed. Carl nodded to Roger's parents to come too, but they shook their heads. They would stay.

The guests began to murmur to one another, stunned and confused by what was happening. Martin, the best man, hurried back to the deck where the disc jockey was set up at the foot of the steps. He quietly whispered to the man and soon after, soft music began to fill the air. The whispering continued but softly.

Amanda looked at the back door.

"Poor Patty," she whispered out loud. "How could Tamera be so cruel?"

"I don't know." Bradley shook his head. "Ever since the day she met Roger she has had it in for him. No one knows why."

"That is awful," Amanda sighed and turned back in her chair to face the gazebo. "I can't believe all the changes back here. The bridge. The gazebo. Did Dad and Mom do all of this?"

"Yes," Bradley nodded to himself. "Mom wants to open up a wedding consulting business and the house and grounds for weddings. She wants to keep herself busy and really enjoys doing weddings."

"That is so neat." Amanda smiled. "I remember our wedding reception here. It was so nice of them to let us use the house. Mom really out did herself with the flowers, food, decorations. Everything was so beautiful."

"Yes, it was." Bradley smiled. He was happy to that Amanda had come. Afterall, he was the one that sent her his invitation. It was a way to break the silence between them. No expectations. Just seeing Patricia get married.

"Ah," Bradley hesitated and looked over at Amanda. She was just as beautiful to him as the day they had met. Her hair was cut in a short almost manly style that was in the right proportions to flatter her rosy cheeks and big brown eyes.

He felt his heart flutter as his hands began to sweat. He had to look away for a moment to gather himself.

"Yes?" Amanda leaned toward him. "You were about to say something?"

Bradley looked over at her.

"You wouldn't want to go out for coffee or something after the reception, would you?"

"I'd love to." Amanda smiled and reached over and took his hand. "I would absolutely love to," she repeated.

Bradley looked down and smiled contented with himself. His plan had worked.

"I wonder what that is all about." Chuck looked over his shoulder in the direction of the house.

Morgan did not turn around. She put her chin in the air and took deep breath through her nostrils.

"I don't know and I don't care," she said flatly. "I'm staying out of this one."

"No. I mean about Bradley and Amanda." Chuck turned away from the house.

"What?" Morgan turned to him and then glanced over her shoulder. "Who invited her?" She said in surprise and wonder. "Oh, this is too much. I can't take this family." She shook her head and settled back in her seat. "They are all a bunch of nuts."

Ariel looked at Mark and shrugged her shoulders as she stood next to Claudia. Mark motioned for her to come to him, but she shook her head.

"I can't believe Aunt Tamera would ruin Aunt Patty's wedding like this," she whispered to Claudia.

"I know." Claudia shook her head. "I feel so sorry for Patty. How embarrassing in front of all of these people. Why didn't Tamera say something sooner?"

"Like for sure!" Ariel slipped back into her air headed speech.

Claudia gave her a curious look and fought the urge to laugh.

"Well, this is taking way too long." Daniel shook his head. "I'm going in there. You stay put," he instructed Nicholas firmly.

"But, Dad," Nicholas pleaded.

"Nick, I am not in the mood. Do as you are told and shut up!" Daniel snapped as he brushed passed Peter and Matthew.

Nicholas looked at Peter and as their eyes met he jerked his head and turned away from them. Folding his arms over his chest he looked as though he were pouting.

Peter smiled to himself at how ridiculous his fifteen year old cousin looked. He turned and looked at Matthew and smiled.

"Thank-you for coming with me," he said and patted Matthew's hand.

"Hey," Matthew looked at Peter and smiled. "Where you go, I go. I want us to be together forever."

"Me too." Peter smiled.

His smile faded and his tone became hushed.

"So, have you told your parents about us yet?"

Matthew rubbed his hands together and let out a sigh.

"No. It's not that easy. They would freak if they knew. I'd be disowned."

"So, what did you tell them? What about Diana?" Peter questioned him.

"I had Monica tell them I found a job out here and would be staying out here. I told Diana we were not getting married and that I wasn't in love with her. If she killed herself, that would be her choice. I would not be made to feel guilty." Matthew looked at Peter and smiled lovingly. "But I don't want you to worry about that. I just want you to get well. I'll tell them in time."

"Okay." Peter smiled. "I love you, Matthew."

"I love you, too, Pete." Matthew winked at him.

Daniel entered the family room unnoticed and looked around. Patricia stood beside Roger and held onto his arm tightly. Daniel could not see her eyes but it was obvious she was crying. The Justice of the Peace shook his head and sighed out loud as he stood between Tamera and the couple.

"I can't believe you are doing this to me," Patricia cried and glared at her sister through her tear-filled eyes. "Why can't you let me be happy for once? Why do you always have to ruin things for me?"

Tamera sighed and looked at her sister. She was

not cold and unfeeling as Daniel had said. She did feel a deep regret over having interrupted Patricia's wedding. She did hope to stop everything before it went this far but Patricia would not listen or return her phone calls.

"I'm sorry, but it's for your own good," Tamera said coldly, lacking any feeling or empathy.

"For my own good?" Patricia nearly screamed at her. "I am an adult. I can decide for myself what is for my own good. I don't need you sticking your fat nose in my business."

Ruth walked over to Patricia and put her arm around her shoulders. She felt anger toward Tamera and at the same time her heart ached for the pain and embarrassment Patricia must be feeling.

"Tamera, this had better be good."

Carl walked over to the Justice of the Peace.

"So, now what do we do?"

The Justice of the Peace shook his head and sighed again.

"First I want to hear the reason why you stopped the wedding." He looked directly at Tamera.

Tamera drew a deep breath and folded her arms over her chest. She looked directly at Roger in a cocky sort of way.

"Shall I tell them or should you?"

Roger glared at Tamera. Even though he did not know her very well, he hated her with every part of his being. Over the years he had struggled with people like her, unwilling to listen to the truth but eager to believe the lies, always out to ruin his life.

"Why don't you tell everyone, since you obviously think you know it all," he said through clinched teeth.

"Mrs. Lynch, enough of these games. What is it?"

The Justice of the Peace asked.

"Okay." Tamera looked at Patricia. "I'm sorry I interrupted your wedding but I had to. You see, Roger was married before."

Patricia shook her head in disgust.

"So," she answered her sister indignantly. "I already knew that. What difference does that make?"

"Did he tell you what happened to her?" Tamera continued. "How after her father had died she inherited all his millions. How she caught him with another woman and was going to divorce him. Then because he didn't want to loose all that money, he strangled her and then tried to cover it up by making it look as though a robber broke into their house? Now he's running from the law."

"Oh, you watch too much TV." Roger shook his head.

"Roger?" Patricia looked at him confused. Her hands beginning to tremble.

"Don't listen to her." Roger put his arm around Patricia.

"Is it true?" Patricia asked him but feared the answer. She wanted so much for him to tell her it was not but began to doubt how well did she really know him.

"Of course it isn't true." Roger answered. He cast a glare in Tamera's direction.

"What happened, son?" Carl asked flatly. "Why don't you tell us all what is going on."

Roger looked over at Carl and nodded his head.

"Okay. It is true. I was married before. We were both young when we were married and so we were very immature. Karen did her share of fooling around and I admit it, so did I. Anyway, our marriage was far from a happy one. We fought a lot. Nothing physical, mainly her screaming and me yelling. We tried marriage counselors with no success. Her father was very rich and he died suddenly. I remember that was the turning point in our marriage. She needed someone to lean on and I needed to feel needed. Her father did leave his entire estate to Karen; only it wasn't millions of dollars as some of the newspapers misreported. I think that is what was the ultimate cause of her death.

"I was away that night at a company dinner we both were to attend. She wasn't feeling well and insisted that I go without her. All I know is that when I came home at eleven that night, the house was surrounded by the police and that's when I found out someone had broken into the house and had killed her. They made off with the money and jewelry from the bedroom safe. I did not kill her."

"Aren't you leaving out something?" Tamera interjected. "The part where she had filed for a divorce that very morning?"

"No!" Roger snapped back at her. "When that story came out in the papers, I contacted her lawyers immediately. They informed me that one of their clerks had come across the papers from months earlier when Karen and I were having trouble. They said she filed them with the state thinking they had forgotten to by mistake. Neither Karen nor I had any knowledge of it. In fact the attorney's contacted the newspapers and had a retraction printed and as things go, no one ever saw the retraction buried on page twenty-six; not front page news!"

Tamera smirked disbelievingly.

"Did you also read about how the scum had raped my wife while he was strangling her? How the tests showed that the semen proved that I did not do it. Did you? Did you?" Roger felt his temper beginning to boil as he tightened his jaw. It was still a painful memory for him even though it had been nearly seven years ago.

Tamera's smirk faded quickly as she suddenly felt embarrassed.

"Did you also check with the police to find out that never once was I ever considered a suspect? I'm not running from any Law. The only thing I've been running from is narrow minded, gossiping old biddies like you and poor journalists who love dealing with innuendo and rumors."

Tamera was speechless. She looked Ruth who immediately turned away. She looked at her father who stared at her with pursed lips, obviously angered by her.

Patricia stepped forward and glared at Tamera through her tears.

"I will never forgive you for this. Never!" She reached out for Ruth and cried silently in her mother's arms.

"Well, as tragic as this all is, this is really not grounds for stopping the wedding," the Justice of the Peace shook his head. "Even criminals on death row can be married and Mr. Ferguson is far from a criminal. So, shall we continue?" He looked at Roger and then sympathetically at Patricia.

"Yes," Roger gave a heavy sigh and smiled at Patricia.

Patricia looked at everyone standing around her and then at Roger. She was so confused by everything that had happened. So many emotions flooded her heart that she was numb.

"I don't know," she said in a shaky voice as she touched Roger's face. "I don't know," she repeated and ran from the room as tears streamed down her cheeks.

"Patty!" Ruth called after her. She turned and glared at Tamera before she hurried after her daughter.

Carl looked at Roger. He could not imagine the pain that he must be feeling.

"Go to her, son," he urged.

Roger bit his tongue to keep himself composed and turned to the Justice of the Peace.

"Please, give us a moment longer. Don't leave."

"You are my only appointment today, Mr. Ferguson. I'll give you all the time you need," he said and smiled sympathetically at Roger.

"Thank-you. I really appreciate that." Roger nodded and then hurried after Patricia.

"Well, are you happy now, little miss know-it-all?" Daniel spoke up for the first time. "You just couldn't keep you mouth shut and your nose out of everyone else's business, could you."

Tamera looked over at her husband and her anger grew.

"Oh, shut up," she hissed and pushed passed him on her way out the back door.

Daniel looked over at Carl and the Justice of the Peace.

"I'm truly sorry about all of this. I tried to keep her under control, but sometimes she is just so bull headed and stubborn."

"Don't I know it." Carl smiled and nodded in agreement.

Matthew leaned over and whispered into Peter's ear.

"Her comes Tamera and she doesn't look pleased."

Peter turned around and watched as his aunt crossed the bridge. Rather than walking up the aisle, she walked around the outside of the chairs to avoid having to walk in front of them. Peter turned back around and shook his head.

Tamera sat down in her seat, two chairs away from Peter, and stared straight ahead.

"So, what's happening?" Nicholas asked quietly.

"Oh, shut up!" Tamera snapped.

Nicholas recoiled as though he had been slapped and then settled back in his chair.

"Tamera is back," Chuck informed Morgan. "Judging from the look on her face, I'd say the wedding is still on."

Morgan looked over her shoulder at her sister. She could see the seething anger in Tamera's eyes.

"I guess so," she nodded in agreement.

Ariel nudged Claudia when she saw Tamera returning to her chair. Claudia nodded silently that she too had seen her. She gave a relieved sigh and looked at the house. The back door opened and Carl, Daniel and the Justice of the Peace stepped out. No one was smiling. Suddenly Claudia felt a sinking feeling in her chest.

"This doesn't look good," she said out loud.

The three walked up the aisle together and then Daniel slipped back into his seat. Carl stopped at the aisle where Roger's parents were seated and filled them in on what had happened. The Justice of the Peace walked over to the gazebo and stood casually and waited for some signal that the wedding was still on.

Carl managed a forced smile and then stood up in front of the assembly. He looked about at all the familiar faces of his family and those of Roger's family as he tried to find just the right words.

Roger knocked lightly on the closed bedroom door. He regretted not telling Patricia everything about his life with Karen, but it was still too painful a topic and not one he liked to talk about. He cursed Tamera under his breath and yet he was relieved that it was all out in the open. If only Patricia could understand. If only she would go through with the wedding. A wave of panic rolled over him as he listened at the door. His thoughts raced. What if she would not marry me? What would I do then? How would I go on?

"Come in," Ruth called in answer to his knocking.

Slowly Roger opened the bedroom door. Ruth sat alone on the edge of the twin bed and looked at him over her shoulder. Patricia stood, leaning against the wall, staring out of the window at the gathering in the backyard. She was not crying, that much he could tell.

"I'll leave you two alone," Ruth said as she stood up.

"Mom, tell them I'll be down in a minute," Patricia said without turning around.

"Okay, dear," Ruth nodded and kissed Roger on the cheek before she disappeared out the door.

Roger felt his cheek and thought about the kiss. He could not tell if that was a good sign or bad omen. He shrugged his shoulders as though shaking off the thoughts and turned his attention back to Patricia.

"Is everything okay?" He asked sheepishly,

wanting to put his arms around her and hold her, but being afraid to.

"Why didn't you tell me about Karen being murdered?" She asked without turning around.

Roger looked away briefly and then turned back to Patricia.

"I guess I didn't want to think about it. I've tried hard to get on with my life and put it all behind me. I guess I didn't want her to come between us."

"And the money? What happened to that?" She continued to question him.

"Well, after Karen's death, I inherited it." Roger felt uneasy about her question.

"So, exactly how much was it, since it wasn't millions?"

"Actually, at the time it was slightly under a million dollars," he answered her question.

"Wow." Patricia responded flatly, without any real feeling. "Then your working in the news room is just for what? To flaunt yourself as a good deed doer?" She looked at him coldly.

"No," he defended himself. "I do it because of the lousy job that was done on me. I want the people of this country to know the truth about what they see and hear. Not just some two bit reporter out to make a name for himself by misrepresenting the facts. If you must know, the money is still in the bank. I haven't touched it. I don't want it and never did."

Patricia turned back to the window. Her mind flooded by conflicting thoughts that argued against each other and her feelings.

"What are we to do now?" She asked softly, again staring out at the gathering below.

Roger took a step closer to her.

"Do you still love me?"

Patricia looked at him with a soft smile.

"With all my heart."

Roger smiled and knelt down on one knee.

"Then Miss Wallace, will you marry me?" He held out his hand to her.

"Yes. I'll marry you Mr. Ferguson." Patricia took his hand.

Roger stood and leaned into her to kiss her. Patricia playfully pulled away and turned her head.

"Not so fast. I don't have a ring on this finger yet," she smiled and showed him her bare hand.

Roger smiled back at her and took her hand and kissed it.

"Well, let's go do something about that."

Morgan was standing next to Carl by the gazebo when Ruth walked up. They both looked at her in hopeful anticipation. Carl noticed that Ruth was not smiling and suddenly felt uneasy.

He greeted her with a quick kiss.

"So, what's the verdict?" He asked.

Ruth drew a deep breath and looked up at the bedroom window.

"I wish I knew. Patty was awfully upset at the news. I don't know."

"Well, thank-you, Tamer," Morgan said sarcastically.

"It's not all Tamera's fault. Although she picked a really lousy time to speak up," Ruth defended her daughter and looked over at Tamera. Deep down she was angry with her but as a mother, she still had to stand up for her even if what she did was wrong.

"So, now what?" Morgan asked.

"We just have to wait," Ruth sighed.

Suddenly the music stopped and everyone turned around to see why. There on the deck at the back door, Patricia stood holding onto Roger's arm. She smiled a reassuring smile to her parents and the music began to play. Slowly the two walked up the aisle as Ruth and Carl took their seats and the bridal party took their places.

"I guess we have our answer," Ruth smiled and gave Carl's hand a gentle squeeze.

The guests applauded wildly as Roger kissed his new wife and cut into their cake. Patricia laughed and cameras clicked all around as Roger lovingly gave her the first bite of the cake. Then it was her turn to feed him. Amid shouts to smear it in his face, she gently fed him his piece. With icing still on his lips, he grabbed her about the waist and drew her to himself and kissed her.

"That is so neat," Peter said to Matthew as he leaned against him. "Wouldn't it be great if one day we could do that?"

"Yeah," Matthew smiled and looked into Peter's brown eyes.

"Oh, don't make me sick," Tamera barked from behind them.

"Aunt Tamera!" Peter jumped nearly losing his balance as he turned around to face her. His head spinning from dizziness due to moving too quietly.

"You two are disgusting," she continued.

"Gee, it seems you just don't know when to quit,

do you." Matthew stood up to her. "I'll tell you what is disgusting. For someone to have such a narrow mind and be so hateful toward people you know nothing about. You are nothing but an ugly overweight bigot."

"I'd rather be a bigot than a faggot like you," Tamera spit. "This is a straight wedding. Why don't you two sissy boys just leave?"

"Maybe we will, when we are good and ready. It would be better than having to put up with the likes of you," Matthew continued to defend himself and Peter.

"And another thing, don't you ever come near my boy, or I'll press charges."

"For what?" Peter gasped in disbelief.

"Think about it," Tamera hissed and walked away.

Matthew watched Tamera as she made her way over to the food tables. His pulse raced in anger. In all his life he had never met someone so full of hate as she.

"And she is your father's sister?" He commented and shook his head in wonder.

"Yeah," Peter nodded his head. "She wasn't always like this. When I first met her she was really nice. I know it's hard to imagine it now."

"Are you okay?" Matthew looked into Peter's eyes again. He looked tired with the dark circles under his eyes. "You look a little pale."

"I'm okay. Just tired, I guess. Maybe we should go sit down." Peter continued to lean against Matthew.

"Good idea." Matthew smiled. "I'll help you to the table over there by the trees and then I'll get you something to eat."

"Thank-you." Peter smiled.

As Claudia stood chatting with Bradley and Amanda, she noticed the conversation Tamera was having with the boys. She strained to hear above the music and dull roar of the many conversations but it was no use. Seeing Peter sitting alone, she excused herself and went over to him.

"So, how are you, dear?" She bent down and kissed Peter's forehead.

Peter looked up and smiled. "I'm okay."

"Are you really?" Claudia asked as she sat down next to him.

"No." Peter shook his head. "What is Aunt Tamera's problem? Have I done something to her and don't realize it?"

Claudia looked over her shoulder at Tamera going through the buffet table.

"No. You haven't done a thing."

"Then why is she so hateful? She even said that if either Matthew or I get near Nicholas, she will press charges. She was implying that we would molest him or something."

"Just ignore her." Claudia shook her head. "She's the type that has to keep things stirred up. Don't let her get to you."

"I'll try, but it's hard not to when she gets in your face like that, Mom." Peter grimaced in pain as his head hurt.

Claudia quickly grabbed him and held him to her chest.

"Peter, honey, please don't upset yourself. It's not good for you."

"What's the matter?" Matthew asked as he approached the table. His blue eyes reflected his fear and deep concern. "Is everything all right?"

Claudia looked up at him and smiled.

"Peter is having another one of his headaches, is all."

Peter sat up and Claudia stood.

"Can I talk to you for a second, Matthew?"

"Sure. Let me put these plates down." Matthew set the plates down and handed the blue plastic silverware and napkins to Peter. "I'll be right back."

Peter nodded. Matthew and Claudia took a couple steps away and leaned against the rail of the bridge. Looking over her shoulder at Peter, Claudia sighed.

"Matthew, please try to keep Peter calm. The doctors say he has to be very careful still and not get his blood pressure up."

"I know, Mrs. Wallace," Matthew nodded. "I'm trying but that Tamera witch isn't helping."

"I know. Thank-you, dear." Claudia leaned forward and kissed Matthew on his cheek. "I'll be right back," she told him, as she spotted Tamera leaving the buffet table.

"What do you want?" Tamera's tone was bitter as she saw Claudia approaching.

"I would like a word with you, dear sister-in-law. That is if you can pull yourself away from your trough." Claudia could feel her own blood pressure rise.

"I have nothing to say to you." Tamera ignored the comment and tried to walk around her.

Claudia grabbed Tamera's plump arm and halted her in her tracks.

"Well, I have plenty to say to you. Get in the house," she ordered.

Tamera was shocked by Claudia's tone. Obediently she set her plate down on the nearest table and headed for the house with Claudia right behind her.

"Look at that, Dan." Carl nudged Daniel and motioned with his head.

Daniel looked over just as Tamera and Claudia disappeared into the house.

"I wonder what that is all about," Carl continued in a speculative voice. "Neither one looked too happy."

"I think I know," Daniel sighed. "Excuse me gentlemen, I have to go tend to my wife."

With that Daniel left Carl and the other men and headed for the house.

The kitchen and family room were a buzz as Ruth, Morgan and a few other women hurried about preparing additional trays for the buffet table. Tamera turned around, feeling a bit relieved upon seeing the others.

"So, what do you want?" She asked defiantly.

"Not here," Claudia glared. "In the parlor."

"Fine!" Tamera retorted and headed for the parlor.

The parlor was empty and quiet. Tamera walked over to the fireplace and turned around to face her sister-in-law. She folded her arms over her chest in an attempt to look superior. Claudia stepped up to Tamera. Her anger mounting inside her.

"Just what is your problem?" Claudia began to interrogate her.

"Problem? I don't have a problem." Tamera played coy. "However, it looks as though you do. You really should try to take it easy." She added condescendingly.

"Don't pull that with me, Tamera," Claudia said firmly. "Ever since the day you found out that my son is gay you have done nothing but harass him and be outright mean to him."

"So," Tamera said condescendingly.

"So, back off." Claudia's tone was threatening.

Tamera looked at Claudia and could see the anger in her eyes. She heard talk around the family about how tough Claudia could be and realized that she was no match physically for Claudia.

"I swear to you, Tamera. If anything happens to my son, I will hold you personally responsible, and I will get even."

"Oh, nothing is going to happen to your little girl," Tamera mocked.

Claudia clinched her teeth and without warning slapped Tamera across the face with all her might. Tamera's head jerked sharply and she almost lost her balance. She quickly covered her reddened cheek with her hand and tried to stop the tears that instantly formed in her eyes.

"That is my son you are talking about." Claudia corrected her. "And the doctors have warned against anything that could cause his blood pressure to raise. All it would take is for him to have a cerebral hemorrhage and I would lose him; and as I said, if anything happens to him, I will get even. Do I make myself clear?" Claudia's jaws were aching from her teeth being clinched so hard. She glared at Tamera not backing down.

Tamera nodded silently, afraid if she said anything her voice would crack and give her fear away. She looked passed Claudia for the first time and noticed Daniel standing in the foyer watching them. From the look on his face, she knew he had heard everything and the anger in his eyes was directed at her.

Amanda smiled and hugged Patricia as they stood

by the gazebo in the back yard. The gentle breeze cooled the late afternoon air around them.

"I am so happy for you. You look absolutely beautiful," Amanda greeted.

"Thank-you, Amanda," Patricia smiled and looked at her. Amanda looked healthy again. The pink was back in her cheeks and the sparkle in her brown eyes. "Ah, did you come with Bradley? I saw you two sitting with each other."

Amanda shook her head a bit confused.

"No. I received an invitation."

"You did?" Patricia said and then realized the surprised tone in her voice. "I mean, of course you did. I'm sorry. Everything happened so fast I had forgotten who everyone was on the list." She smiled.

"That's understandable." Amanda flashed an uncertain smile back. "I remember when Bradley and I were married. I was so happy that I had mom's help with everything, otherwise I'm sure I would have overlooked something."

"Yes," Patricia smiled having nothing left to say and wondering who had sent the invitation

Amanda sensed the uneasiness of the situation and began to fidget with the empty punch glass in her hand.

"Well, I guess I'll go get myself something to drink. I'm just so happy that you have finally found yourself a man. I'll see you later."

Patricia smiled and watched as Amanda walked away. As her smile faded she could not help but wonder what Amanda meant by that comment. She shrugged it off and greeted another guest with a hug.

Daniel stood in the foyer after Claudia left the

parlor and wondered if he should speak to Tamera. His mind was flooded with memories from years ago, similar fights and arguments, tears and pains. Slowly he walked into the parlor and took out his wallet.

Tamera watched her husband in silence. Daniel removed an old worn photograph from his wallet and then sat down on the love seat and just stared at it. Tamera's curiosity grew and she slowly walked over to him and sat down beside him.

"What's that?" She asked sheepishly.

Daniel wiped his mouth and gave a slight sniff as he struggled to keep his tears to himself. He handed her the picture.

Tamera looked at the photograph and smiled at the familiar face of Daniel at sixteen. She had seen that picture before. In fact a larger one rests on their mantle at home in their living room. She handed the picture back to Daniel.

"So, why are you looking at yourself?" She asked with a smile.

"It's not me," Daniel said flatly.

"What?" Tamera looked at him in surprise. "Of course that's you."

"No, it's not." Daniel looked up at her. His expression was serious, his tone dry. "I never told you this, but this is my twin brother, David."

"What?" Tamera nearly laughed in disbelief. "You're joking."

"I am serious," Daniel clinched his teeth and looked back at the photograph. "I have an identical twin brother."

Tamera was shocked. She could not believe what she was hearing. After all these years, how could she have not known about this? She looked at Daniel.

"Why didn't you tell me this a long time ago?"

"Because it was something my family never talked about," Daniel began. "This photograph was taken of the two of us when we were both sixteen. Mom tore David out of the picture and threw it away. I dug it out of the trash and hid it."

"Why?" Tamera was confused.

"Because David is a faggot, as you so eloquently put it." Daniel looked over at her with a cold disgusted look.

Tamera recoiled from the sharp tone in his voice.

"About two months after this photo was taken, David told me that he was gay. He had known for years that he was attracted to boys, men, but he continued to play the straight game. At first he would actually go out with girls although none of them ever stayed with him for very long. Then he met this guy and we began the charade. We would leave the house saying we were going out on a date with our girls and we would meet his male friend two blocks away. They would then drop me off with my date at the theater and come back later to pick us up. I did not mind, because we would cover for each other on many things.

"But then one night it all fell apart. The other boy's parents confronted my dad and mom when we were out. They had found a picture of David and a love note from him in their son's back pack. Well, when we got home there was a huge fight. My parents were more concerned about what the neighbors' might say than they were about how David felt. He was forbidden to see the boy again and my parents had him admitted to a psychiatric hospital to straighten him out. The day he went into the hospital, my parents forbid us to ever say his name again. They threw out all of his belongings and tore up all his photographs. That's when I realized, they had no intention of getting him out. To this day they say they only have two children, my sister and myself.

"Anyway, three months later, the hospital called and said that David ran away. We haven't seen or heard from him again." Daniel gave a heavy sigh and put the picture back into his wallet.

"Oh, Dan," Tamera breathed and put her hand on his shoulder. "I'm so sorry."

Daniel pulled away and glared at her.

"No you're not."

Tamera sat back, shocked at his reaction.

"How can you say that?"

"What do you mean, 'how can I say that?' You know damn well how I can say that." Daniel felt his temper grow. "Look at the way you are treating Peter and Matthew. You are just as ignorant and bigoted and pigheaded as my parents; and the worst part of it is, you are raising our son to be just like you." Daniel stood up. "I've had enough. I'll pack my things and be out tonight. I'm going to find my brother."

"No, Dan," Tamera pleaded and reached for him.

"Don't touch me. I can't even stand the sight of you right now."

Daniel turned around and walked out the front door.

Tamera sat stunned. In her mind she kept replaying Daniel's words over and over. Still they were not sinking in. Daniel would not leave her. They had weathered much worse than this and survived. He was not serious, she thought to herself. Then slowly the realization of his words began to stir doubts in her mind.

"Dan?" She said softly, uncertainly. "Dan?"

Tamera slowly rose to her feet and walked into the foyer. Her hands shook with fear at the idea that he may have been serious about leaving her this time. She reached for the door knob and opened the door.

"Dan!" She called as she stepped out onto the front steps.

The sound of a car engine starting sent a wave of panic washing over her. Suddenly the tears welled up in her eyes as she realized he was serious. Her heart pounded as she ran down the front walk.

"Dan!" She screamed. "Stop. Please, stop!"

Their tan sedan slowly pulled away from the curb and headed down the street.

"Dan, no!" Tamera screamed. "I'm sorry," she cried and fell to her knees in the grass of the parking strip.

Patricia walked out the back door dressed in her purple cotton summer dress. She kissed Roger and they stood together looking out at the assembly. As if giving a silent signal, Patricia looked at her bouquet and bounced it in her hand. It felt a lot heavier than she thought it would and she wondered if she would have enough strength to toss it over her head. Slowly all of the single women stepped forward and huddled together at the foot of the deck stairs.

"Aren't you going to see if you can catch the bouquet?" Amanda asked Claudia playfully.

Claudia smiled at Amanda.

"Only if you try," she teased.

"Well, we are single eligible women." Amanda cocked her head.

"True," Claudia nodded in agreement. "Okay. Let's give it a shot."

Claudia and Amanda walked over to the small cluster and stood in the back. Claudia really did not want to do this and she felt slightly embarrassed by being there; afterall, she had been married before. However, it was nice to see Amanda laughing and having fun.

Patricia smiled when she saw Claudia and Amanda join the group.

"Is everyone ready?" She called out looking directly at the two of them.

"Yes!" Came their shouted response.

For a brief second Claudia's eyes met Patricia's and suddenly she realized what Patricia had in mind. She quickly looked away as she felt butterflies in her stomach and her pulse beginning to race.

Patricia turned around and prepared herself to throw her flowers over her head with all her might. It had been years since she had thrown a football on her high school powder puff team and this bouquet weighed a lot more than the football. She wondered if she would have enough strength to lob it as far as she needed to.

"Okay, on the count of three," she called out. "One. Two. Three!" She swung the flowers with all her might then turned around quickly to see where they went.

The bouquet flew high into the air over the heads of the cluster of women. Patricia smiled as Amanda and Claudia realized it was headed their way. Both women backed up to try to catch them. They kept backing up and backing up unaware that the swimming pool was getting closer and closer. Patricia screamed to warn them but it was too late. Both women grabbed the bouquet and immediately toppled into the pool.

Patricia ran down the steps and pushed through the crowd of women as Amanda surfaced with the bouquet, laughing.

"I got it," she said proudly holding the dripping flowers over her head.

All at once the entire assembly applauded and laughed with the two of them. Bradley bent down and offered Amanda his hand. He carefully helped her out of the pool so as not to soak himself in the process. Meanwhile, Ruth hurried over with two large towels and gave both Amanda and Claudia one.

Bradley looked into Amanda's eyes and laughed.

"So, I guess this means you are the next in line to get married."

"Not necessarily." Amanda looked at him bashfully. "Bradley, I have a question."

Bradley smiled nervously, he hated it when she said that. It always meant he had been caught at something.

"Sure," he said reluctantly.

"Mom tells me that you moved out of the house, but haven't sold it. Why?"

Bradley looked away sheepishly.

"Well, I - I don't know. I guess I'm just not ready to close that chapter of my life yet."

"You sent me that invitation, didn't you." Amanda said bluntly.

Bradley looked at her in shock.

"Who told...?" He smiled guiltily. "Yes. I confess. I sent you the invitation. I was hoping you would come if you thought that Patty sent it to you."

Amanda smiled and put her hand against the side of his face.

"I would have come even knowing you sent it, you silly boy."

Bradley bit his lip and fought back his joyful tears.

"Amanda, I'm so sorry. I have been such a fool. Could you ever forgive me?"

Amanda felt a warmth grow inside her chest. She never doubted that he would come back to her. The doctors had told her to be patient and they were right.

"There is nothing to forgive." She shook her head. "We both went through a very difficult time."

Bradley could neither stop his tears nor hold back his smile.

"Amanda, I love you so much."

"I love you, too," Amanda smiled.

Without thinking, Bradley wrapped his arms around Amanda and pulled her soaked body next to his. He did not feel the wetness seeping into his suit and even if he had, he did not care. He kissed Amanda as he had never kissed her before. Then he pulled himself away and knelt down before her.

"Amanda, will you marry me?" He asked her still holding her hand.

A full smile spread across Amanda's lips as a lump formed in her throat.

"Yes, Bradley. I'll marry you," she choked.

Bradley stood up and took her in his arms and lifted her off the ground. They kissed and he spun her around.

Peter nudged Claudia as she toweled off. They both smiled as they looked across the pool at Bradley and Amanda.

"I guess the right one did catch the bouquet." She put her arm around her son and hugged him. Peter shrinked back from the dampness of her dress.

Ruth closed the front door as the last of the guests drove off. She smiled to herself as she reflected on the events of the day. Everything considered, the wedding turned out fairly well for Patricia and Roger. It would certainly be memorable.

Carl walked up behind Ruth and wrapped his arms around her. He kissed the back of her neck and turned her around.

"Well, Mrs. Wallace, now the last of our children is married, what do you say we go upstairs and relax in a nice hot tub together?"

Ruth looked into Carl's eyes and smiled at him.

"Why, Mr. Wallace, whatever do you have in mind?"

"Come along, my dear, and I'll show you." Carl took Ruth's hand and led her up the stairs.

"But what about the mess down here?" Ruth protested.

"It can wait until later." Carl tugged at her playfully.

"Okay, dear." Ruth smiled at her husband.

The Announcement

The cold December wind howled through the barren branches of the oak trees in the front yard. The ground was frozen solid and the few left over leaves from autumn rattled against the blades of grass as they were blown across the lawn. The left over pine wreath rocked as it hung on the front door.

Morgan turned the collar of her heavy, brown winter coat up as she and Chuck walked up the front steps. She could see her breath in the midday air as she exhaled. She was not pleased about being summoned out into these elements, out of her warm home, without any explanation.

"This had better be good news," she said as her teeth began to chatter.

"I'm sure it is." Chuck smiled at her and knocked on the front door.

"Oh, no one could hear that," Morgan snapped at Chuck. "Let me." She rang the doorbell.

From inside the house she could hear Kevin crying

and knew that Ariel and Mark were already there. The sound of footsteps coming nearer seemed to make Morgan colder. She shivered.

"It's about time. Someone could freeze to death out here," she complained.

"Morgan, it's not that cold." Chuck laughed to himself.

The front door opened and a rush of warm air greeted them. Morgan instantly bolted into the foyer, nearly knocking over her mother. Ruth looked at Chuck, who shrugged, and then over at Morgan and smiled.

"Well, hello, Morgan," she greeted and closed the front door. "Hang up your coats and come on into the family room. Everyone is here and waiting."

Chuck watched as his mother-in-law disappear into the family room. He turned to Morgan and handed her his coat to hang up. She recoiled at the thought.

"I'm not your slave. You know where the coat rack is." She tossed the coat back at him.

Chuck shook his head. He could tell it was going to be one of those days again. He hung his coat on the brass coat rack beside the front door.

"Great." Morgan strained to peer into the family room. "We're always the last to hear about everything."

Chuck took her arm and whispered in her ear.

"Well, if we had left when I wanted to we wouldn't have been the last ones here. Now, come on."

The two of them walked into the family room and looked around. It was true everyone was present, Patricia and Roger, Claudia, Peter and Matthew, Ariel and Mark, baby Kevin, Bradley, Amanda, Benjamin, Nicholas and Tamera. Almost everyone, Chuck thought to himself.

"Come on in," Carl welcomed them from his chair next to the fireplace. "Get yourself warm."

Morgan noticed that everyone appeared to be in a good mood. That fact seemed to calm most of her fears, but she could not help but remember the last time she was summoned to the house. It was over a year and a half ago and the news was not good. Not wanting to delay the suspense any longer, she walked over to an empty chair opposite Carl by the fireplace and sat down.

"So, now that I'm here, what's going on?" She said, more than asked.

Carl looked over at Ruth and smiled. He always could count on Morgan to be impatient. He then looked at Bradley who nodded his head.

Bradley looked around the room at the faces of his family. Slowly he stood up and took a deep breath. He straightened his deep navy blue slacks and long sleeved matching sweater. Letting his breath out with a heavy sigh, he grinned from ear to ear.

"I want to thank-you all for coming," he began. "You all know how rough it has been for Benji, Amanda and me this passed year."

Patricia looked at Roger and smiled. Memories of seeing Amanda and Bradley at their wedding three months ago came flooding back. Roger looked at Patricia and smiled an uncertain smile. He had no clue as to what was going through her head. He looked back to Bradley.

"At first I started drinking again, but after talking with Morgan, I stopped that and went back to A. A. I thought that I was ready to get on with my life. So Benji and I moved out of the house; but that didn't help.

There is a prayer we say every meeting at A.A.. It says we have to accept the things we can not change and change the things we can. So," Bradley continued to smile and looked over at Amanda..

"Come on," Morgan interrupted. "What is it? Don't tell me, you two are dating again."

Bradley frowned at Morgan for interrupting him.

"No. We aren't dating again."

"Oh, good," Morgan sighed out loud, louder than she had realized. Seeing everyones' shocked expressions, she quickly added, "Oh, no offense, Amanda."

"None taken, Morgan," Amanda said through clinched teeth and smiled. She was never very comfortable around Morgan. Perhaps it was because she always seemed too much the tomboy and Amanda hated that. Still, she did not dislike Morgan as a person.

"Well," Bradley sighed. "May I continue without any more interruptions?" He glared directly at his oldest sister. He scratched his short, dark-brown hair. "Great. Now, I've lost my train of thought." He sighed heavily not hiding his disgust. "Last week Amanda and I took a trip to Reno, Nevada. While we were there, we were married. There, I said it." He looked down at Amanda and smiled. She smiled back at him.

"Congratulations." Claudia put her arm around Amanda as they sat on the couch. "I'm so happy for you."

"Thank-you." Amanda smiled.

"All right, Brad. You sly devil," Roger grinned. "Way to go!"

All at once the family room was filled with laughter and the chatter of everyone talking at once.

Ruth looked over at Tamera who sat quietly apart from the rest of the family at the breakfast nook table.

Tamera stared at the family not thinking about anything. Just void of all emotion. Her blue eyes were red and tired from many sleepless nights. She did not even try to hide the dark circles with cosmetics as she normally would have.

Slowly Ruth walked over to her.

"Is this seat taken?" She asked as she sat down in the chair next to Tamera. Tamera did not reply.

"You look as though you are a million miles away." Ruth tried to catch Tamera's eyes.

"I wish I were," Tamera answered flatly.

"What is wrong, honey? Do you want to talk about it?" Ruth asked trying not to pry.

"No. Everything is fine. Nothing is wrong. Life is wonderful," Tamera shrugged and appeared to be a bit annoyed that Ruth would even think that her life was less than heavenly bliss.

"Tamera," Ruth noticed her daughter's sarcasm and lowered her voice. "I'm your mother. I know when you are lying. There is something wrong. What is it dear?"

Tamera looked at her mother for the first time since Ruth had sat down.

"I don't want to talk about it right now," she said flatly. Her blue eyes began to tear. She quickly stood up and left the room.

Ruth shook her head and sighed at her daughter. The happy chatter of family, as they huddled around Bradley and Amanda, brought back the smile to her lips. She stood up and addressed the family.

"Now it's my turn to share a secret," she beamed.

The entire gathering became silent. Everyone turned to look at Ruth. Their faces reflected expressions of shock and curiosity. Ruth laughed out loud.

"It's not that kind of a secret," she said. "Amanda and Bradley, everyone else too, come into the dining room."

Amanda looked at Bradley curiously as they walked through the kitchen and into the dining room. Her eyes lit up and a smile spread across her lips as she looked on the table. There on the lace covered table sat a small wedding cake, complete with bride and groom. Two candles burned on either side of the cake, the smell of sulfur still in the air from the match stick Ruth used to light them.

"Surprise!" Ruth and Carl beamed at their son and daughter-in-law.

Bradley gave his parents a confused look.

"How did you know about our secret? I thought we hid it well?"

Carl laughed at having a secret from his son.

"It wasn't easy. Believe me."

"Amanda, Bradley," Ruth interrupted. "Why don't you two go ahead and start cutting the cake? I'll get the coffee and juice."

"Sure, Mom," Amanda nodded and started around the table.

"Wait." Bradley halted his mother. "Aren't we supposed to cut the first piece together?"

Ruth smiled at her sentimental son.

"Yes, that's right."

Everyone applauded as Bradley and Amanda gave each other the first bite of their cake. Ruth looked around the room at her children and grandchildren. Her smile faded when she looked at Tamera.

Tamera stood off by herself, leaning against the archway into the foyer. Her long blonde hair pulled back by her scarf as though done quickly. Her mid-calf length blue denim dress also looked as though it had been thrown on without a care. Definitely not Tamera's usual manner. Ruth could tell that there was more bothering her daughter than she was being told; however, Ruth knew in her own time, Tamera would tell her. Ruth turned around and went back into the kitchen to get the coffee and juice and some glasses.

"So, Mark," Chuck walked over to his son-in-law. "Have you thought any more about the trucking idea we talked about last week? What's the word with your appeal to the courts?"

Mark's hands began to sweat as he drew a deep breath. He had thought about his father-in-law's idea. He also considered his own ideas, hopes and dreams and how going into business with Chuck would affect them. Mark looked at his wife. Ariel nodded and gave a slight shrug and smile as though telling her husband, "Go ahead."

Mark turned back to Chuck and tightened his lips in an almost frown.

"Not as good as I thought it would go. The District Attorney is claiming since my parents bodies were found along with illegal drugs, then under some law they had every right to confiscate all of my parents' property and funds. My attorney is arguing that since my parents were never arrested or charged with any crime that law would not apply. He's also pointing out that still does not give them grounds to seize my personal funds and property. My parents had the house and a rather large trust set up in my name as well as one for Kevin."

Chuck listened eagerly and nodded, not in agreement but just that he had heard what Mark had said. He then looked Mark directly in the eyes.

"Were they trafficking drugs, son?"

Mark understood Chuck's challenge. It was not about their true innocence. It was about whether or not he could win. Mark knew he had to look him directly in the eyes and without flinching or hesitation, otherwise Chuck would see through his guise.

"I don't know," he answered just soft enough and with the right tone to be believable.

Chuck smiled compassionately at Mark and put his hand on Mark's shoulder.

"You have been through enough already losing both your parents at once. I'm really sorry you have to go through this too. I hope you win and things start settling down again." He smiled and winked at his daughter before walking over to Carl.

Ariel looked at her father and then at Mark.

"Why did you tell him that?"

Mark smirked at his father-in-law across the room.

"Ariel, if your father knew we won our case, then he would be hitting me up to back him in his new trucking scheme. We have our own dreams and ambitions. We have our own plans for that money, remember? We want to buy a house of our own and start up our music store. If I tell him the truth, then they will all be for nought. We will never see them happen. Do you understand?"

"Yes," Ariel agreed with her husband as she rocked Kevin in her arms. "But, honey, he's going to find out sooner or later."

"True." Mark smiled and kissed Ariel's cheek. "But if it's all the same, I'd rather it be later. For now, let it's keep it our little secret, okay?"

"You..." Ariel smiled at him and shook her head.

Tamera stood silently and watched Peter and Matthew across the room. Thoughts of Daniel's face as he left her filled her mind. Her hard heart began to soften. She began to think about how she had been treating her nephew and his friend. She asked herself, why? She could not find a reason for her hostility toward them. They had never done anything to her. In fact they had continued to be nice to her despite everything she had said to them. It wasn't that. She told herself she was doing it to protect her son; but deep down, she knew that was not true. She thought maybe it was that she was afraid of what others might say to her if they knew. Over the passed six months, however, no one, not even the neighbors, had ever said a single word to her about them. What bothered her so much about it? She wondered to herself as she stared at them.

Peter smiled at Matthew as he slowly, carefully, sat down in a chair against the wall. Matthew smiled back at him and said something into Peter's ear. Immediately Peter blushed.

Suddenly, an image flashed in Tamera's mind and she had her answer. She turned around and walked into the parlor.

Roger cuddled with Patricia as they sat next to each other at the table. His short beard tickled as he kissed Patricia's soft neck. She pulled away and smiled at him.

"So, do you think we should tell them?" He

whispered loud enough for only her to hear.

Patricia looked around the room.

"Why not? Everyone is here except for Dan."

Suddenly Patricia's mind caught up with her words. Her curiosity grew instantly like a balloon giving way to the first burst of breath. She looked around the room again for Tamera but not finding her, turned to Nicholas.

"Give me a minute," she said to her husband and left him at the table.

Roger watched Patricia confused by her sudden departure. He shrugged to himself and shook his head. He would never understand this family. He continued to eat his cake.

"Hi, Nick," Patricia greeted as she leaned against the wall next to Nicholas.

"Hi, Aunt Patty," Nicholas returned with a smile.

"How's everything going?" She tried not to sound like the reporter she was as she began her questioning.

"Okay, I guess." His answer was less enthusiastic, as his greeting was.

"Oh, that bad." Patricia frowned at him then smiled. "So, how is your dad?"

Peter looked up at his aunt. Immediately his heart ached and a lump grew in his throat. He struggled to fight back his tears. Afterall, a fifteen year old boy does not cry and especially in front of grown ups.

Tamera stood quietly and looked at the photographs on the mantle. Her eyes stopped when she saw Morgan's and Chuck's wedding photo. She recognized herself immediately. How she let her mother talk her into being Morgan's bride's maid, she could not remember. The only thing she knew was that she could not tell her mother or Morgan why she did not want to and why she disliked Chuck so much.

As she stood motionless she searched her heart. Her anger was gone. Her pain over what had happened was dead. She felt nothing, nothing at all. It happened so long ago that it seemed as though it had happened to someone else.

"Still millions of miles away?" A soft voice came up from behind her.

Tamera jumped and spun around to face her mother. Her heart pounding in her chest.

Ruth smiled and almost laughed.

"I'm sorry. I didn't mean to startle you."

"You didn't," Tamera lied. "Well, maybe a little. That's okay."

Ruth walked over to the love seat and sat down. She looked at her daughter and patted the cushion next to her.

"Come, sit down," she ordered, more than asked.

Tamera obediently did as she was instructed.

Ruth took a deep breath and let out a heavy sigh as she touched Tamera's hands as they rested in her lap. She gave them a gentle squeeze and Tamera responded silently by taking hold of her mother's hand.

"Honey, I know something is bothering you," Ruth spoke softly. "Why don't you talk to me about it."

Tamera looked at her mother. Her thoughts went in all directions. Her emotions were a confused pool within her that swept through her in waves and then were gone.

"I don't know how," Tamera answered Ruth as tears filled her eyes.

Ruth put her arm around her daughter and could not help remembering the frail little girl from years gone by. As a child Tamera always wore her heart on her sleeve. Whenever she cared about someone, she cared very deeply and as a result she was always being hurt. Many were the times Ruth would sit with her in that very room with her arms around her daughter, comforting her. Now was no different.

"It's okay. You can tell me anything. You know that I love you and that will never change."

Tamera looked up at Ruth as tears fell from her eyes.

"It happened so long ago, but it still hurts as though it were yesterday. I tried to forget; to say it happened to someone else, but I can't. I've never talked about it to anyone."

Ruth was becoming confused and more concerned by the way Tamera seemed to be skirting around what was bothering her.

"It's okay, dear," Ruth reassured her. "You can tell me."

Tamera looked into her mother's soft, brown eyes.

"You have to promise not to tell anyone, not even Daddy. He would be so upset and you know his temper."

"But honey, he's my husband and your father," Ruth protested. She had never kept a secret from Carl in all their forty-one years of marriage. She did not want to start now.

"Mom, promise me," Tamera pleaded.

Ruth looked around the room as though looking for a way out of the promise. She looked at Tamera and her heart melted. She touched Tamera's puffy cheek and smiled reassuringly.

"If it is that important to you, I will keep this between you and I." Ruth conceded.

Tamera nodded to herself.

"I don't know how to say it any more gently, so I guess I'll just say it. When I was fourteen until I was fifteen, I was sexually abused." Tamera's voice trailed off as the words seemed to stick in her throat. It was the first time she had heard those words associated with her and suddenly it all became painfully real.

Ruth was shocked by what her daughter had said. Her heart pounded on the edge of panic and pain. She looked away as though to catch her breath and absorb the words she had heard. She quickly looked back at Tamera and hugged her close to her chest.

"Oh, honey, I'm so sorry," she apologized not knowing what else to say. For the first time in her life she did not know how or what to do to help her daughter.

Tamera ignored the apology.

"For years I tired to convince myself that it was all happening to someone else. Whenever it happened, I tried to disassociate myself from it. Almost as though I would leave my body and watch from a safe distance what was happening until it was over. Then I would shower and scrub myself until I was raw. I felt so dirty. Even in my clean clothes, I felt dirty." Tears filled Tamera's eyes as she remembered, but they did not fall.

Ruth listened and her heart ached as she tried to remember where she had been during those years when her daughter needed her. She realized she was there, only she assumed Tamera's obsession with cleanliness was just a product of being a teenager. How could she have been so wrong? She wondered to herself silently almost blaming herself.

"Who did this to you, dear?" Ruth took Tamera's face into her hands and looked directly into her tearing blue eyes.

Tamera tried to look away.

"I don't want to say." She tried to convince herself. "If I told, more innocent people would be hurt. I couldn't live that."

Ruth looked at her daughter understandingly but her mind began to search wildly all the members of her family. She knew that most child abuse happened from those inside the family circle. One by one she eliminated everyone until her thoughts turned to Carl. Her pulse quickened as she remembered Tamera's insistence in having her promise not to tell him. Suddenly she began to doubt her husband and her heart began to break.

"Tamera, you have to tell me dear," Ruth said near tears. "I have to know for my own peace of mind. I can't go on suspecting everyone. Please tell me."

Tamera realized at that moment what her mother was thinking and nearly gasped.

"Oh no, Mom. It was not Daddy. It was Chuck," Tamera's voice trailed off again.

Ruth heaved a relieved sigh and hugged Tamera gratefully. They held each other, quietly consoling themselves.

"I've been doing a lot of soul searching these past few months," Tamera finally spoke up as she sat back. She looked at her hands as though they somehow held her thoughts and words. "I know everyone thinks I'm a mean, heartless witch."

"Oh, I don't think so," Ruth tried to reassure her.

"It's true," Tamera protested. "Patty hates me. Roger wont speak to me. I realize now why I have been so mean to Peter and Matthew. It's not their fault, but seeing them for some reason has brought back a lot of painful memories. I guess I just struck out at them unfairly for it."

"You know, it's not too late to start mending fences." Ruth smiled slightly at her daughter. "I know for a fact that Peter does not hate you. As for Patty and Roger, give them time. I'm sure they will come around."

"There's more, Mom." Tamera looked at Ruth. "Daniel left me the day of Patty's wedding. We had been fighting for months. He said I was becoming a cold hearted bigot and he couldn't take it anymore. I don't know where he is and I haven't heard from him since."

Again Ruth was stunned. Tamera and Daniel had been through so much over the years. They were the last ones Ruth would have thought to split up. She did not know what to think.

"Well, Daniel is an intelligent man. I'm sure wherever he is, he is fine. Maybe he just needed some time for himself. I'm sure he'll be back. Don't worry too much," Ruth tried to reassure Tamera. "However, when he does come back, you two should talk and you should tell him what you told me. He'll understand."

Tamera tried to smile but deep down she had her doubts about how understanding Daniel would be.

"I'll try."

Bradley cornered his father in the kitchen. The

steam from Carl's cup of freshly brewed coffee was almost a distraction to Bradley as they stood almost face to face.

"Come on, Dad," Bradley whispered. "How did you find out about Amanda and me? We didn't tell anyone we were going."

Carl smiled at his son. He loved teasing Bradley and remembered years ago when he and Ruth had brought him home from the hospital. He would lay on the couch with Bradley asleep on his chest. Then, he would playfully poke him in the tummy. Bradley would grimace without waking up. Carl would touch Bradley's soft button nose and pat him on the back. Those were days long ago but never forgotten by Carl.

"Think, boy." Carl poked Bradley in the stomach playfully. "You did tell someone."

Bradley cocked his head and looked at his father. He searched his memory for the name of the person he supposedly told but he came up empty.

"No, Dad. I didn't tell a soul." He shook his head confidently.

Carl grinned and then looked very serious.

"Where did you leave Benjamin?"

"With a neighbor, Catrina, but I only said we were going away for the weekend and would be back." Bradley admitted.

"What about Amanda?" Carl smiled loving his little game.

Bradley thought for a moment. At first he was ready to dismiss the whole idea that Amanda had said something, but then doubts began to creep up. He was not upset at the thought that she may have told. He was more curious about how his father knew Catrina.

"She could have," Bradley admitted and then began his own interrogation. "So, how do you know Catrina?"

Carl looked at his son and recognized that look in his eyes.

"Oh, don't even think that," he laughed. "Your mother ran into them at the grocery store. She told your mother and that's how we found out."

Bradley nodded his head. Finally the secret was out. He had his answers and he was satisfied.

Claudia sat quietly beside Patricia at the breakfast table in the nook and thumbed through the photographs from Patricia's and Roger's wedding. The pictures had turned out quite nicely. The photographer did a very professional job; even capturing Amanda and her as they tumbled into the swimming pool holding onto the bride's bouquet.

"That is a wonderful album." Claudia smiled and closed the book. "Thank-you for sharing it with me."

"No problem." Patricia smiled proudly. "Afterall, you were the matron-of-honor, you should be the first to see them."

"Well, again, I thank-you," Claudia nodded.

"So, now that Peter is graduating in a few months, have you thought about what you will do?"

Claudia looked toward the dining room and then back at Patricia.

"I've tried not to think about it," she admitted softly. "Peter wants to get an apartment with Matthew right away. I don't blame him. I understand. It's just hard letting him go. He's so young and after all he's been through, I'm just worried."

Patricia put her hand gently on Claudia's and looked into her brown eyes.

"I know this is going to be rough on you, but it is bound to happen sooner or later. Just like it was for our parents when we moved out, so it will be for us when our children go out on their own."

"I know, but it is so hard," Claudia sighed. She fought back her tears as a feeling of loneliness overwhelmed her.

Carl sat down at the dining room table across from Peter and Matthew. He looked around the room as Nicholas and Patricia, the only others remaining there, walked into the kitchen. He turned his gaze to Peter. He smiled to himself at how much Peter reminded him of Steven. The same sparkle in his brown eyes. The same cowlick over his right eyebrow. A tear came to his eyes as he remembered the story he told Steven about how he came to have that silly cowlick. It helped the story to be more believable when he took Steven to see the cows on his father's farm in the country. Steven was so afraid the cows would lick him again, he would not go near them.

Carl looked at Matthew and suddenly he did not know what to think. He never understood the how a man could be attracted to another man, he did not want to really, but it did not bother him as much as he had thought it would. Matthew's love of sports, fishing and hunting helped break the stereotype in Carl's mind of what a gay man was like. He really did like Matthew, too.

"So, Pete," Carl looked at his grandson. "How are you doing?"

Peter looked at his grandfather. The two had barely
spoken since the incident upstairs nearly seven months
ago. He felt embarrassed and ashamed for what he had
done.

"I'm doing okay, Grandpa," Peter nodded slowly.

"You are still having trouble walking I noticed,"
Carl tired to speak softly trying not to sound prying.

"Yes," Peter nodded. "I also have been having
headaches, but Grandpa, please don't worry. I'll be
okay."

"I know, son," Carl smiled. He looked at Matthew.
"So, how are things at work?"

Matthew looked up at Carl and smiled.

"Things are going pretty well. I can't thank-you
enough for getting me that security job. Working
nights gives me a chance to take some classes at the
community college during the day."

"Well, I'm just glad I could help. It's nice to know
they still remember me down at the plant. Usually after
you retire, you are forgotten immediately. So, what are
you taking?"

"Right now just some basic required courses. I
haven't decided on a major yet," Matthew nodded in a
so-so manner.

"You have time. Just be sure it will be something
you enjoy doing. I sure did enjoy working at the plant
but even that got old after twenty-five years. The last
five were about to drive me crazy, but it was worth it."
Carl looked back at Peter. "Hang in there, son. I love
you."

"Thank-you, Grandpa." Peter smiled. "I love you,
too." He watched as Carl stood up and walked out of
the room. Slowly he took Matthew's hand and gave it a

gentle squeeze. He looked into Matthew's eyes. Matthew smiled and gently leaned closer to Peter and tenderly kissed him on the forehead. Peter closed his eyes at the touch of Matthew's soft lips.

"Ahem." Tamera pretended to clear her throat as she stood in the threshold between the foyer and the dining room.

Matthew and Peter both jumped and looked at her. Matthew sat back in his chair and defied her with his angry eyes. Peter's cheeks blushed as he looked at his aunt, realizing he had been caught in an act of showing public affection.

"I'm sorry to disturb you," Tamera's voice was unusually soft.

Peter looked at Matthew puzzled by Tamera's tone. He looked back at her.

"That's okay, Aunt Tamera."

Tamera sheepishly entered the room and stood holding the back of the chair at the head of the table. Her hands sweat as she tried to find her words. She looked at the table cloth and took a deep breath. Slowly she raised her eyes and looked at them both.

"Can I talk to you both for a moment?" She asked and actually waited for a reply.

"Sure," Matthew spoke up and gestured toward the chair. "Have a seat."

Tamera sat down immediately and folded her hands on the table in front of her.

"Peter, Matthew," she began. "I know I have gone out of my way to be mean to you both."

"I'll say you have. You've been a regular bitch toward us," Matthew scoffed bitterly.

Peter quickly put his hand on Matthew's to silence

him. He realized the tone in his aunt's voice was different, softer, meeker. He wanted to hear what she was about to say.

"I deserve that." Tamera nodded. "I tried to tell myself I was justified because I was protecting my son, but that was not true. It's just that seeing you two together brought back some painful memories that I have tried to forget. I guess I misdirected my anger toward both of you and I'm sorry. I hope you both can forgive me and we can be friends again."

Peter looked at Matthew who sat expressionless, stunned by Tamera's seemingly sudden change in personality. A smile spread across Peter's lips and he turned back to his aunt.

"Sure, Aunt Tamera. Apology accepted and everything is forgotten."

"Thank-you," Tamera smiled slightly and nodded. With that she turned around and left the room.

Peter looked back at Matthew who sat staring blankly at the wall, deep in thought.

"What is it?" He asked.

"I wonder what memories she is talking about." Matthew looked at him. "What is her secret? Do you think she was a lesbian?"

"Aunt Tamera?" Peter laughed. "You have to be kidding."

"Then what?" Matthew ignored Peter's laughter.

The smile faded from Peter's lips as he began to think about what his aunt had said.

"I don't know," he answered softly.

Claudia leaned against the doorpost of the back door and stared out at the cold wintry scene across the back yard. The tall oak trees stretched their naked branches toward the sun as though begging for its warmth to return. Steam rose from the swimming pool that remained uncovered and unprotected from winter's bitter cold. The lawn chairs and picnic tables were put away for the season. The yard looked so bare and almost lifeless. Claudia shivered at the sight.

Deep in her ears the words of the doctor echoed in her head. Words that she wished she could erase. She had asked for a second opinion, but even that came back with the same painful news.

Ruth noticed Claudia standing alone deep in thought. Slowly she walked over to her. Of all of her children's spouses, she felt more on an equal with Claudia. Not like mother and daughter-in-law, but more like peers. Perhaps it was because she had never known Claudia as Steven's wife.

"Penny for your thoughts," Ruth spoke softly as stood beside Claudia and stared out the back window with her.

Claudia looked at Ruth and pretended to smile.

"I'm not even sure if they're worth that much," she sighed.

"Something troubling you, dear?" Ruth asked as she slowly turned to face Claudia.

"You could say that." Claudia nodded in agreement.

"Peter?" Ruth guessed.

Claudia looked at Ruth surprised.

"Yes. How did you know?"

"I'm a mother, too. I recognize the look." Ruth smiled empathetically. "Do you want to talk about it?"

Claudia looked around the room. The family had all regrouped in the family room and were busy chatting with one another. An occasional burst of laughter broke the constant drone but then vanished just as quickly.

"Sure." Claudia nodded.

"Let's get a cup of coffee and go in the other room," Ruth invited. "I've noticed that Peter doesn't seem to be getting better. He still has difficulty walking at times."

"Yes," Claudia agreed and set the coffee cups on the counter and then closed the cupboard.

Ruth filled them with coffee.

"How is he doing with getting around school?"

"He uses a cane of sorts," Claudia confessed and stared at her coffee.

The two women walked into the parlor and sat down; Ruth on the love seat and Claudia in the winged back chair across from her.

"So, what do the doctor's think? Will this be permanent?" Ruth continued their conversation.

Claudia drew a deep breath and held it for a few seconds as she tried to maintain her composure. A lump grew in her throat and she thought about the doctor's words again.

"Ah," she fumbled to find the words the doctor used. "The doctors have found that there are splinters from the bullet and possibly bone fragments that have lodged in Peter's brain near his ears. They are putting pressure on those areas. That is the reason he gets dizzy and also has been having those headaches."

Ruth set her coffee cup down on the coffee table in front of her.

"Oh, poor Peter," she sighed. "Did they say if there is anything they could do to help him?"

Claudia looked down and then set her coffee cup on

the table too.

"Yes," she nodded. "The doctors are recommending surgery. They say they could successfully remove the fragments and splinters but whenever you are dealing with the head and brain, there is a fifty-fifty chance of..." Claudia's voice trailed off.

Ruth bit her lip as thoughts of the worst filled her mind. She shook her head as though to shake them away.

"So, what are you going to do?"

Claudia looked up at Ruth. Her eyes were filled with fear and tears.

"I am leaving it up to Pete," she answered. "We had a long talk with the doctors and he knows all the risks. Peter refuses to have the surgery until after he graduates from high school. The doctors advised against waiting that long but Peter wont hear of it. He wants to finish school first."

"What about you?" Ruth looked at Claudia. "What do you think?"

That was all Claudia needed to hear. The tears began to fall down her cheeks.

"I am so scared," she confessed. "I have never been this frightened in all my life, or felt this helpless. I have to admit, I haven't tried very hard to sway him into having the operation sooner."

"Oh, Claudia," Ruth sighed and shook her head. She could not begin to understand the pain that Claudia was feeling. In all of her years as a mother, she was never faced with this type of situation.

"The doctors have scheduled surgery immediately after the graduation ceremony. We will leave the auditorium and go straight to the hospital." Claudia looked at Ruth as she coolly informed her of the arrangements. "I would appreciate it if you and Dad would be there with me."

Ruth stood up, as did Claudia. The two met and embraced in a tight hug.

"Of course, dear," Ruth whispered in Claudia's ear. "We all will be there, and when he is well enough, we will celebrate not only his graduation, but also his recovery."

"Thank-you, Mom." Claudia closed her eyes and continued to hold Ruth tightly.

Patricia slowly walked over to Roger and put her arm around him as he continued to talk with Carl in the family room. Roger winked at her and smiled. She kissed his cheek and then looked at her father.

Carl stopped mid-sentence and looked at his daughter. He could tell by the look in her brown eyes that she had something up her sleeve. He had come to notice her subtle clues while she was growing up.

"Okay, Patty." He raised his head. "Out with it. What are you up to?"

"Me?" Patricia played innocent. "Nothing," she teased and looked at Roger. "Can we tell them now?"

Roger looked at his father-in-law and then around the room. Everyone appeared to be present and accounted for.

"Sure. Why don't we."

Roger and Patricia turned around to face the majority of the family in the room.

"Everyone," he raised his voice over the din. "May I have your attention for just a moment. Patty and I have an announcement to make."

Ruth quickly looked at Carl and smiled. Her mind raced as she anticipated the announcement. She had been hoping for months that Patricia would move back from Seattle. It was such a long way away and Ruth had missed being able to see Patricia whenever she wanted.

Tamera looked at Patricia but kept her head down. Patricia still had not forgiven her for disrupting her wedding. Every time she had tried to get in touch with Patricia she failed. Patricia would either hang up on her or just not answer the telephone when Tamera would call her. She wanted so desperately to tell her sister how sorry she was and how bad she felt for what she had done. Even Roger would not speak to her.

"Well," Patricia smiled and looked about the room. "I just want everyone to know, that I am not just getting fat. Roger and I are adding another grandchild to the family. We are going to have a baby!"

There was a collective gasp and then applause at the news. The room burst again with happy chatter as everyone congratulated Patricia and Roger.

"Oh, honey, that is wonderful." Ruth hugged her youngest child. "When are you doing this?"

"I'm due in June," Patricia beamed.

"Congratulations, son." Carl shook Roger's hand. "I can't tell you what a thrill it will be for you and Patricia to have a child. It will be beyond your wildest dreams. Children fill your life with joy, laughter, happiness. You will think about and do things you thought you had forgotten. Like what if felt like to tie your own shoe for the first time. When you teach that little one, all those memories will come back. It's truly wonderful."

"Thanks, Dad." Roger nodded proudly.

Slowly Tamera made her way up to Patricia. Just as Patricia turned from hugging Morgan, their eyes met. Slowly Patricia smiled and reached out her arms to hug her sister.

Tears fell from Tamera's eyes as she quickly hugged her sister and held her close.

"I'm so happy for you and I am so sorry about what I did."

Patricia gave Tamera a gentle squeeze and then released her. She looked into Tamera's blue eyes. All her anger was gone.

"Enough is enough," Patricia smiled. "I forgive you and we won't speak of it again. Besides, we are sisters."

Tamera cried and hugged Patricia again.

"I love you, Patty," she choked.

The sound of the front doorbell chiming, caught everyone's attention. Ruth looked at Carl curiously.

"I wonder who that could be?" She speculated.

"I'll get it!" Nicholas shouted as he ran into the foyer.

"Yes?" He greeted as he opened the front door and froze. A chill ran up his spine as he looked at the visitor. His heart pounded.

"Dad!" He shouted and threw his arms around his father's neck.

Tamera jumped when she heard her son cry, "Dad". She quickly ran into the foyer just as Nicholas pulled the visitor into the house. Tamera stopped and looked at her husband.

"Dan," she smiled and began to cry. She rushed over to him and wrapped her arms around him. She closed her eyes and pressed her face against the side of his. Something pricked her cheek but she didn't care. She took a deep breath and realized his cologne smelled differently. She then realized he was not hugging her back, but standing rigidly. Slowly she released her hold on him and pulled away. That is when the sparkle from his diamond stud ear ring caught her eye. He looked like Daniel.

The front door opened and another man, identical to the man in front of Tamera, stepped inside.

Nicholas stepped back and shook his head confused.

"No. No," he repeated. "What's going on?"

Daniel dropped his coat onto the floor and rushed over to Tamera and took her in his arms. He kissed her with all the passion he had on their wedding day and held her tightly in his arms.

Tamera was still in shock and kept staring at the identical stranger behind Daniel .

Daniel released his wife and looked around the room at the shocked faces of his family. He smiled and stepped back beside the man that looked just like him.

"Everyone," he greeted. "I'd like to introduce you to my twin brother, David."

Nicholas shook his head in disbelief as though he were dreaming. His mouth still open in shock and his eyes fixed in a dead stare at his uncle and father.

"David," Daniel held out his hand to Tamera. "I'd like you to meet my wife, Tamera."

For the first time David smiled. Tamera noticed that even his smile was identical to Daniel's. He held out his hand and took Tamera's giving it a soft squeeze.

"I think we have already met," he spoke softly.

"And, this is our son, Nick." Daniel motioned for

Nicholas to come to him.

"Hi, Nick," David greeted. Then shook the boy's hand.

"Ah, hi." Nicholas was still confused.

Slowly Daniel went around the room and introduced the family to his brother. Daniel could tell by all of their shocked expressions that he had some explaining to do.

"I know you all have questions and I'll be happy to answer them," Daniel offered. "But first I'd like a moment alone with Tamera. Nick, will you take your uncle into the family room. We will be there in just a few minutes."

"Okay," Nicholas hesitated.

"Come on, David." Carl and Ruth each held out a welcoming hand to him and ushered the family back into the family room.

Daniel ushered Tamera into the parlor and over to the love seat. From the look in his eyes, Tamera knew that the situation between them was still strained. She sat down obediently and without a word.

Daniel looked at his wife. He remembered his parting words nearly four months ago and he still meant what he had said. The only difference was his anger was gone.

Tamera fidgeted as she sat next to her husband. She fought the urge to throw her arms around him and hold him. Her heart pounded nervously beneath her chest and echoed up into her ears. The silence only added to the throbbing pulse.

"Tamera," Daniel broke the silence and looked away from her gaze. "There is something I need to say."

"No," Tamera interrupted him as her fear and

anxiety grew rapidly inside her. "Please, let me go first. I've been doing a lot of thinking about what you said before you left."

Daniel looked at her again and raised an eyebrow.

"And..." he urged her to continue.

Tamera slumped and looked at her hands in her lap for a moment and then back at her husband.

"You were right. I was being unfair and totally unreasonable and I'm sorry. I realize now why I was acting that way and I have changed. I've already apologized to Matthew and Peter. I am sorry, truly sorry, Dan," Tamera's words trailed off.

Daniel took a deep breath and looked away from her for a moment. He still had his doubts as to whether or not she had actually changed, but he was willing to accept her at her word, for now. Truth be known, he did miss her and while he was away had not stopped thinking about her.

"I accept your apology," he nodded. "I must admit too that I am sorry for what I said. I was hurting and angry but that is all behind us now."

Tamera smiled and threw her arms around Daniel. They kissed each other and all their pain from their months of separation were gone. Tamera did not want to let go but finally settled back.

"So, how did you find David?" She asked as she cuddled Daniel's arm.

"It wasn't easy," Daniel admitted. "I contacted a company, Seekers of the Lost. They took the little information I had and came up with a list of people with the same name. One by one they narrowed it down to a man in San Francisco but by the time I got there, he had moved. So, I talked to his former landlord and found out his forwarding address. We met up in Philadelphia. Come on, let's go into the other room and we can all talk about it."

Tamera stood up with Daniel and the two started into the foyer. Suddenly, Tamera stopped and tugged on Daniel's arm. He turned around to face her. Tamera smiled as she looked into his brown eyes.

"I love you, Dan," she breathed.

"Me, too," Daniel returned.

The Graduation

The mid-May sun shone brightly in the clear blue sky high above the high school campus. The groundskeeper had done a wonderful job mowing the lush, green lawns between the parking lot and gymnasium. The flower beds were in full bloom and pruned to perfection as only he would do. The eighty year old man, in his faded blue coveralls, went about his work on his hands and knees pulling the tiny weeds from the far edges of the flower bed; seemingly unaware of the many people that passed by him.

Slowly Peter stepped up to the curb and looked around. He had no feeling toward the school he had attended for nearly two years. The school that had harassed his friends and him unrelentingly. Even the faculty had turned a blind eye toward the teasing and at times physical torment. He drew a deep breath and let it out as though cleansing himself of those memories. He was just happy to finally be through with all of it.

Claudia stepped up to Peter's side and proudly put

her arm around him. What a strange twist of events had happened. Who would have thought that twelve years ago, her son would be graduating from the same school as his father. She smiled as she remembered Steven and wished that he could have been there to see his son.

Matthew handed Peter his cane and mortarboard. His blue eyes sparkled with pride as he watched Peter put on his blue cap with gold tassel. He took Peter's hand in his and gave it a reassuring squeeze.

"Congratulations, Peter. You've made it," he smiled.

"Oh, not quite yet," Peter teased him. "I still have yet to get my hands on that diploma. Then it's, 'Good-bye and good riddance to Washington High.'"

Claudia smiled and ignored her son's comment. She knew of all his trials there but did not want to dampen the joyousness of the moment.

"Well, I guess I should be going. I'm supposed to meet with the rest of my so called classmates in the cafeteria." Peter looked at them both. "You two better go on in and get seats."

"Okay, dear," Claudia nodded and kissed Peter's cheek. "Just as soon as your grandparents arrive."

"Do you want me to help you?" Matthew offered.

Peter turned to his companion and put his hand gently on Matthew's cheek.

"No, Matt," he spoke softly. "I'll be okay."

Matthew closed his eyes and leaned against Peter's touch.

"Okay," he conceded.

Claudia took Matthew's arm as they watched Peter walk off toward the school building.

"He's doing so much better, isn't he," Matthew

exclaimed as he noticed Peter barely using his cane.

"Yes," Claudia nodded in agreement. "Who would ever know just how bad he has it."

Ruth and Carl walked up behind Matthew and Claudia. They had watched Peter leave as they pulled into the parking lot. Ruth's heart ached as her mind momentarily flashed back almost twenty years ago. She remembered watching Steven run off with his friends, all talking excitedly at once. How happy he looked. She was so proud of him. He had worked hard in school becoming the student body treasurer and editor of the Spectrum, their yearbook. She sighed as the memories faded and were replaced by the present.

Carl looked at the old school building and thought back to his graduation day so long ago. Only the school building then was the size of the gymnasium alone. It had long since been torn down and replaced by the newer one that stood before him. The third generation of Wallace's to graduate from George Washington High. His chest swelled with pride.

"Well, are we all set?" Ruth asked as she put her arm around Matthew's.

Matthew jumped a little and smiled.

"Hi, Grandma," he said as he looked at Ruth.

Ruth smiled at the sound of Matthew calling her "Grandma". He had never done that before. She was surprised at how, deep down, she really liked it.

"Hi, son," she returned. "Well, let's get inside."

"What about the rest of the family?" Carl looked back toward the parking lot.

"We can save them seats." Ruth winked at Matthew and held fast to his arm. "Come on, Carl."

Carl walked over to Claudia and offered her his arm.

She took it and the four of them walked into the gymnasium.

The thundering echo of the gathering inside hit their ears with almost a deafening blow. Ruth looked around the large open room. Long banners hung down from the ceiling on either side of the rows of chairs. Large posters of photographs of the various members of the class taken throughout their four years were adhered to the brightly colored cloth banners along with slogans Ruth did not take time to read. Instead she excitedly searched for the face of her grandson. She turned away from the last one disappointed. Suddenly the banners were ugly to her. Just examples of the vanity of an elite group of graduating students.

Carl called to her from a row of chairs he stood over protecting as a mother hen her nest. She quickly joined him and tried to forget about the banners.

"Do you think we have enough?" Ruth asked as she counted up the chairs.

Carl looked over the chairs again.

"I think so," he nodded and then turned to Matthew. "Hey, son, why don't you go outside and see if the others are here yet."

"Yes, sir," Matthew answered and then hurried off to find the rest of the family.

Ruth sat down next to Claudia and noticed that she was looking at a piece of paper from the hospital.

"So, how is he?" Ruth asked sheepishly, knowing that it was a very sensitive subject.

"Oh, he's doing fine." Claudia smiled at her mother-in-law. "Better than I am."

Ruth tried to smile reassuringly as she looked at Claudia. She noticed amid her long brown hair that was neatly pulled up in a Gibson style a few gray hairs were beginning to show. Beneath Claudia's brown eyes were dark shadows from worry and her lack of sleep. Even in her loose fitting, brightly colored, silk dress it was obvious that Claudia had lost weight. Something she did not need to do.

"He's going to be fine." Ruth put a gentle hand on Claudia's.

Claudia looked over at Ruth and tried to smile.

"I keep telling myself that," she said and bit her lip to keep from crying. "I'm so glad you are here." She hugged her mother-in-law.

"I'll always be here for you," Ruth whispered into Claudia's ear.

Matthew spotted Tamera as she walked across the parking lot toward him. His opinion of her was still guarded even though she had apologized to them last winter. Still, something deep down made him feel uneasy. Maybe it was his own secret that haunted him and his fear that by letting it out, those he loved would act just as she had. He shrugged it off for the moment and focused on the ceremony at hand.

Tamera turned around half way to Matthew and called for her son, Nicholas, to hurry up. Nicholas had been lagging behind. He did not want to come to his cousin's graduation, not because of Peter being gay. It was just that he found the whole idea boring. He resented having to wear a suit and especially a tie.

"Afterall, I am not the one graduating," he had tried to argue with his mother before she put her foot down.

Despite his complaining, he looked sharp in his gray pin striped suit. His brown hair was just recently trimmed and neatly combed.

"Not a bad looking young man," his uncle David had commented seeing Nicholas all dressed up.

"Now, remember, just sit still and be quiet," Tamera instructed Nicholas as she took his arm.

"Like I was going to make a big scene. I'm sure," Nicholas scoffed.

"Hi, Aunt Tamera. Hi, Nick," Matthew greeted as the two approached him on the sidewalk. "The rest of the family is inside about half way up the center isle on the right."

"Thanks, Matthew," Tamera smiled. "By the way, how is Peter? Is he worried about the operation later this afternoon?"

The words hit Matthew hard, nearly taking his breath away. He had tried all morning to forget about what was going to happen that afternoon . He was surprised that he had almost succeeded, but now, it hit him like a blow to the gut. All his fears and anxieties tearing apart his insides.

"He's doing fine," Matthew managed to speak. "He's just taking one thing at a time. Right now, he's graduating. He's not thinking about anything else."

"That's good." Tamera smiled. "Let him enjoy his successes."

"Yes," Matthew nodded. "Go on inside. I have to wait here for the rest of the family." Matthew tried to change the subject and ushered them along.

He watched in silence as Tamera and Nicholas disappeared into the gymnasium. Damn her. He thought to himself as his fears returned. He thought about all the "what if's" that could happen. All the things that could go wrong with the operation. Peter was so calm when the doctor went over the possibilities with them all. He did not flinch when the doctor said he could end up with permanent brain damage resulting in his inability to walk without a cane; or when he said he could possibly die. The only time Peter showed any sign of uneasiness was when he was told he could end up with a severe case of brain damage that would leave him bedridden for the rest of his life. That was something he could not bear to think about. Neither could Matthew although he had resolved in his heart that should it happen that way, he would stand by Peter.

Matthew turned away from his thoughts as Daniel and David approached. Matthew quickly looked at each ones left ear, to see who wore an ear ring, the only way to tell them apart.

"Hello, David." Matthew held out his had to the tall, handsome man with dark brown hair and brown eyes. If he were not already committed to Peter, Matthew felt he could really get to like that man. As David took his hand, Matthew felt a shiver run up his spine. David had a firm handshake, obvious by his toned muscular arms that were hidden beneath his long sleeved, white shirt.

"You look very nice, Matthew." David smiled at the young man. Even though he was old enough to be Matthew's father, he had always been attracted to blonde, blue eyed, athletic built men and Matthew was no exception. Still, he respected commitment and Matthew was definitely committed to Peter.

"Thank-you." Matthew felt his face blush.

"Well, I guess we should be getting inside, don't you think?" Daniel smiled noticing Matthew's rather obvious attraction.

"Yes." Matthew turned away from David.

As the three men started for the gymnasium, Daniel heard his name being called. He stopped and turned around to see Morgan and Chuck hurrying across the parking lot toward them. Daniel clinched his teeth at the sight of them and turned around.

"Come on," he said to the other two. The three men proceeded into the gymnasium.

Morgan slowed to a walk upon seeing Daniel's blatant slight. Her first reaction was anger and she set her jaw. She knew she had not done anything to warrant being treated in such a manner and she did not like it one bit.

"Hurry up!" She snapped at Chuck.

The seats inside the gymnasium filled up rapidly as the clock ticked away the seconds before the ceremony was to begin. Ruth looked down the row at the faces of her family. Everyone had finally arrived and anxiously awaited the graduation to get underway. Ruth noticed that Amanda had brought a gift with her, wrapped in blue and gold paper. She smiled at her daughter-in-law's thoughtfulness and yet wondered if she realized they were all going to the hospital directly after the ceremony.

Patricia sat uncomfortably in her seat between David and Roger. She shifted her weight and tried to get a more comfortable position, but it did not help. She rubbed her very pregnant stomach. Only two weeks from her due date, she hoped it were over already. She did not like being pregnant as much as she thought she would. Regardless of the pain of child birth, she wanted the baby out, now. Roger smiled at Patricia and put his arm around her. She nestled against him and kissed his cheek.

The sound of the band coming alive brought immediate silence to the gathering. Everyone looked around to see what was going to happen. Slowly, from the back of the gymnasium, first the Principal and then his assistant walked into view. Behind them the guest speaker and the senior class faculty kept up the slow paced procession. Finally, in single file, the senior class walked up the isle.

Claudia looked through tear filled eyes at the many faces of the students for Peter. She gasped with joy as their eyes met. They both smiled proudly at each other.

Peter held fast to his cane as he slowly walked up the isle. He felt a bit dizzy and light headed with all the excitement. He looked over at Matthew and slowly, deliberately blinked. Matthew smiled and did the same. Their private signal to each other. Once passed the aisle where his family was seated, Peter continued up the steps onto the raised platform and stood by his chair until the rest of his classmates had finished filing in. Then, as though as one, they all sat down.

Claudia listened to the lectures as first the vice principal and then the principal spoke. Their words did not register as her thoughts were fixated on the operation that awaited her son that afternoon. She tried to stay focused on the ceremony but it was no use. She looked over at Peter and smiled.

The applause echoed loudly throughout the gymnasium as the guest speaker, who turned out to be from the local scholarship foundation, awarded six students with a scholastic achievement scholarship award. Peter watched oblivious to the whole affair. His head was beginning to spin inside worse but he tried to stay focused. It is just all the excitement. He tried to tell himself.

The applause continued unceasingly as one by one each student stepped forward and received their diploma. Claudia took Matthew's hand and held it tightly as Peter stepped forward and accepted his diploma. Again, he looked over at Matthew and blinked. Matthew smiled proudly and winked at him.

The vice principal stepped forward after all the graduates had returned to their seats and announced that the P.T.A. had arranged for a reception to be held in the cafeteria immediately after the ceremony. That having been said, the band struck up again and Pomp and Circumstance filled the gymnasium. Everyone stood and applauded the graduates as they filed out of the building.

Ruth looked at Claudia and gave her a hug.

"So, is everyone meeting at the hospital?" Bradley asked Morgan who sat next to him.

"As far as I know," she answered matter-of-factly.

"How are you doing?" Roger looked at his wife.

Patricia sat rubbing her round stomach. She had continued to be restless during the ceremony and felt sorry for those around her for distracting them. It could not be helped.

"I'm okay," she replied uncertainly. "I think."

Roger gave her a curious look.

"Pains?"

"No." Patricia smiled. "I just feel funny. That's all. I can't seem to get comfortable."

Roger nodded, relieved at the news. With only two weeks before the baby's due date, he was still very nervous about the whole birthing thing. He agreed to be with Patricia during it, but he was not so sure he could handle the sight. Despite Bradley saying it was the most beautiful experience he had ever had, somehow, the look on Amanda's face said otherwise. Even the doctor warned him about the realities. There would be blood. Roger was definitely not looking forward to that.

The waiting room at Dwight Memorial Hospital was warm and peaceful. The wall sconces were dimmed, casting a soft glow on the powder blue walls. The blue paisley print, upholstered chairs were inviting. Even the live, green plants and a bouquet of fresh, spring flowers added to the feeling of calm.

Chuck rested his arm around Morgan's shoulders as they sat on the small couch. Occasionally he would look over at Tamera and Daniel who sat directly across the room from him. Tamera kept her head down although she knew he was watching her. Daniel knew it too and tried to stifle his rising anger.

Bradley and Amanda sat next to Mark and Ariel watching Benjamin and Kevin play on the floor. Bradley smiled as he could not believe that Kevin was already a year old. Time had flown by so quickly. He looked over at Amanda and kissed her forehead.

"I love you," he whispered.

Amanda smiled back at him without a word.

"My, aren't we all a bunch of gloomy guses," Patricia said as she walked into the room. "I guess I'll just have to liven up the party a tad!"

"Oh, Patty," Morgan sighed. "We aren't here to party."

"Well, we aren't here for a funeral either," Patricia retorted. "So, lighten up guys."

Patricia and Roger walked over and sat next to Tamera and Daniel.

"So, where's Nick?" Patricia asked as she looked around the room.

"He's down at the cafeteria with David," Tamera replied lifelessly. She did not want to be there, much less talk to anyone. She just wanted it to be over and to go home.

"Oh," Patricia nodded and gave Roger a shrug as though telling him she gives up.

"Aunt Patty," Ariel spoke up. "Have you and Uncle Roger decided on a name for the baby?"

Patricia smiled at her niece. Happy that at least someone was willing to try and bring some life into the gathering. She looked at Roger for a moment who gave her one of his smirks.

"Well, we are still discussing it," Patricia admitted. They were not fighting although it was the first test of their new marriage. Their first disagreement. "We've narrowed it down to Jessica Marie if it's a girl. If it's a boy, I want name him Roger Steven."

"But I want to name him, Steven Colin," Roger interrupted and smiled at Patricia.

"Wow," Ariel breathed. "They are both really good names, but I have to go with Uncle Roger's choice."

"Traitor." Patricia playfully glared at her niece.

Ariel laughed.

"I like yours, too," she tried to cover up. "But, Steven Colin Ferguson has such a nice ring to it."

"I guess it comes down to who gets their hands on the birth certificate first." Patricia laughed at Roger.

"I guess so," he replied.

Peter lay silently on the gurney in the prep room. His hand trembled as he held onto Matthew's hand tightly. He looked into Matthew's blue eyes and tried to see the calmness he could always count on. It was not there this time, only concern and fear. He tried to smile. Matthew did the same.

"No matter what happens," Peter spoke softly yet firmly. "I want you to know that I love you with all my heart and soul and will always love you."

Matthew fought hard to hold back his tears. A lump rose in his throat and he felt his vocal cords tighten. He nodded, fearing to speak and break his concentration.

"You have been everything to me," Peter continued to look lovingly at Matthew. "I have never been so happy in all my life as I have this passed year with you."

"Stop it," Matthew found his voice. "Nothing is going to happen to you. You will be fine. You'll see. We will have many years together. Don't talk like that."

A single tear fell from Matthew's eye and he wiped it away quickly.

"You are going to be okay," Matthew repeated more for himself than for Peter.

"That's right, honey." Claudia stepped up to the side of the gurney. She looked at her son and barely recognized him with his head shaved. All of his beautiful thick brown hair, gone. She looked at the tubes that ran from the i.v. bags down into the back of Peter's hand. Her heart ached as she looked at him.

"You'll be out in no time and everyone will be here waiting for you," she smiled.

"Excuse me." A voice from behind them interrupted. "It's time to get him down to surgery."

Claudia turned around and gasped as she looked at the nurse. She was not ready to let Peter go. Not just yet. She looked back at Peter, forgetting to hide her worry. It was too late, Peter saw her expression and a fearful tear flowed down the side of his face.

"I love you, Mama," he said and reached for her.

Claudia bent down and hugged her son, holding him tightly to her chest. Tears escaped her tightly shut eyes and dampened her cheeks.

"I love you, Peter," she whispered into his ear. She gave him one last squeeze and a kiss, then let go and left the room in a hurry.

"Come back to me, dear man of mine," Matthew whispered into Peter's ear as he hugged him.

"I will. I promise," Peter replied and kissed Matthew's soft lips. "I promise," he repeated and held Matthew's face in his hands. "I love you."

"I love you, too," Matthew breathed. "Forever."

Peter looked at his grand-parents for the first time. He smiled at them.

"Take care of my mom, for me."

"We will, son." Carl winked. "Now, don't you worry about anything; just think about getting better."

"You will be fine, Peter." Ruth patted his hand and then stooped down and kissed his forehead. "You will be fine. See you in an couple hours after you are through in there."

"Okay, Grandma." Peter smiled. "I love you both," he called to them as they left the room.

Ruth walked into the hallway just outside the prep room. She was greeted by the sound of Claudia crying and the sight of her as she held onto Matthew. She glanced over at Carl whose eyes were red with tears. He shook his head and headed down the hall toward the waiting room. Ruth knew the look in Carl's eyes. He hated hospitals and much more seeing one of his own in them. She turned back to Claudia and walked over to her.

"Claudia," she spoke softly yet firmly. "Stop it. Peter is going to be just fine. This is not good. You have to be strong."

Claudia looked at her mother-in-law and fought hard to suppress her tears and worries. Her throat tightened as she swallowed back her tears.

"Okay," she breathed. "I'll try, Mom."

"That's my girl," Ruth smiled. She put her arm around Claudia as Matthew released her.

"Now, let's go get something to drink and then join the others," Ruth said as she led Claudia down the hallway toward the cafeteria.

Matthew stood silently and watched them disappear then slowly he leaned against the wall and slid down to the floor. He folded his arms over his knees and rested his forehead on them. He could not cry. He could not think. Just images of Peter laying on the gurney and looking up at him flashed in him mind. Slowly he looked up at the door across the hallway.

"Come back to me, dear man, please," he begged softly.

Ruth sat quietly next to Carl and watched through the glass wall of the waiting room as Claudia paced in the hallway. She sighed out loud and shook her head. She understood Claudia's uneasiness and inability to sit and wait. It was even difficult for her to do. She looked away.

Patricia sat next to Roger and rubbed her round stomach. Ruth watched as she noticed Patricia grimace occasionally as she continued to rub herself.

"Are you okay?" Ruth asked Patricia.

Patricia looked over at her mother.

"I'm not sure," she replied honestly.

Suddenly a sharp pain in her groin took Patricia's breath away. She lunged forward and gave a guttural moan.

"Mom!" She gasped and looked over at Ruth.

Ruth recognized the look and immediately jumped to her feet. Morgan, Tamera, Amanda and Ariel also recognized what was happening and tried to mask their smiles with looks of concern.

"What is it?" Roger leaned forward and tried to get Patricia's attention. "What's the matter?"

"Get a wheel chair and nurse in here right away," Ruth ordered and looked at Roger.

"Why? What's wrong?" Roger looked at his mother-in-law confused.

"You are about to become a father." Ruth looked at him and saw all the color drain from his face. "Oh no." Ruth barely got the words out when Roger collapsed in a dead faint on the floor at Patricia's feet.

"Bradley, get the nurse in here," Ruth ordered as she helped Patricia to her feet and into the hallway.

Carl immediately revived Roger and helped him back into his chair. He tried hard not to laugh at his son-in-law who sat bewildered in front of him.

"You okay?" Carl smiled.

"What happened?" Roger asked groggily. His head still in a daze.

"You passed out, my man," Chuck laughed and slapped him on the back.

"Chuck, be nice!" Carl snapped and shot Chuck a glare.

"Sorry, Dad." Chuck hid his smirk and returned to his chair across the room.

"I've got to go with Patty," Roger said with a bit more confidence.

"No. You should stay here. Ruth is with her. They will be fine," Carl assured him.

Roger did not put up any arguments. He sat back in his chair and tried to calm himself. Every now and again feelings of guilt, at not being by Patricia's side, crept up but he immediately dismissed them as Carl's words echoed in his ears.

"Well, isn't this great!" Morgan spoke up in her usual sarcastic tone. "This family never ceases to amaze me. Nothing is ever simple is it?"

"What's that supposed to mean?" Tamera looked at her sister.

"For starters, Peter is in the operating room as we speak and now Patricia is on her way to the maternity ward," Morgan continued her tone. "We never can have things simple. Just one thing at a time. Nope. They all have to happen at once."

"Oh, mother," Ariel sighed. "Aunt Patty didn't do this on purpose."

"No one said she did!" Morgan snapped at her daughter. "I'm just stating a fact. That's all."

"Well, fact or not, I don't care to hear it," Ariel

mimicked her mother's tone.

David looked down the hallway, feeling out of place in the conversation. His eyes came to rest on Matthew who continued to sit outside the prep room door on the floor.

"I'll be right back," he told his brother and left the room.

Slowly he walked down the hallway not taking his eyes off the handsome young man. He had noticed Matthew sneaking a look at him over the passed six months. He pretended to not notice but he had. David could not help but be flattered by it. Afterall, he was twice this boy's age and then some.

"Come on," David spoke as he looked down at Matthew and held out his hand.

Matthew slowly looked up at David. His blue eyes still dry but filled with worry. Cautiously he reached up and took David's hand.

"Let's go get a cup of coffee," David invited.

"Okay," Matthew nodded, relenting to the advice of his elder.

Daniel sat in the suddenly quiet waiting room and looked at Chuck across the room. As he did, he could not help but hear Tamera's words and see her tears as she told him about what had happened to her all those years ago. Tamera had made him promise not to say a word to anyone, but he found it difficult to just sit silently.

Daniel looked at his wife and she looked at him. Instantly she knew what he was thinking about. She put a calming hand onto his. He looked at her hand and then back at her blue eyes.

"Please," she spoke softly. "Keep this secret for me."

Daniel nodded, giving in to the wishes of his wife and stifled the feelings inside his chest.

The cafeteria was quiet. The lunch rush was over. Only two nurses occupying a booth along the wall remained. They sat quietly sipping their coffees and reading their newspapers.

Suddenly there was a loud bang as the kitchen door swung open. A busboy pushed his metal cart into the room and froze as he looked surprised to see Matthew and David standing at the counter.

"Sorry about the noise," the busboy apologized and then went about cleaning the tables.

"Oh, pay him no mind," the short round woman at the cash register said as she took David's money for the two coffees.

Matthew and David walked over to a clean table on the opposite wall from the women. Matthew sat down and stared at the dark brew in his cup. He was not hungry or even thirsty. He was numb with worry.

David sat across from Matthew and studied the young man's face. He could tell that Matthew was worried. It was only obvious. He wondered if his face showed as much when he sat in a similar chair two years ago.

He looked through Matthew as he remembered the blonde haired, blue eyed man he left behind. He smiled unconsciously at the memories. John was so full of life, always laughing and so optimistic, even up to the end. He never complained once about the many days and weeks he had to spend in the hospital during his therapy. The painful shots and procedures, he endured them all to prolong his life. To give them one more day to be together. Then finally the day came and he had to go.

David looked at the emerald and diamond ring on his little finger. The one John had given him on their ten year anniversary together. He was so sentimental. Always the romantic. A tear fell from David's eye. He quickly brushed it away and hoped that Matthew had not seen it. Afterall, he was there to cheer Matthew up not worry him more.

"Peter will be just fine," David spoke softly and reached across the table and patted Matthew's hand.

Matthew looked up and nodded without smiling.

"I know he will. I just worry about him."

Matthew reached into his pocket and took out a small box. David recognized it immediately. It was a jewelry box. Matthew opened it and stared at its contents.

"When he wakes up, I'm going to give this to him," he said out loud, more to himself than to David. "I'm going to ask him to be my life partner. I love him so much."

David smiled as he looked at the gold wedding band with a row of five small diamonds.

"That's wonderful. I hope you two will be as happy as John and I were."

Matthew looked up at David. He had never mentioned a man in his life before. Only because of what Tamera had told him did he even know that David was gay. He suspected it, but never talked about it.

"John?" Matthew asked not trying to pry.

"Yes," David smiled. "John was my life partner.

We met of all places at the bus stop one rainy winter evening in San Francisco. There was just something about him that clicked with me and I with him. Right that very night, we went out on our first date. We were together for ten years."

"What happened?" Matthew heard himself ask before he realized it. "I'm sorry," he quickly apologized. "It's none of my business."

David smiled again. It had been a long time since anyone had asked. It almost felt good to be able to speak of him again.

"It's okay. David passed away a couple years ago. He died from complications from AIDS. I used to tell everyone it was cancer, but I guess I was just in denial."

"I'm sorry to hear that." Matthew now took David's hand.

"It's okay," David breathed in and told himself as much as telling Matthew.

Matthew looked at David curiously. He hesitated to ask, but did anyway.

"What about you? Are you HIV positive?"

David nodded his reply and hung his head for a moment, not out of shame or self pity, but for finally admitting it to himself.

"Yes. I am," he said out loud and looked up. "I have tested positive and so far have not had any problems. I haven't told anyone. Not Daniel or Tamera, so please, let's keep this between us. Our secret for now. I don't want anyone to dote on me or pity me."

"I understand," Matthew nodded. "Thank-you for telling me about John and you. It's encouraging."

"Don't mention it." David winked. "You and Peter

are going to be just fine. Are you going to have a ceremony, you know, family and friends."

Matthew smirked and shook his head.

"I don't think that would be a good idea."

"Why not?" David pulled back and looked at him.

"Well, my parents don't know I'm gay. If they did they would be furious."

"I see," David nodded. "You know, if they can't handle it, that is their problem, not yours. You just have to remember to be true to yourself."

The words struck a memory in Matthew's mind. He smiled as he remembered Peter's and his conversation a year ago.

"Pete said those same words to me a year ago," he told David.

"Good advice," David nodded.

Matthew smiled.

"Excuse me," the soft voice of a woman interrupted Claudia's thoughts as she continued to pace in the hallway outside the waiting room.

Claudia looked at the woman dressed in a dark brown fur coat. The light caught the diamond ear rings that hung from her ears beneath her dyed black hair. Her eyes were hid behind a pair of dark sunglasses. Claudia looked at the gentleman at the woman's side. Dressed in a business suit, he looked a bit more approachable.

"Yes?" Claudia replied looking directly at him.

"We were wondering if you could tell us were we could find Claudia Wallace?" The man spoke up.

"Well, you have found her. I am Claudia," Claudia answered him and held out her hand to greet him. He politely took it and then released it almost as quickly.

"What can I do for you?" She asked.

"We're looking for our son, Matthew. His sister told us we could find him here," the woman spoke up in an almost arrogant tone.

Claudia turned around and looked into the waiting room. She looked down the hallway and then back at the couple.

"He was just here an hour ago. You could wait in there. I'm sure he'll be back soon," Claudia answered them a bit distracted.

The woman looked into the room at the many faces and manner in which everyone was dressed and froze in her tracks.

"I think I'll just wait out here," she said with a rather condescending tone.

"Leslie Murphy, get in there," the man ordered. "I've had enough of your attitude for one day!"

"Don't start with me, Raymond," Leslie challenged her husband.

"Not another word from you," Raymond snapped and shook his finger in her face. "March."

Leslie walked into the waiting room and looked around for a place to sit.

Ariel quickly picked up Kevin and his toys from the floor and the chair beside her to make room for Leslie. Leslie smiled a forced smile and turned around to sit in the chair nearest the door.

Nicholas stood up and gave his chair to Raymond. He walked over to the empty place next to Ariel and sat down.

"So, how much longer is this going to take?" Nicholas fidgeted.

"I don't know. Aunt Claudia said Peter's operation

was only going to be an hour or so, I thought. I don't know about Aunt Patty. Uncle Roger and Grandpa have been gone for about a half an hour."

"These things take time," Tamera spoke up. "We just have to wait."

"Well, I'm tired of waiting," Nicholas moaned.

"Here." Tamera dug into her purse and pulled out some money. "Take this and get me a soda. Get yourself something too." She handed him the money.

"Okay," he answered her reluctantly and left the room.

"Ohmygod!" Matthew gasped as he walked with David toward the waiting room.

"What's the matter?" David asked as he strained to look ahead of them.

"My parents are here," he answered just as his parents stepped out of the waiting room.

"Remember, be true to yourself," David reminded him and patted him on the back. He continued down the hall.

"Matthew." Leslie rushed to her son and threw her arms around him.

"Mother," Matthew replied and gave her a quick obligatory hug.

"Son," Raymond nodded stoically.

"Father," Matthew answered in just the same manner. "Why didn't you tell me you were coming? How did you know I would be here?"

"Your sister told us, first of all; and secondly, you haven't been keeping in contact with us yourself," Leslie answered with a bit of annoyance in her tone.

"I've been kind of busy," Matthew replied.

"So we hear," Raymond spoke up for them. "Your sister also told us you haven't been home for weeks. She said you were staying with the Wallaces?"

"Well, yes." Matthew nodded sheepishly.

"The Wallaces," Leslie repeated out loud as she suddenly began to remember. "Wasn't there a boy back home you used to hang around named Wallace?"

Matthew sighed out loud.

"Yes, mother. His name is Peter. He and his mother moved out here a couple of years ago. Right now he is in surgery."

"Oh my," Leslie shook her head. "That's too bad. Why don't we all go out to dinner now and catch up on what you have been doing."

"I can't right now. I need to stay here," Matthew lowered his voice as he looked over at the waiting room. How he longed to be inside with them at that moment.

"Nonsense, boy," Raymond scoffed. "He's got family here. He doesn't need you."

Matthew felt his anger spring to life at the sound of his father's words. He looked at his father with rage in his eyes.

"Don't ever say that again."

Raymond stiffened his back and stood straight up.

"Don't you take that tone with me, boy."

"Then don't tell me what to do. I'm twenty years old. I'm not a boy anymore. I'm a man. I have my own life, now," Matthew snapped back.

"You may be twenty, but you are still my son, and I will not have you talk to me in that tone of voice," Raymond clinched his teeth and lowered his voice.

"What's so important that you need to stay here?" Leslie interrupted the argument.

Matthew looked at the floor and then looked at his mother. All his life he had always done what they had expected him to do regardless of whether or not it was what he wanted. He had always tried to please them out of fear of being cut out of their will as they had so often threatened him. Any feelings of love for them were gone. Even the fear of them was gone. He no longer cared about their will or their money. He had found something, someone more important to him.

"I'll tell you why I have to stay here," Matthew answered her. "Because the man I intend to spend the rest of my life with is in that operating room right now. That is why."

Leslie looked at the door behind them confused and then back at Matthew. He could tell she was lost.

"What?" Raymond's voice echoed down the hallway. The loudness even surprised him. He lowered his voice. "What are you telling us? You are one of those sissy boys?"

"Gay, Father," Matthew answered him. "If you must label us, we prefer to be called, gay."

Raymond cocked his head and looked at Matthew out of the corners of his eyes. He gave a disbelieving cough.

"Call it what you want. It is still obscene," He sneered.

"Oh, honey, all you need is a good woman." Leslie put her arm around Matthew's.

Matthew pulled back and shook his head.

"No. Don't you people ever listen. I don't want a woman. I am gay. I am in love with Pete. I want to spend the rest of my life with him. Just leave me alone."

Claudia cautiously walked over to the three, hearing Raymond's loud voice down the hall.

"Is there something wrong?" She spoke softly.

Raymond looked at Claudia angrily.

"This is all your fault," he snapped. "You and your disgusting son."

Claudia looked confused.

"Now-"

"Just what kind of a house do you run, lady?" He interrupted her. "What kind of a mother are you?"

Claudia recoiled at the harshness of his words. She was totally caught off guard. She looked at Matthew as though asking him to tell her what was going on.

"Well, I hope you are happy," Leslie snapped at her. "You have allowed your son to turn our son against us and into some kind of a freak."

Matthew turned to his mother.

"So, is that what you think of me?"

Leslie ignored her son and stayed fixed on Claudia.

"We have lost our son today and I hope you lose yours," she cursed.

Instantly, reflexively, Claudia slapped Leslie across the face, knocking her dark glasses off. Leslie quickly retrieved them and put them on.

"Don't you ever say that to me again," Claudia spoke up in an firm tone. "As for you, Mr. Murphy, just what kind of father are you? You obviously don't know much about the goings on in your own household. If you did, you would have known about your son and mine years ago. So, don't preach to me, you self-righteous pompous ass."

Without further word, Claudia turned around and left the three standing. She fought hard to hold back her tears and pain, not wanting to give them the satisfaction of knowing how much they hurt her. She rounded the corner of the adjoining hallway and burst into quiet sobs as she collapsed against the wall.

Matthew stood in disbelief at seeing this cruel, inhumane side of his parents. He had never known them to be so hateful. He smiled proudly as he thought how Claudia handled herself with them.

Raymond turned back to his son and breathed a deep breath.

"So, what is it going to be? Are you coming home with us or are you staying?"

Matthew shook his head and smiled.

"You just don't get it," he said calmly. "I am staying."

"That is fine." Raymond set his jaw. "Stay then, but know this, you will be written out of our wills when we get back home."

Matthew shook his head and laughed out loud.

"Go ahead. It is obvious to me now, you care more about your damned money than you do about me. You always have. Well, I don't care about your money and I don't care about you either. Bury your money with you both. That is your child."

"Oh, Matthew," Leslie gasped and covered her mouth.

"It's true." Matthew did not back down.

"It's a boy!" Came the shout from the waiting room. Matthew looked over his father's shoulder and smiled as the waiting room began to stir with excitement.

"All right, Aunt Patty," he said out loud.

"Aunt Patty?" Leslie questioned.

"Yes. You see, Pete's family accepts me for who I am, not who they think I should be; unlike you two, my own parents."

"It is because we are your parents that we can't," Raymond answered, his tone much softer. "We had so much hope, so many dreams for you, boy."

"But they were your dreams, not mine," Matthew answered his father calmly. "You never once asked me what I wanted to do with my life. You just assumed I would be just like you. Follow in your footsteps right into the family business. Well, I don't want to."

"You are making a big mistake," Raymond answered and put his hands on Leslie's shoulders.

"Well, I disagree and it is my life." Matthew stood his ground.

Raymond bit his tongue and nodded.

"Come on, Leslie," he said and he steered her away. As they reached the elevator, he turned back to Matthew. "We'll be staying at the Hilton, if you change your mind."

Matthew laughed and shook his head as he watched his parents disappear into the elevator.

"You just don't listen," he said out loud to himself.

"So, how did it go?" David asked as he walked up behind Matthew.

"Not as I had thought it would," Matthew shrugged and turned around to face him. "Or even hoped."

"Well, just remember, we are all here for you. We all love you and Peter. You are part of our family now."

Matthew looked into David's brown eyes and smiled.

"I sure could use a hug, right now," he admitted.

David took Matthew in his arms and held his firm body against his chest. David closed his eyes as a feeling of warmth filled him inside. A feeling he had not felt since John . It felt good to hold a man again. It felt good to hold Matthew.

David opened his eyes and let go of Matthew so quickly that Matthew looked at him curiously.

"Is something wrong?" Matthew asked.

"Ah, no," David lied and looked away avoiding Matthew's eyes. "Let's go see the others."

The waiting room was all astir as Matthew and David joined the family. Claudia walked over to Matthew and put her arms around him.

"You okay?" She asked and smiled at him for the first time that afternoon.

"Yes," he replied. "Thank-you so much for being there for me."

"Anytime," she nodded. "You are like my own son, now. Part of my family."

"Thank-you." Matthew said and kissed Claudia on the cheek.

"So, how are Patty and the baby?" Tamera asked Ruth.

"Patty is fine and the baby is too. He's beautiful." Ruth smiled proudly.

"So, what did they name him?" Ariel spoke up over the noise.

"Patty relented and they named him Steven Colin," Carl informed the family.

"I knew it." Ariel grinned happily.

"When can we see them?" Morgan pressed as everyone stood in a huddle in the center of the room.

"In a few minutes." Ruth halted the small mob.

"Patty is a bit tired and wants to spend a few moments in quiet with Roger and Colin."

The family continued to talk at once. Everyone was so caught up in the excitement of the new baby that for a split second, they had forgotten about Peter. Even Claudia and Matthew listened happily to the chatter and were swept away by the moment.

No one saw the doctor standing in the doorway. Still dressed in his powder blue scrubs. Slowly he reached up and removed his cap and looked at the joyful huddle in front of him. He bit his lip as he searched for Claudia and Matthew.

Ruth glanced over at the doorway and saw the doctor. Their eyes met briefly and she felt a shiver run up her spine. She froze.

Slowly the room fell silent as everyone turned their attention to the doctor in blue.

He cleared his throat.

"Excuse me, is Claudia Wallace here?"

Claudia jumped when she heard his voice and stepped forward through the gathering.

"How is he? Can I see, him?" Claudia talked excitedly as she rushed to him. She ignored the look in his eyes. Refusing to see it. She grabbed his arms and held on tight.

"Ah, Mrs. Wallace," the doctor tried to avoid her eyes and her grasp. "Please sit down for a moment."

Matthew's heart sank at the sound of the doctor's voice. He suddenly felt as though he could not breathe. His head became dizzy. The room began to close in on him.

"I need some air," he panted and bolted from the room.

Daniel looked at David. Their eyes met and David understood. Without a word, David ran after Matthew.

"Matthew, wait!" David called to him as he reached the parking lot.

Matthew stopped and leaned back against the side of his car and bent down. His shoulders shook as he sobbed and tried to catch his breath. No. This could not be happening. He took the ring box from his pocket and looked at it through his tear filled eyes.

"No," he whispered out loud.

"Matthew." David repeated softly as he caught up with him. Gently he placed his hand on Matthew's shoulder.

Immediately Matthew stood up and hugged David and continued to cry.

"He can't be. He promised me he'd come back. He promised. He can't be."

"It's all right, Matthew," David consoled him. "It wasn't his fault. He would have come back to you if he could have."

David held tightly to the firm young man. It felt good to hold him. Without thinking, he gently kissed Matthew on the side of his head.

Matthew drew back, confused. His mind was blank as he looked at David. He was not upset about the kiss. In fact, he did not know what to think or feel. He just stared into David's deep brown eyes.

David looked into Matthew's tear filled blue eyes and his heart began to beat faster. He was not thinking of anything, just how beautifully handsome the young man in front of him was. Slowly he leaned forward. To his surprise, Matthew leaned into him. Their lips found each others and pressed tightly together in a passionate kiss as they held each other.

The waiting room was cold and quiet. Everyone had found a chair and was seated. Ruth sat next to Carl and held onto his hand tightly.

"I'm sorry, Mrs. Wallace," the doctor shook his head as he crouched beside her chair. Even after twenty years in practice, he had never become used to delivering bad news. He hated that part of his job.

"No," Claudia said firmly and directly, drying her tears. "Tell me when I can see him."

"He'll be moved into the I. C. U. shortly," the doctor continued. "But, Mrs. Wallace, he won't know you are there."

Tears filled Claudia's eyes on their own again. Her heart ached and her stomach tightened. She began to pant and her eyes could not focus on anything as she searched the room for someone to hold.

Ruth quickly rushed to her side and took her into her arms. Ruth could feel Claudia's trembling and she held her tighter.

"He is going to make it," she whispered into Claudia's ear. "You have to believe that. You heard the doctor, his coma is temporary. He will wake up."

Claudia pulled away from her mother-in-law. She looked at the woman she had come to trust deeply and prayed that it was true.

Ruth looked out of the window at the darkness of the night. Finally the day was over. She sighed to herself.

"Come to bed, dear," Carl beaconed her.

Slowly she walked over to their bed and sat down.

Her white cotton nightgown hung loosely on her tired shoulders. As she sat on the edge of the bed, she continued to look out of the window.

Carl lay silently watching his wife. Gently he reached up and began to rub her back with the back of his hand. Ruth moaned as she felt herself relaxing against his touch. He smiled to himself and sat up on his knees behind her. His bare chest was just inches behind her head. He slowly began to massage her shoulders with both hands. She responded by laying back against him and closing her eyes.

"How could I have been so blind?" Ruth reflected.

Carl raised an eyebrow.

"Blind?" He repeated.

"Yes." Ruth sat forward a bit. "It's funny. You raise five children and you think you know them, what goes on in their heads. Only to find out, you really don't. You were oblivious to their internal pains and torments all those years. I thought we didn't keep secrets from each other. That we were honest and open, but these passed two years have really made me stop and think."

Carl listened and stopped rubbing her shoulders.

"First Steven. Why didn't he tell us about Claudia? I think it is sad that he died and never even knew he had a son. Poor Peter, look what his secret resulted in. Then, Morgan having an abortion then living with the torment. Tamera and Daniel keeping it quiet about Nicholas' adoption. I just don't understand it, I should have known," Ruth sighed and crawled under the covers.

Carl laid back down. He wrapped his arm protectively around his wife and kissed her forehead.

"Ruth, it's not your fault. We did the best we

could. You know, I guess when you think about it, we all have things about ourselves that we don't tell one another. Our little secrets. They aren't meant to hurt anyone. It's part of what makes us individuals. I guess the difficulty comes in knowing which secrets we should let go of and which secrets need to be kept."

Ruth looked up at Carl.

"You don't have any secrets, do you?"

Carl smiled at her.

"After forty-six years of marriage, you know all there is to know about me. I have no secrets." He kissed her.

"That's good." Ruth smiled contentedly and closed her eyes.